9/11
ORDINARY PEOPLE:
EXTRAORDINARY
HEROES

NYC - THE FIRST BATTLE IN THE WAR AGAINST TERROR!

Colonel Will G. Merrill Jr., U.S. Army retired

http://ordinarypeopleextraordinaryheroes.com/

ISBN: 1456312219
ISBN-13: 9781456312213
Library of Congress Control Number: 2010916195

Cover photograph courtesy of FDNY

Dedicated to the men and women of the FDNY, NYPD, PAPD and other agencies who, as first responders on September 11th, 2001, ran toward the devastation at Ground Zero knowing that their duty was to save the lives of others even at the risk of their own. They added a whole new meaning to the sterling reputation for courage for which their organizations are so justly famous.

Contents

Acknowledgements

Special mention should be given to some people who were kingpins in their assistance. My wife, Barbara, has been especially helpful with my "passion" as she rightfully calls the writing of this book; not only encouraging me to postpone other priority projects, but also offering constructive suggestions, traveling with me and helping me edit this four-year-long project. My children have also been very supportive and helpful. Mike has been my technical consultant. Bill, even while stationed in Iraq, has introduced me to important people. They, along with Mary and Susan have also helped me with editing and suggestions on how to improve Ordinary People.

Jim Boyle, two term president of the Uniformed Firefighters' Association, was uniquely helpful in introducing me to many key people including FDNY Fire Commissioner Sal Cassano and Congressman Peter T. King. Commissioner Cassano, Congressman King, Mayor Rudy Giuliani, and Deputy Chief Anthony R. Whitaker, Port Authority Police, among many others, were very gracious with their help and added so much to Ordinary People.

Retired Navy Captain Jim Mathews, a native of Brooklyn who worked at 90 Church Street before the Towers were built, spent many hours not only assisting with the editing of the manuscript, but encouraging me with his enthusiasm that these stories of valor must be told to our countrymen. Readers will unknowingly thank him for his ability as a master of the English language to clearly and concisely help edit this work.

My deepest thanks go to the many people that have assisted me in the writing, interviewing and editing of Ordinary People. I wish to thank the following listed in alphabetical order by last name:

Mrs. Marge Arce, Mother of David Arce, firefighter FDNY

Deputy Inspector John Argenziano, NYPD

Mrs. Joanne Barbara, widow of Assistant Chief of Department Gerard Barbara, FDNY.

Firefighter (retired) Bob Beckwith, FDNY

Division Chief FDNY (USMC Col) (retired) Charles Blaich

James Boyle, two term president of the Uniformed Firefighter's Association

Firefighter Sean Brookridge, FDNY

Tim Brown, Office of Emergency Management, NYC

Captain Mike Brunton, FDNY

Captain Thomas Brunton, FDNY

Deputy Chief of Department NYPD (retired), Salvatore Carcaterra,

New York City Fire Commissioner Salvatore Cassano

Monsignor David Cassato, chaplain, NYPD

Mrs. Eileen Cirri, widow of Lieutenant Robert Cirri, PAPD

Firefighter (retired) Thomas Cooleen, FDNY

Jefferson Crowther, father of Welles Crowther

Lieutenant Peter Culkin, FDNY

Monsignor John Delendick, FDNY chaplain

PAPD Lieutenant (retired) Alan DeVona

Chief (retired) James "Dixie" Duggan, FDNY

Stephanie Folwell, Friends of Firefighters Foundation

MaryAnn Foote, Soldiers' Angels

Mrs. Shirley Foreman, Mother of PAPD Officer Donald A. Foreman

"Fireman Jack" (retired) FDNY and Delores Fortmeyer

Firefighter Jim Fortmeyer, FDNY

Edward Fusco, President, Brooklyn Breakfast Club (retired firefighters)

Mayor Rudolph Giuliani

Firefighter Mark Grillo, FDNY (Formerly NYPD)

Firefighter Ken Haskell

Beth Hatton, Executive Assistant to Mayor Giuliani, widow of FDNY Captain Terry Hatton and mother of Terri Hatton

Captain (retired) Daniel Hill, U.S. Army

Lee Ielpi, FDNY (retired) now President, September 11th Families' Association

Division Chief Jay Jonas, FDNY

Chief of Department, FDNY Edward Kilduff
Congressman Peter King, Chairman, Homeland Security Committee
Lieutenant (retired) Mickey Kross, FDNY
Lieutenant David Lim, PAPD
Steven MacDonald, medically retired police officer, NYPD
Barbara Mahon, Family Liaison Officer PAPD
Rose Mazza, mother of PAPD officer Kathy Mazza
Capt (retired) George McGann, FDNY
Battalion Chief James McGlynn, FDNY
Janet McGuire, American Red Cross
Firefighter Thomas Meehan, FDNY
Chief of Department PAPD (retired) Joseph Morris
Senior Detective John Pesce, NYPD (retired)
Firefighter Chuck Pettignano, FDNY
John Picciano, Chief of Staff (retired), New York Police Commissioner
Firefighter (retired) Danny Prince, FDNY
Lieutenant Bill Reddan, FDNY, Squad 252
Susan Rescorla, widow of Rick Rescorla
Captain Glenn Rohan, FDNY
John Shimansky, PAPD Officer, retired.
Firefighter Charlie Stevens, FDNY
Mrs. Thelma Stuart, widow of PAPD Officer Walwyn Stuart.
Lieutenant Brian Sullivan, FDNY.
Firefighter Joseph Torrillo, FDNY (retired)
Chief (retired) Christopher Trucillo, PAPD
Firefighter (retired) Don Van Holt, FDNY
Captain (retired) John Vigiano, FDNY
Attorney Michael Weinstock, volunteer firefighter
Deputy Chief PAPD (retired) Anthony R. Whitaker
Firefighter Matt Yellick, chauffeur Ladder 107, FDNY
I deeply apologize if I have inadvertently missed someone!

Introduction

"Ordinary People: Extraordinary Heroes" vividly recalls for us the catastrophic legacy of the most destructive terrorist attack in our country's history. This book snaps the events of that day, the Pearl Harbor of our generation, into razor-sharp focus. The stories are told with amazing clarity, not by journalists, but by heroic firefighters, police officers, and civilians who survived and prevailed. In doing so they saved the lives of countless others while confronting deadly danger. They answered, without hesitation, the call to a war zone as deadly as the best Marine or Army infantry units have ever faced. Their heroism was already in place before the emergency gear and fire helmets were pulled on. The history of 9/11 is not simply a story of tragedy perpetrated by evil. It is the triumph of courage that shows the determination of our people to prevail over adversity. It was, all in the same day, our worst day, and our finest hour.

These men and women have brought us all a special gift with their interviews. Their words are so poignant because they have had years to reflect on every detail of their experiences, and decided that they were now ready to share them. Not one of them could recall that day at Ground Zero without choking memories and heartache, of friends and comrades among the 343 FDNY firefighters, thirty-seven Port Authority police officers, and twenty-three officers of the NYPD who perished while performing their sworn duty to protect and to serve. A thread of consistency running through these interviews is the repetition by so many participants of the clear need to go immediately to where they could be of most help, regardless that it was also the place of the greatest danger.

The senior leadership of these organizations was on the front line of battle that day. Among the fatalities were the chief of the FDNY, deputy fire commissioner of the FDNY, other senior FDNY chiefs, and the superintendent and chief of the Port Authority Police.

Clear in the minds of each American who remembers 9/11 must be the hard resolution that 9/11 will never be allowed to happen again. Some of those who will read this book are now old enough to understand better the events of the day. It is a lesson those generations of Americans yet unborn must also come to know. That powerful early resolution of "Never Forget!" must remain strong.

The larger issues in our society and our government are how we must treat terrorism, the defense of our country against it, the sacrifices we must make to ensure the safety of our people and our way of life. All of these depend on our moral courage as a nation to parallel the great physical courage of those who were at Ground Zero on 9/11.

On May 1st, 2011 Usama Bin Laden was brought to justice. Our country's tracking him down and killing him serves as a wakeup call to all terrorists. "If you come after America, we will get you, no matter who you are, where you are or how long it takes."

Freedom isn't free. Every citizen of the United States has a role in this fight. We must all stand up to our responsibilities. There is no other way.

Peter T. King
Member of Congress

Prologue

"He stands in that unbroken line of patriots who have dared to die that freedom might live and grow and increase its blessings. Freedom lives and through it he lives— in a way that humbles the undertakings of most men."

Harry S. Truman in a letter to the father of Marine Corporal Qvistgaard, killed in action in Korea on October 26, 1952.

Rick Rescorla and Dan Hill had met in Africa in the 1960s and became lifelong friends[1]. In 1990 Rick, a retired army colonel employed as vice president for security of Morgan Stanley Dean Witter, asked his friend Dan to help him assess the risk of terrorist actions against the World Trade Center. The request was based on the requirement that Dan's class had while in the Army Infantry Officer Advanced Course at Fort Benning, Georgia, to write a plan on how to attack the United States from the Soviet Union. Dan Hill proposed that during the 1970 State of the Union message presentation when Congress, high-ranking military leaders, the president, vice president, and other notables in the U.S. Government were assembled, a suicide cargo plane loaded with high explosives or a nuclear weapon would strike Capitol Hill. This would be coordinated with nuclear strikes on Cheyenne Mountain in Colorado, the nerve center of U.S. nuclear response and antimissile/antiaircraft defense for the entire country. American command authority would be devastated, and U.S. options for a retaliatory counterstrike would be greatly reduced. Dan Hill's ability to think from the enemy's perspective would prove a chillingly accurate and effective one

---

1   Except as otherwise noted this account is based on the author's interview with Daniel Hill.

that would later go unheeded by some, but would save many lives in the largest company located in the World Trade Center.

After surveying the Dean Witter offices, Dan and Rick went to the basement parking garage. No security guards. No ID check. Delivery trucks drove in and out at will. Dan's analysis was that the way to bomb the World Trade Center (WTC) would be to steal a truck, paint it with an office supply company logo (everyone expects office supply trucks to make deliveries to the WTC), and load it with a bomb composed of ammonium nitrate and diesel fuel. The truck could be driven into a lower parking level and set to explode after the driver had left. The truck could be stolen so there would be no "paper trail" (i.e., credit card or driver's license information). The explosive components were easily obtainable on the commercial market without raising suspicion or being traceable.

Rescorla went to Port Authority of New York and New Jersey officials responsible for WTC security at that time and presented their findings. The Port Authority had come up with a similar scenario, but no significant security measures were taken[2].

On February 26, 1993, a truck bomb exploded in the basement of the Twin Towers. With some difficulty, Rescorla shepherded the Dean Witter employees out of the building, going down stairways with flashlights he handed out. Six people were killed and three hundred wounded in the attack. Evacuation of the building took four hours[3]. Ramzi Yousef, the Sunni extremist who planted the bomb, later said that he had hoped to kill 250,000 people[4].

Rick called Dan Hill in St. Augustine, Florida, again to ask for his help. Dan flew to New York City immediately. They went to the blast scene and found that no one had determined how the attack had been conducted because investigators couldn't get access to where the truck had been parked. Dan purchased some rope and snap links from a sporting goods store and the two men rappelled into the crater using techniques Dan had learned in the U.S. Army Ranger School. They found the chassis of a truck. Dan, from the odor, immediately identified the explosive as a mixture of ammonium nitrate fertilizer and diesel fuel. This same explosive was later used by

---

2   *Heart of a Soldier*, p. 176.
3   *The 9/11 Commission Report*, p. 280.
4   Ibid., p. 72.

Timothy McVeigh in the April 19, 1995, Oklahoma City bombing, which he had patterned after the 1993 attack on the World Trade Center.

After ascending from the hole, Dan and Rick were criticized by the FBI for "contaminating the scene." Twenty Dean Witter employees were injured, mostly by smoke inhalation, in the 1993 attack.

This terrorist bombing resulted in heightened attention to security practices in Morgan Stanley offices. Even so, some people complained about having to perform fire and evacuation drills. Some senior executives avoided participating in the arduous walk down the staircase to the ground floor.

A year later Rick again asked Dan to come to New York City to assess the situation. They surmised that since the truck bombing had not been completely successful—the tower remained standing and only six people had been killed—terrorists would try a different approach. Now, with iron gates over the parking garage and strict ID procedures, Dan said, "It's got to be from the air." Rick agreed. Their analysis was that an attack would most likely be by an international cargo plane filled with explosives. They did not expect two planes, nor did they anticipate that these planes would be domestic flights loaded with fuel for a cross-country flight, with fuel as the catalyst for the explosions. They had, however, broken the code on the likely method for the next attack.

As he had done prior to the truck bomb, Rick insisted that the people in his company prepare for such an attack. The security staff was expanded. Evacuation drills were held more frequently. Fluorescent tape and emergency lighting had been installed in the stairwells by the Port Authority, which had also placed emergency generators and smoke evacuation fans in the buildings. IDs were checked. Barriers were installed to prevent vehicles from running into the buildings, and dogs were used to detect explosives[5].

At 8:47 a.m. on September 11, 2001, a hijacked commercial passenger aircraft struck the North Tower of the World Trade Center. Sixteen minutes later a second aircraft struck the South Tower.

---

5   Chief Christopher Trucillo, PAPD (retired), interview with the author November 3, 2009.

World Trade Center and NYC Skylines-photo by author

Chapter One
The World Trade Center Attacks

"We believe that the worst thieves in the world today and the worst terrorists are the Americans. Nothing could stop you except perhaps retaliation in kind. We do not have to differentiate between military and civilian. As far as we are concerned, they are all targets."

Usama Bin Laden[6]

American Airlines Flight 11 departed Boston's Logan airport at 7:59 a.m. on September 11. It had a crew of nine, including two pilots, and eighty-one passengers for a total of ninety people on board. Even though there were more passengers than normal for a Tuesday morning on this flight, there were many empty seats on the aircraft, designed to carry 158 people.

At 8:24 a.m., a radio transmission from Flight 11 said, "We have some planes. Just stay quiet and you'll be OK. We are returning to the airport." This was followed a few minutes later by another transmission saying, "Nobody move please. We are going back to the airport. Don't try to make any stupid moves."[7]

Flight attendant Betty Ong was the first person aboard the plane to report the hijacking. In her twenty-five-minute phone call, she reported that a passenger, probably a thirty-one-year-old man who had served four

---

6   *The 9/11 Commission Report*, p. 47.
7   Ibid., p. 19.

years in the Israeli military,[8] had been stabbed in business class. Several witnesses reported that he may have attempted to disrupt the hijacking, as no other passengers, except crew, had been injured at this point. Betty Ong's relatives later described her as a "take-charge" person. After hearing a recording of her phone call, they said that she was very calm.

Another flight attendant, Madeline (Amy) Sweeney, called the American Airlines Systems Operations Center (SOC) at 8:44 a.m. and also reported the hijacking. During her call she was asked to look out the window to see if she could see where they were. She replied, "We are flying low. We are flying very, very low." Then she screamed, "Oh my God! We are flying way too low!" Then her call was lost. Amy Sweeney was the mother of two children, ages four and six.[9]

Retired FDNY Lieutenant Roy Sutherland had started a new career as a ticket agent for American Airlines in Raleigh, North Carolina. Somehow, he doesn't understand how—perhaps the flight attendant dialed the wrong number—Roy received a phone call from a flight attendant on American Airlines Flight 11 who told him that the flight had been hijacked. He passed the information on to the American Airlines authorities.[10]

At 8:47 a.m., forty-eight minutes after takeoff, American Airlines Flight 11 crashed into the North Tower of the World Trade Center.[11]

Fifteen minutes after Flight 11 departed Logan airport, it was followed by United Airlines Flight 175. About a half hour later, five terrorists, using mace, the threat of a bomb (probably false), and knives took over the aircraft. A flight attendant and a passenger both reported in phone calls that the hijackers had killed both pilots. A short time later, passenger Peter Hanson called his father and told him that the flight had been hijacked and that an attendant had been stabbed. He also said that the plane was making strange moves and that someone may have been killed. At about the same time, a United Airlines employee received a call from a male flight attendant informing him that the airplane had been hijacked, both pilots had been killed, and a flight attendant stabbed. He said that the hijackers were flying the aircraft.

Peter Hanson called his father again at 9:00 a.m. and told him, "Things are getting very bad on the plane. Passengers are throwing up. The plane is

---

8   Ibid., pp. 585–587.
9   *Portraits*, "Madeline Amy Sweeney," p. 586.
10   "Fireman Jack" Fortmeyer, interview with the author.
11   *The 9/11 Commission Report*, p. 594.

making jerky movements. I don't think the pilot is flying the plane. I think we are going down. I think they intend to go to Chicago or someplace and fly into a building."[12]

Brian Sweeney, thirty-eight years old, another passenger, left a voice-mail message for his wife confirming that the plane had been hijacked. Brian had attended Boston University on a football scholarship. After graduation he joined the Navy, attended Naval Aviation Officer Candidate School and flew F-14s during the 1991 Persian Gulf War. He later taught at the U.S. Navy Fighter Weapons School.[13] Brian called his mother and told her, "The passengers are thinking about storming the cockpit." Mrs. Sweeney turned on her television set immediately after the call and watched as her son's plane, United Airlines Flight 175, crashed into the South Tower of the World Trade Center at 9:03 a.m. loaded with 76,000 pounds of fuel at a speed of 587 miles per hour.[14]

The most challenging of fires to fight, other than those involving explosive materials or dangerous chemicals, are those in high-rise skyscrapers. Each tower had 110 stories and was 1,350 feet high. The World Trade Center complex contained seven buildings, including the Twin Towers, all connected by an underground concourse. There were ninety-nine elevators and three stairwells in each tower.[15] The devastating crashes that occurred on September 11 in what had once been the world's tallest buildings presented the toughest fires possible. Most elevators were not working, and people were at risk to use them once the building was hit. Firefighters said that jet fuel had penetrated some elevator shafts, spreading fire and blowing out windows, creating chaos and confusion on the lower floors among people evacuating the buildings. Some stairwells were destroyed and impassable, both for people trying to get out of the building and for rescue workers trying to climb up the passageways.

Frightened people descending stairways only forty-four inches wide to escape the inferno had to go down single file as they passed firefighters carrying breathing apparatus, protective clothing, and other gear weighing up to one hundred pounds, going up the stairs. People trapped on upper floors, desperately trying to breathe, broke windows and hung their heads

---

12   *The 9/11 Commission Report*, p. 7.

13   www.dem.com/ajec/brian.

14   *The 9/11 Commission Report*, p. 600.

15   Ibid., p. 278.

and upper bodies outside to draw in a few more breaths of air. Some waved pieces of clothing, desperately trying to signal people on the ground, hoping and praying for a miracle that, somehow, someone could rescue them, while realizing that there would be no way out.

Then, as the heat, the flames, and the smoke overcame them, some jumped or fell noiselessly until they hit the concrete or asphalt below. Both firefighters entering the buildings and people fleeing the towers were in danger of being struck by people jumping from high floors, preferring a sudden death to being burned alive. People on the ground described the noise made by the impact of the bodies as sounding like bombs hitting. Witnesses said a pink mist rose from the area where the bodies hit the pavement below. Firefighters and police directed people escaping from the buildings to passageways where they were less likely to be struck by falling bodies or debris.

Senior FDNY officers immediately concluded that this wouldn't be a firefighting operation, but rather a rescue mission.[16]

Survivors in or near the Twin Towers tell similar stories. The loudest rumble they ever heard was when each of the towers fell. The roar resembled a massive express train approaching. Running and crawling under vehicles, people were seeking shelter, hiding in doorways, going into buildings through broken-out storefront windows to escape the tremendous cloud enveloping them. Pitch-black darkness at ten o'clock in the morning on a bright, sunny day. Amazement at still being alive, and sometimes, wondering if they were, in fact, still alive. Calling for friends and companions in the total darkness. Finding some and not finding others. Crawling in the dust, careful not to fall into a void. Wondering where they were. Seeking doorways or stairs to exit the black buildings. Some trying to get outside, then finding that they were already outside. As the cloud gradually dissipated, they felt as though they were on a surreal moonscape, completely devoid of color. The whole area was buried inches deep with powdery gray dust. Vehicles were overturned and thrown about by the force of the tremendous wind created by the crashing towers. Massive fire trucks were burned and crushed, covered with ashen dust. Firefighters saw no office furniture, file cabinets, and desks, as they had found in previous building collapses. Everything was pulverized except the papers. Papers everywhere. People found documents from the Twin Towers miles away in Brooklyn and throughout the city. Workers in nearby stores

---

16   *The 9/11 Commission Report*, p. 290.

handed out dust masks and water bottles to dazed survivors of the devastation as they slowly worked their way through the streets out of the chaos. They would find their way home with no taxis, no buses, no subways as firefighters and policemen directed them to safety.

Even after the South Tower fell, the second one hit and the first to collapse, the firefighters stood their ground. A group of three N.Y. policemen and three firefighters had gone up to the fifty-fourth floor when they felt the North Tower shake as the South Tower collapsed. One firefighter received a radio message ordering him to evacuate the building. He replied, "We're not f#%!ing coming out!" The firefighters did convince the policemen, who had no breathing apparatus or protective clothing, to leave, which they did reluctantly. "One firefighter stopped to take a breath, and we looked each other in the eye," said Louis G. Lesce, making his way down from the eighty-sixth floor in the first tower hit. "He was going to a place I was damn well trying to get out of. I looked at him thinking, 'What are you doing this for?' He looked at me like he knew very well. 'This is my job.' "[17]

An FDNY chief said, "I would never think of myself as a leader of men if I had headed north on West Street after the South Tower collapsed." Three highly respected senior firefighters helped rescue people, both civilian and firefighters, from the Marriott Hotel in the complex. Some firefighters stood watch near the remaining tower and told civilians and firefighters leaving the building when they could run so that they wouldn't get hit by people jumping or debris falling. Deputy Chief Pete Hayden, directing the firefighting effort, said, "Some companies did hear us and didn't come down." In other cases, when they called specific battalions, they got no replies due to poor communications.[18]

Engine 54 and Ladder 4 of Battalion 9, located in New York's "Hell's Kitchen," lost twelve men on 9/11.[19] Ladder Company 7, from Twenty-Ninth Street in Manhattan, had been out on another fire when they were called to Ground Zero. The six men responding were never seen again.

Lieutenant Kevin Pfeiffer, with his men from Engine 33, reported to his brother, Battalion Chief Joe Pfeifer, the first battalion fire chief on the scene. Kevin wasn't supposed to be there that day. He had taken two weeks' vaca-

---

17   Dean E. Murphy, "Honoring the Rescuers," *New York Times*, http://www.nytimes.com/library/national/091101rescuers.html.

18   "Facing the End," *Time*, September 24, 2001, p. 69.

19   http://www.galenfrysinger.com/fire_engine_54_new_york_city.htm.

tion to prepare for the fire department captain's test. Joe told his brother that the fire was reported on floors seventy-eight or eighty of the North Tower. Kevin and his crew from Engine 33 headed up the stairs.[20] After the South Tower collapsed, and after he was finally able to make his way out of the destruction and massive cloud of dust and smoke that resulted, Joe tried several times, unsuccessfully, to contact his brother in the North Tower. Then the North Tower collapsed. Engine 33 was missing. Kevin was killed.

Ladder Company 105 and Engine Company 219, from Dean Street in Brooklyn, were among the first companies to respond. Seven died. Vincent Brunton, a twenty-two-year veteran of the FDNY and captain of Ladder 105, and two of his brothers had established themselves as a firefighting family, as so many FDNY career firefighters were. "Vinnie" and his two brothers, Tom and Mike, also captains, were career firefighters before 9/11. One nephew, Tim, has since become a firefighter.[21] Vinnie, as are his brothers, was a leader. Five firefighters from that crew were killed in action that day. Firefighter Frank Palombo, Ladder Company 105, from the same station, left his wife, Jean, and ten children, eight boys and two girls, ages one to fourteen.[22] Jean would look at Frank at the dinner table and find him with tears in his eyes. He would say, "I'm so fortunate to have all of these children."[23] A memorial service was held for Frank Palombo on October 20, 2001.

When Ladder 105 was dispatched to Ground Zero, another company, Ladder 107, was "relocated" to its firehouse to cover in 105's absence. Firefighter Matt Yellick, the chauffeur, or driver, said that as they were en route to the Dean Street firehouse where 105 was assigned, they were followed by Engine 214, which was being relocated to Bedford Stuyvesant at the same time. Engine 214 volunteered to go to the WTC and went there instead of to its relocation fire station. All of the crewmembers of Engine 214 except the chauffeur were killed when the towers collapsed.[24] Police Officer John Perry was at the NYPD headquarters filling out his retirement papers. When he saw the Twin Towers struck, he took back his badge and went to Ground Zero. He was last seen helping people reach safety.[25]

---

20   *Report from Ground Zero*, p. 37.

21   Tom and Mike Brunton, interview with author, September 11, 2007.

22   Jean Palombo, interview with author, September 11, 2007.

23   *Portraits*, p. 380.

24   Matt Yellick, FDNY firefighter, interview with author.

25   John Picciano, NYPD Chief of Staff, interview with author.

People fleeing collapsing Tower-photo courtesy of FDNY

Chapter Two
The Commander and the Patrol Sergeant

"The concussion from the explosion knocked me right on my butt and I ended up face down in the street."

Captain Anthony R. Whitaker

Port Authority Police Department (PAPD) Captain Anthony R. Whitaker and Sergeant Alan DeVona were a team, working together much like a military commander and his most senior sergeant. [26] Each morning they would meet in the mall section of the World Trade Center before the 6:45 a.m. roll call. After the roll call on September 11, 2001, Captain Whitaker went to the lobby of the North Tower and Sergeant DeVona started on his normal routine and was working at the police desk in World Trade Center Five, near the North Tower.

Captain Anthony R. Whitaker— Port Authority Police Department

Captain Anthony R. Whitaker, raised in Brooklyn, was standing in the underground shopping mall adjacent to the lobby of the North Tower on the morning of September 11, 2001. As commander Port Authority Police at the World Trade Center, it was his custom to stand near the lobby every

---

26   Chief Anthony R. Whitaker, interviews with the author.

morning at 8:30 for about thirty minutes to watch people rush from the subways and the street to their offices. In uniform and wearing his hat, he would nod and greet people. Although he didn't know the names of the thousands of passersby, he recognized many of their faces. He was showing "command presence," partly to assure the public that the PAPD police were on duty and also to set an example for his subordinates. This particular morning, foot traffic was noticeably lighter, which he attributed to city elections being held that day.

Suddenly, he heard a loud roar and felt something warm on the left side of his face. Looking up, he saw a gigantic fireball surging from the lobby of the tower. The ball of flame rushing toward him looked to be pushing people before it, while others appeared to be caught in the flames. Instinctively, he pivoted to his left and ran down the passageway between the Twin Towers. As he ran, a "voice" told him, "You won't make it down the hallway!" He darted into a corridor leading to a freight elevator. He grabbed the security guard stationed there and pulled him to cover at the end of the corridor. As the flames swept by, Whitaker fell, struck his head and was knocked unconscious.

Minutes later, and only partly conscious, he rushed back down the darkened hallway toward North Tower. In the strange, now quiet hallway and darkness, he saw an eerie scene as two figures fully engulfed in flames ran toward him. Whitaker froze as he tried to comprehend the scene unfolding before him. The phantom-like figures, no clothing, no skin, flesh badly burned, didn't make a sound as they approached and ran silently by.

As Captain Whitaker stumbled down the hallway toward the lobby where he had been, the inner voice said, "Don't look down!" He obeyed and, as he walked, he realized he was stepping on things—soft things— and he heard crinkling, crushing noises. He was walking on human bodies and body parts in the darkness. As he approached the North Tower, having worked at John F. Kennedy Airport for more than eight years, he recognized the smell of jet fuel.

Whitaker didn't know what had happened with the fireball coming into the lobby, people in flames, human bodies all over the floor and the building in darkness. He didn't know that a commercial plane had hit the building. Nor did he understand then that the ball of fire had come from flaming jet fuel cascading down the elevator shaft, then rolling into the lobby. He realized, however, that the situation was beyond control and there was only one thing to do—evacuate the entire World Trade Center. He couldn't immediately transmit this message as other traffic jammed the Port Authority command radio net. He heard Police Sergeant Alan DeVona instructing the police desk to evacuate Buildings Five and Six. As soon as there was a break in the radio traffic, he countermanded that order and directed, "Evacuate the entire complex! That means all seven buildings. Get everyone out of here!" Unfortunately with the chaos, damage to radio transmitters, and the incompatibility of radios among many agencies, the evacuation order was delayed in reaching all of the emergency workers in the various buildings.[27]

The scene in the lobby was chaotic. People being evacuated were hurried through the underground shopping mall beneath the plaza to avoid being hit by falling bodies. In Captain Whitaker's words, "Hundreds of people were jumping to their deaths. It was like rain falling!"

From the Fire Control Desk (located in all New York City high-rise buildings), he could hear breaking glass as people dived from the upper stories of the building and crashed to their deaths through the glass-covered entrance. Police and firefighters rushed people through the mall to the Eighth Avenue subway station, where they could walk underground to Chambers or Fulton streets and exit safely. He met three other PAPD officers, Donald Foreman, Nathaniel Webb, and Walter McNeil, friends who had been assigned to the Holland Tunnel. Whitaker was puzzled that they were there so quickly. In his still-dazed state, he asked them how they got there so quickly. He then realized that he'd been unconscious longer than he thought.

After seeing the evacuation under way, Captain Whitaker watched the FDNY setting up a command post in the North Tower with firefighters mustering and starting the long, arduous trek up the tower stairs. He briefly talked with a fire chief and then was ordered to go to the South Tower to assess the situation there. Whitaker led his three colleagues to the unmanned fire control desk in the South Tower lobby. He directed Foreman and McNeil to set up communications between the WTC, the PAPD, and the NYPD command organizations.

---

27   Some people reported that they heard public announcements directing them
to remain in their offices. These were most likely made by civilian fire safety directors
appointed by their companies.

An FDNY officer, an emergency medical technician (EMT), and a PAPD officer, Bruce Reynolds, assigned to the George Washington Bridge, entered the lobby from the door on Liberty Street with a gurney. From the size of the body on the gurney, Captain Whitaker judged it to be a female. He said, "I don't know if she was dead or alive, but she was burned to a crisp." Whitaker noted that the skin tone of Reynolds, a black man, was an odd purplish color and he was obviously having difficulty. He asked him if he was all right. Reynolds replied that he was having trouble breathing. Whitaker ordered the other men to carry the gurney and for Officer Reynolds to get some rest.

At the fire control desk, an FDNY captain came over and said, "I need a PAPD officer with a radio to come with me into the tower." Whitaker ordered Nat Webb to accompany the captain. Webb wanted to remain to work with the other police officers and challenged the order, "Why me?" Whitaker replied, "Because those other two guys (Foreman and McNeil) are setting up communications. That leaves you." As Webb, who was not happy, accompanied the captain, he looked back at Whitaker and the two had a silent eye-to-eye conversation. Webb said, "Please, can't you get someone else to do this?" Whitaker silently replied, "I'm sorry, but this is important and you must follow my orders. If there was someone else, I'd send them, but there isn't, and I have to stay here." The FDNY captain, Officer Nat Webb, and fifteen or twenty firefighters entered a freight elevator and headed upstairs to assist with the evacuation. Whitaker never saw them again.

Two minutes later, Whitaker got a radio transmission from PAPD Chief William Hall directing him to meet at a footbridge. He told McNeil and Foreman, "I have to go talk to the chief. I'll be right back. Get those lines in and keep them open!" Instead of going out the door to Liberty Street, the shortest way, the "voice" said, "Don't walk on Liberty Street!" Instead he hurried back through the lobby, crossed the mall, and headed toward the footbridge near the Deutsche Bank building.

When he arrived, the chief wasn't there, so he radioed him and learned he was at a different footbridge on West Street connecting the Federal Building to the World Financial Center. Whitaker went back through the mall to the PATH[28] escalator in the center of the area. Sergeant Martin

---

28   Port Authority Trans-Hudson Corporation (PATH), a subsidiary organization of the Port Authority.

Duane was directing the evacuation there. Although hundreds of people were streaming out, there was no panic and no apparent injuries. Assured that the evacuation was going well, he hurried over to a corridor in Building Five, which housed some Port Authority offices, financial companies, and government agencies. PAPD Police Officer Clinton Davis ran past him to the emergency (storage) room looking for Scott Air Paks (breathing apparatus for emergency workers). Davis picked up as many air packs as he could carry and went back up the escalator. Then Sgt. John McLoughlin, who had been working at the Port Authority Bus Terminal, came in and asked if Captain Whitaker had keys to the emergency room. When Whitaker replied that he didn't, McLoughlin left.

Whitaker met Geoffrey Wharton, chief of the Silverstein transition team, on the corner of Church and Vesey streets. (The transition team was coordinating the transfer of operations of the World Trade Center from the Port Authority to Larry Silverstein, who had bought control of the World Trade Center two months earlier.) He was concerned about team members on the eighty-eighth floor and wanted to go into the tower to help them. Whitaker convinced Wharton that he would not be able to help them, and told him to go north on Church Street. Still feeling the effects of his concussion, Captain Whitaker might have blacked out, as the next thing he remembered was standing under the footbridge at West Street, where he met one of the PAPD Emergency Service Unit officers who was taking shelter under the footbridge. Whitaker heard what sounded like explosions as jumpers' bodies hit the sidewalk. He knew that the officer was under the footbridge for protection from the bodies, pieces of steel, chunks of concrete and shards of glass that were raining down. He crossed West Street and went to a truck bay at the World Financial Center. A fire truck pulled up, and he suggested that the firefighters set up an emergency center there and said, "We'll start funneling people over here to get them away from the building." A dazed woman in her forties stumbled towards them. She was in a stupor as she walked past Whitaker. All of the flesh had been burned off her smoking body. The firefighter ran over, set her on the ground, and started to treat her.

As he walked towards Liberty Street, Captain Whitaker looked back at the North Tower and saw the gaping hole and raging fire. He called the World Trade Center police desk and repeated his order for a complete evacuation of all seven buildings in the complex. He started back toward the

South Tower, but, again, heeded the "voice" which told him not to walk on Liberty Street, and instead he walked back one block away, with the Saint Nicholas Greek Orthodox Church between him and the South Tower.[29] He walked through the church's parking lot toward the Tower entrance.

Suddenly, Whitaker heard the high-pitched whine of jet engines looked up and saw a low-flying commercial airliner coming down along the Hudson River toward the Brooklyn Bridge. It made a complete circle and only sixteen minutes after the first plane hit the North Tower, this plane dove right through the South Tower. Finally, he understood it was no accident and New York City was under attack. He said, "The concussion from the explosion knocked me right on my butt, and I ended up face down in the street. You could feel the heat even at ground level. Then debris started raining down. I must have blacked out again. When I came to, I saw someone standing in front of a building. He said, 'Come this way! Come this way!'" Whitaker ran toward the building where the man, a security guard, had opened a door to the lobby of the building. Whitaker dove in along with two or three other people. He lay on the floor for a few minutes, then asked the security guard if there was another way to get out of the building. The guard took him to a truck dock at the back of the building. There were hundreds of people there who, when they saw his uniform, anxiously started badgering him with questions. He had no answers but replied, "Stay calm. We'll get through this. Whatever is going on, we'll get through it." The security guard led him to the back door on a side street, and Whitaker started back toward the WTC complex.

Still on his way to rendezvous with Chief Hall, he saw the two towers in flames and confusion in the plaza. Captain Whitaker states that the experience with the 1993 truck bombing set the stage for what happened in 2001. Since the tower struck in February 1993 withstood the effects of the explosion, many people did not think that the Towers would collapse on 9/11. Many first responders did as they had done in 1993.

When he met Chief Hall, hundreds of police and firefighters were standing in the intersection awaiting instructions. Chief Hall decided to walk up Vesey Street toward Church Street between Building Seven and the main complex. Although he had an uneasy feeling, Whitaker said, "OK," to the senior officer and the two men started walking. As they passed the truck

---

29   This church was destroyed later that day.

bay of Building Seven, they heard a tremendous noise, like a gigantic animal groaning. Looking up, they saw the South Tower collapsing. As the structure fell, it created a hurricane force wind. Whitaker dove into the open doors of the truck bay of Building Seven, where hundreds of people had already congregated. Suddenly the truck bay went black and the wind was blowing at fifty or sixty miles an hour like a tornado inside the bay. Whitaker got to his feet and grabbed the shoulders of someone holding on to a post. He held on for dear life as he was pelted with debris. The chalky dust that came with the wind clogged his eyes, nose, mouth, and ears. When the wind finally subsided, it was so dark that someone said, "The doors must have closed." In the darkness, a group of people formed a line holding on to the person in front of them, and someone led them out of the bay through the doors, which were still open, to a nearby office building and into a bathroom. Whitaker, a black man, looked into a mirror and, he said, "I was a mess! I looked like a gray ghost." He cleaned up as best as he could and went back into the street, where he met a good friend, Alan Reiss, director of the World Trade Department. He asked Reiss, a trained engineer, "Do you think the North Tower will fall?" Reiss looked at the tower and matter-of-factly replied, "Oh yeah. It's going to fall."

Minutes later as he was looking up at the tower, Whitaker saw a slight movement of the large antenna that stood on top of the building. He ran back to where Reiss was standing and said, "Alan! We better get out of here! The building is going to come down, and I mean right now!" He ran to the intersection where policemen and firefighters had congregated and said, "Get the hell out of here!" He ran over to the PAPD command bus at the curb and ordered the driver, "Get the bus out of here! The building is coming down!" He ran by several fire trucks and told the firefighters, "Get out of here!" Some left, others stayed. He then directed PAPD officers in the area to leave. He and Reiss started running north on West Street. They made it about a half a block when they heard the same loud ominous groan. Whitaker looked over his shoulder in time to see the antenna on top of the building begin to waver. Then he saw the tower collapsing and a new cloud forming and racing toward them up West Street. They instinctively realized that they couldn't outrun the cloud, so they hit the ground near the curb and hugged each other as the cloud rolled over them. After the cloud passed, they got to their feet and stumbled along until they came to the Port Authority command bus which Whitaker had ordered to move away earlier. He led Reiss to the bus and then guided some civilians to the relative safety and clear air inside. Cars were exploding everywhere as red-hot pieces of steel from the tower pierced gas tanks. Police in the area at first thought that bombs were exploding. He directed the bus to move to safety on Chambers Street.

Chief Whitaker doesn't remember much that happened after that. Other people who were there have told him that he is fortunate he can't recall all of the details. Years later, a PAPD friend of his with vivid memories spent much of his time sitting on a park bench or a couch, watching TV under heavy medication, still suffering from posttraumatic stress disorder (PTSD).

Regarding the "voice" that kept giving him instructions, Chief Whitaker said, "I feel lucky and I feel blessed. Although I was raised as a Catholic, I am not real religious, but I am a believer. I definitely know whose voice I heard more than once that day that told me, 'Don't go that way, go this way!' I followed the instructions and advice that I received although I knew of a quicker way to get to where I was heading. I've always believed in God, and he was definitely with me on that day, and not only for me. He was there for a lot of other people as well."

Chief Whitaker said there were between 100 and 150 PAPD contract civilian guards on duty within the WTC complex. Every single one of them stood his or her post and did his or her utmost to get people out of the area. One woman, an attorney, was carried downstairs in a wheelchair by some of these guards. She still works for the Port Authority.

Donald Foreman, Whitaker's best friend and classmate,[30] and Walter McNeil, the PAPD officers setting up communications in South Tower, were killed. Their bodies were found at the fire control desk they were manning. Nathaniel Webb, who accompanied the fire captain into the tower, was also killed. The remains of Bruce Reynolds, the officer who Captain Whitaker had directed to rest, were found where Whitaker left him. The firefighter and the emergency medical technician, who were also carrying the gurney with the burned woman, were killed. Their bodies were recovered, although the woman's remains were never found. Sgt. John McLoughlin, who had asked for the keys to the emergency storage room, was buried alive in the rubble and was rescued the following day. Clinton Davis, the

---

30   Anthony Whitaker and Donald Foreman had planned to retire together.

officer who was looking for the Scott Air Paks, was killed. Sergeant Martin Duane, who directed the evacuation through the mall, survived. Chief William Hall, who was with Captain Whitaker when the first tower fell, also survived.

Rescue and recovery operations started immediately. The PAPD worked twelve-hour days from September 11 until May 30, 2002. Captain Whitaker commanded the night shift from 6 p.m. to 6 a.m., alternating with Inspector Joseph Morris, who commanded the day shift. Whitaker worked beyond his twelve hours as often as he could. Not married at the time, he plowed into the work to alleviate his "survivor's guilt" and the grief that he felt from losing some of his best friends. While his memories of September 11 are incomplete, he has vivid recollections of the period following. He recalls that a fire truck that had been parked on Liberty Street was recovered four stories underground. He also remembers the dump trucks used to clear debris in the months afterward. "One of the things that haunts me to this day," he said, "is all those dump trucks. I didn't know that there were that many dump trucks in the world." He is also haunted by not knowing how many of the people that had passed him every day in the lobby on their way to work did not survive. With the World Trade Center gone, there was no place to go back to see familiar faces coming and going.

Captain Whitaker attended as many memorial services for his fellow officers as he could. Others would come up and thank him. He would ask, "What for?" and they would respond, "You saved my life!" Sometimes their stories would trigger a memory, but often he had no recollection of the incidents they would relate.

PAPD Sergeant Alan T. DeVona

On the morning of September 11, 2001, Sergeant DeVona made an arrest of a man aggressively soliciting money and charged him with disorderly conduct and resisting arrest.[31] Two Port Authority Police officers processed the arrest, one of whom was Police Officer Uhuru Houston. As DeVona was leaving WTC Five and preparing to go down to complete related paperwork, he heard an explosion. The building rocked violently. He immediately called for emergency PAPD units to respond. Officer Anthony

---

31   Lieutenant Alan DeVona, interview with the author.

Basic and DeVona stepped outside, and Basic reported over the radio, "Possible aircraft hit the upper ten stories of the North Tower!"

DeVona observed that a plane had struck the tower, but he thought that it was a private plane. He did not comprehend that it was a terrorist attack. He directed officers Murray, Brady, and Maggett at the police desk to contact every available unit in the city and contact the central police desk to initiate a full mobilization. He ordered the officers to prepare for the evacuation of the North Tower. He then went onto the plaza, where he saw balls of fire falling from the sky. As he and Police Officer Basic ran across the plaza, they realized that they should have gone through the building, as they had to dodge bodies and building parts falling from the sky. They went into the North Tower to the predesignated command center.

DeVona stepped out onto the VIP Plaza adjoining the tower, where he was shocked to find bodies scattered about. He doesn't know if these were "jumpers" or passengers that were on the plane. He saw a woman standing in the lobby holding on to her purse. She was severely burned. When a fire truck arrived with Chief Pfeiffer, he escorted the woman to the firefighters. Then he went back into the command center to coordinate the rescue effort with FDNY Chiefs Pfeiffer and Hayden. Chief Pfeiffer asked DeVona which stairwell would be best to use, and DeVona replied, "Stairwell B—it goes all the way to the top; the other two end at the seventy-sixth floor." Firefighters started up the stairs.

Emergency calls started coming in from the Windows on the World restaurant, where people were trapped. Sgt. DeVona replied that firefighters were on their way up. Meanwhile, Port Authority police were evacuating people from the lower floors through the Church Street exit near the police desk in World Trade Center Building Five. As more PAPD officers arrived, DeVona assigned them to duties, some to respond to the police desk, others to assist in the evacuation. Two six-man teams of NYPD officers from an Emergency Services Unit (ESU) arrived and followed DeVona's suggestion that they go into the North Tower to assist in rescue operations. A PAPD ESU team, also with six men, arrived and he directed them to also go into the North Tower.

DeVona heard explosions. He looked toward the FDNY firefighters in the lobby. Their heads would turn toward the canopy outside of the building as they heard the explosions. DeVona finally realized that the noises were the sounds of bodies hitting the canopy over the entranceway of the building. Blood splattered like rain, and soon covered the windows.

Port Authority Superintendent of Police Fred Morrone told Sergeant DeVona that he was going upstairs. As he and Inspector Anthony Infante headed up, Infante glanced over at DeVona and smiled, as if to say, "Don't worry! We'll be all right."

Amidst the chaos a report came in that there was another plane inbound, probably due to the report of the hijacked aircraft headed toward Washington, D.C. Then another report came in of a possible missile fired from the rooftop of the Woolworth building. DeVona asked his police desk to check with the NYPD for verification, and it was found to be false.

Fifteen police officers, firefighters and civilians were standing near the thirty-foot-long command desk when they heard what sounded like the eerie rumbling of an approaching train. Not knowing what it was, DeVona looked toward the mezzanine and was shocked to see an ominous black cloud coming toward the window. He jumped under the four-foot-high desk as all the windows were blown out and a tornado-like wind tore through the building. DeVona was shielded from the flying debris but was engulfed in the cloud of dust. Then everything went black. He was coughing violently. His life did not flash before his eyes. He didn't think about God. In his blackened world he was thinking, "I'm going to die by choking to death! A stupid way to go—not like you're dying trying to save someone or doing something meaningful."

As the dust settled, he blew his nose and tried to get on the radio. There was no communication. He turned on his powerful Streamlight flashlight, and it sliced a beam of light through the darkness. He saw a man and a woman, one—he doesn't remember which—with a foot injury. In the building where he worked, he didn't know where he was. He said a quick prayer and led the pair, the injured person's arm around his shoulder, to the left, feeling his way along a wall. They stumbled over a ground-level window frame into the street, where he ran into a fire truck in the darkness. As the three worked their way to the north, the black of night slowly turned to gray. As they walked, it got lighter until they could see. They met an EMS crew, and DeVona turned the pair over to them.

When the air cleared, he turned around and looked back. He saw the skeleton of what had been the South Tower, the first time he realized the building had fallen. He met Inspector Timothy Norris, who was in tears.

19

Norris said, "There must have been thousands of people killed!" DeVona replied, "Whatever they did to us, we'll get back at them!"

Captain Anthony Whitaker, Sergeant Alan DeVona, and Alan Reiss, a Port Authority civilian, were on West and Vesey streets when Reiss said, "Building One (the North Tower) is going to fall!" Moments later, the building started to tremble, and then it slowly fell, picking up speed as each floor crashed through the one below. Reiss said, "Cover up!" and the group ducked down. It wasn't as scary this time. They knew what to expect. When the air cleared they headed north and broke into a high school, where a group of people, primarily PAPD officers, congregated. Their cell phones weren't working, so they found a pay phone and a firefighter was able to get through to his family. The firefighter took the names of DeVona and some of the others and asked the person that he was speaking with to call their families to let them know they were all right.

Two police officers from LaGuardia or JFK airport said that they had to go back to the site. Chief William Hall stood up on a table with a bullhorn and said, "Give me your attention! I'm in charge here and no one is going back until I tell you to go back!" The Port Authority policemen then went north to the Manhattan Community College on West Street and Duane Street, where they set up a command post in the gym.

Police Officer Houston, the man processing the arrest when the first plane struck the North Tower, was most likely killed when the South Tower fell, because his body was recovered in the corridor of Building Four next to the South Tower. One of the two NYPD ESU teams and the PAPD ESU team that Sergeant DeVona directed into the North Tower were all killed. Superintendent of Police Fred Morrone and Inspector Anthony Infante were also among those that fell. The people in the Windows of the World restaurant that called for help after the North Tower was first hit all died.

Anthony R. Whitaker was later promoted to deputy chief of the Port Authority Police Department and retired in December 2010.

Patrol Sergeant Alan DeVona was promoted to lieutenant in June 2002. But he was deeply troubled by internal demons created by memories of the officers that were lost—many good friends following his instructions. He tried to project the image of strength, but he found himself overreacting to situations and breaking into a cold sweat when facing such things as bomb threats, which were not uncommon. He had great difficulty sleeping. The memories of decomposing bodies and the stench of death were constant reminders of the horrors of 9/11. His family life suffered as he poured himself into his work. Then on March 1, 2003, he felt a crushing blow. A female Port Authority sergeant, experiencing personal problems, went into the restroom of the New York City Port Authority bus terminal and blew her brains out. DeVona took charge of the gruesome scene, secured her weapon, recovered the body, took the necessary photographs, and supervised the transfer to medical authorities. While she did not have a role on 9/11, her suicide overwhelmed Lieutenant DeVona. On April 15, 2003, he worked his last shift as an active police supervisor. He went on medical leave due to post-traumatic stress disorder and retired on September 4, 2004.

For years, hopelessness and depression consumed DeVona. He gained weight until he weighed 265 pounds. For two years he was heavily medicated, but when he determined it wasn't helping, he talked to his doctor and they discontinued the medication for depression. His wife and three children were troubled by his behavior but never gave up on him. At last, Alan DeVona considered that the only way out of his despondence would be to end his life. These thoughts had weighed heavily on him soon after 9/11/01. Then, almost five years later, he called Ed Finnegan, a retired police officer friend, a heroic figure on 9/11 responsible for saving many lives that day. Ed saved another life that day when he discussed the ramifications of the act that Alan was about to perform. Ed told Alan of the devastation that the family and friends of a suicide victim experienced. After their conversation, DeVona's strength of character came through. He decided, in his words, "to be the master of my demons and to never allow them to rule me." He went to work memorializing the lost heroes of the PAPD and constructed a memorial to them in his backyard, planting thirty-seven holly trees, one for each of the PAPD officers killed on 9/11. He lost weight. He understood that his depression had been destroying his family, and he worked to improve his relationship with them. His medication now only consists of Xanax to control panic attacks and Ambien to help him sleep better. (He states that "sleep is a gift.") He acknowledges that while he is not yet out of the forest, he now has a compass and a flashlight.

DeVona was in contact with other people from the Port Authority who were deeply troubled. Friends, knowing of his recovery, told him of others suffering from depression. Recognizing their symptoms, he tracked them down. He told them how his life had balanced on a razor's edge and expressed his fears of where they were headed. He went on to describe the impact that taking one's own life had on those around them. He told of the police sergeant that killed herself at the bus terminal. He delineated the effect that it had on him.

On December 20, 2009, Alan DeVona received a phone call from a jubilant man. He had met the man in October 2007 when he and retired 9/11/01 First Responder Officer Eric Bulger were building a reflection pond at the 9/11 memorial that Eric had built.

Eric told Alan that the man still worked for the Port Authority and was still deeply troubled by the loss of his friends on 9/11. "Alan, will you please speak to him?"

When they spoke, Alan recognized the signs of impending doom from the look on the man's face and the words he spoke. It was like looking into a mirror of the past. DeVona spoke bluntly to him and told him about the horrors he overcame when he realized the consequences, and that it was not his decision, but God's. The man said, thankfully, that no one had ever spoken to him before so directly.

After their conversation, during which they wept together, DeVona repeatedly told him, "Don't you do it!"

The man decided to go on living. Now, just before Christmas, he had found his place in life, through faith in God, and was enjoying life, his family, and his grandchildren. He then told Alan that on the day they had met, he had already decided he would end his life that day. He asked Alan what he thought of his news. Alan DeVona told him that conversation was the best Christmas present that he had ever received.

Statue of Rick Rescorla-photo courtesy of Dan Hill

Chapter Three
—Rick Rescorla

"Today is a day to be proud to be an American. Tomorrow the world will be looking at you!"

Rick Rescorla on September 11, 2001, as he supervised his company's evacuation of the South Tower

Cyril (he disliked the name and later changed it to "Rick") Rescorla was born in Hayle, a Cornwall seaport on the southwest coast of England, in 1939.[32] During his childhood, this region of England was used to marshal American troops preparing to invade Normandy. As a boy in 1942–43, Rick became fascinated with American soldiers who were going in convoys to a training area near his home. Once, the American soldiers held a party for the children, and another time Rick even got a ride in a jeep. He admired these friendly American soldiers as they trained for the grim business of combat. This admiration was to become a major factor in shaping his future.

When he came of age, Rick joined the British army initially as an infantry paratrooper with the British First Parachutist Regiment. Then, after first serving in British Army Intelligence in Cyprus, he joined the Colonial Police Force in Northern Rhodesia, now Zambia, but a British territory in 1961.

---

32   Daniel Hill and Susan Rescorla interviews with the author.

The CIA had hired Daniel Hill to pose as a mercenary working for the independence of Katanga in the Congo. Dan was selected because of his previous experience in the U.S. Army Ranger School and as a U.S. Army undercover agent who infiltrated into Hungary, smuggling weapons for "freedom fighters" during that country's ill-fated 1956 revolution. Dan, who spoke fluent German, sat in the back of a truck loaded with cases of beer concealing high-powered World War II German Mauser sniper rifles he was bringing to rebel Hungarians. Passing checkpoints, Dan let the freedom fighters answer questions while he sat unobtrusively in the rear.

When Dan's role as a Katangan mercenary ended (because American and European interests withdrew their support) he purchased a small car and drove to Northern Rhodesia. He stopped at a small town to watch a rugby match. After the game, the winning team, whose star was Rick Rescorla, went to a local pub to celebrate their victory.

Dan introduced himself to Rick and said, "Good game! I'd like to buy you a beer."

Rick replied, "You're a Yank!" and the two started on the road to become lifelong friends.

Rick offered Dan a place to stay, and after a few days, Dan joined the Rhodesian Colonial Police Force while still working for the CIA as an independent contractor. The colonists wanted to secede but the Rhodesian government threatened military action if they tried.

After a time, Great Britain, which supported the government, prepared to send in the British Army. Rick and Dan, not wanting to fight against Rick's countrymen, decided to leave Rhodesia and, in 1962, went to England. Rick joined the Metropolitan London Police Academy and was assigned to the Scotland Yard Flying Squad, a SWAT-type organization. Dan returned to the United States and started a construction business in Nevada.

They remained in contact, and both prospered. After about a year, however, they were bored and missed military life. They, as Dan said, made a joint decision to "dump civilian life, enlist in the U.S. Army, and apply for Officer Candidate School (OCS)."

Dan, now married, moved his wife and two small children to New Jersey near his wife's parents. Rick, with Dan as his sponsor and expressing intent to join the U.S. Army, immigrated to the United States. Dan had been an enlisted aide for General Hugh P. Harris in 1957 who was now the commanding general of the U.S. Continental Army Command. Because of the men's exceptional experience and backgrounds, General Harris gave them his support and both Dan and Rick were able to join the U.S. Army under an option to attend OCS after successful completion of basic training.

Dan was required to repeat basic training since he had been out of the Army for three and a half years. They were in the same basic training class at Fort Dix, New Jersey, and, because of their prior military service, were soon made "acting NCOs" even though they were privates (E-2). They helped shape new recruits into soldiers. At night they studied endlessly, not basic training material, but military lore (Von Clausewitz' *On War* and works on Napoleon, German Generals Rommel and Guderian, North Vietnamese General Giap, and Mao Tse Tung, for example) that one would find at the Army's Command and General Staff College or the Army War College—advanced military courses that promising lieutenant colonels and colonels aspire to attend. They vigorously applied themselves to physical conditioning regimens, exercise, and swimming. The two would run five miles with fifty-pound packs full of sand on their backs. When they arrived at OCS at Fort Benning, Georgia, Dan in July, Rick in November of 1964, they already far surpassed the physical conditioning level that graduates were required to attain.

With years of training, outstanding physical fitness, prior study, and military experience, OCS was "a fun time and a snap." Dan was two classes ahead of Rick, as Rick's application took longer to process because he was not yet an American citizen. Dan finished first in his OCS class and Rick finished in the top 10 percent in his. The two then went separate ways, although they maintained contact, even visiting each other in Vietnam.

Rick was assigned to the First Air Cavalry Division and Dan to the First Brigade (Separate), 101st Airborne Division. While his contemporaries played cards and read pocket books on the voyage to Vietnam, Rick studied the Vietnamese language. Wounded early in his tour, Lieutenant Rescorla could have been evacuated to the United States but went back the following day to lead his men.

When Rick asked why his platoon always got the more difficult and dangerous missions, Captain Diduryk,[33] his company commander, replied, "I want to get the job done."

---

33   Captain Diduryk was killed in action in 1968 during his second tour in Vietnam.

Later, in the fierce battle of the Ia Drang Valley, Rick established himself as a heroic platoon leader.

After that battle, General Hal Moore (then a lieutenant colonel), author of the book *We Were Soldiers Once, and Young* said of Rick, "He was the best platoon leader that I have ever known!"

During his tour in Vietnam, Rick earned a Silver Star, two Bronze Stars, and a Vietnamese Cross of Gallantry with Gold Star—all awards for bravery in combat, in addition to his Purple Heart.

Returning to the United States a few months apart, Rick and Dan were assigned as senior tactical officers at OCS. Rick, now eligible, became a U.S. citizen in 1967.

"Rick was a sensitive and compassionate man," Dan Hill said. "He was too close to his troops, knew too much about them. Even though Rick's troops had the lowest killed-in-action (KIA) and wounded-in-action (WIA) rates, every casualty ate away at him."

He once told Dan, "The level of our inefficiency and incompetence is measured and paid for by the men who are killed or wounded."

Because of this, Rick left the active army in April 1968. He enrolled in the University of Oklahoma to study creative writing, while also joining the Oklahoma National Guard where he ran the Officer Candidate program.

He applied for a job teaching hand-to-hand combat to Drug Enforcement Agency (DEA) agents. The DEA recruiter told him he didn't stand a chance of getting that job because there were more qualified candidates. "More qualified?" Rescorla asked. "How are they more qualified?" The recruiter rattled off a list of people with awards for black belt karate, judo, etc. Rick said, "I'll tell you what. I have a bear pit not far from here that the National Guard uses. Come out there with your more qualified applicants and have us all jump into it. You will know who is most qualified when the last man standing climbs out." Rick was the last man standing and got the job.

He earned both bachelor's and master's degrees in literature, and a degree in law. Following this he taught law at the University of South Carolina, then he took a position in security with the Bank Administration Institute (BAI), which provided services for small banks. He soon established a reputation as a top-notch security professional and was hired by Continental Illinois Bank, the fifth largest bank in the nation, and in 1977 became vice president for security.

In this job, he discovered that a senior officer of the bank was spending a lot of money. This executive owned a large second home and expensive automobiles. He was taking his family on costly vacations to exotic ocean resorts. Rick's investigation revealed the officer was involved in fraudulent loans, costing Continental millions of dollars. Rick asked Dan, as a consultant, to assist in the investigation. They went to the Cayman Islands, where they obtained the records of the individuals involved. The evidence resulted in the bank official being charged, indicted, and convicted. As a result, the Treasury Department took over the bank in a high-profile seizure to prevent losses and erosion of public confidence.

Officials at Dean Witter then offered Rick a position as security director at their headquarters in New York. Rick moved to Morristown, New Jersey, and in 1985, Dean Witter moved to the South Tower of the World Trade Center. Later, when Dean Witter merged with Morgan Stanley in 1997, Rescorla became the director of security for Morgan Stanley, with his office still in the World Trade Center.

Rick Rescorla, now a colonel in the U.S. Army Reserve, moved from Chicago to New York City. Seeking a position with the New York Army National Guard, Rick filled out the necessary forms, brought in his military records, and took the other actions necessary to transfer from the Army Reserve to the National Guard. Soon after, a lieutenant colonel from the N.Y. National Guard headquarters called him to arrange an interview. Colonel Rescorla arrived at the National Guard headquarters in Albany, New York, at the appointed time. The same lieutenant colonel who had arranged the interview ushered him into a room where five full colonels were seated behind a long table. Rick reported to the colonel who was obviously in charge, who then asked Rick to be seated in the lone chair facing the table.

The colonel in charge welcomed Rick and said, "Well, let's get down to the business at hand."

Rick then excused himself for interrupting and asked, "Just what is the business at hand here, gentlemen?"

The colonel, president of the Board of Officers, replied, "Oh, haven't you heard? We're here to evaluate you for your request to transfer to the National Guard."

He looked over the room, inspecting the pressed uniforms, the well-shined shoes, the polished brass, and the silver eagles on the shoulders of the members of the Board of Officers. He saw that not one of the "evaluators" wore a patch denoting service in combat on the right shoulder of his army green uniform. Not one wore an award for valor.

Rick said, "Gentlemen, there is nobody present here that is qualified to evaluate me."

There was a short embarrassed silence, followed by some obvious indecision and mumbling among the Board of Officers.

Finally, the president of the board said, "Colonel Rescorla, will you excuse us for a few minutes?"

Rick replied, "Certainly, gentlemen," and returned to the outside office.

About fifteen minutes later, the president came out and asked Rick to return to the meeting. Now, there were six officers behind the table. The new addition was wearing the two shiny silver stars of a major general—the adjutant general of the State of New York. Rick reported to the general and was again asked to take a seat.

The general spoke: "Colonel Rescorla, you are correct. By military or academic or civilian achievements, nobody here, including me, is qualified to evaluate you. Based on experience and proven achievement if you were to join the New York National Guard, you would be more qualified to wear these stars that are on my shoulder than I am. What do you suggest we do in this situation?"

Rick replied, "Sir, unless the governor is prepared to make me his adjutant general and you are willing to change those two stars for one, I believe the only option left is for me to retire. I have over twenty years' military service as the record shows."

The general then said, "I see that your record fails to point out one of your obvious fine qualities, Colonel Rescorla."

"And what would that quality be, sir?" Colonel Rescorla asked.

"You possess the biggest set of balls I've ever even heard of," smiled the General. "My staff will be at your disposal to expedite your retirement papers."

Colonel Rick Rescorla thanked the general, saluted, and returned to his work in the World Trade Center. Rescorla retired from the Army in 1990 with the rank of colonel.

Dan, in the meantime, had retired from the Army and moved to St. Augustine, Florida, where he worked as a contractor building homes, restaurants, and other buildings in Florida. The two men spoke frequently by telephone and visited each other often.

Then, on 9/11, the hijacked aircraft struck the North Tower. Designers of the buildings, construction of which was completed in 1973, had engineered them to withstand a direct hit by a Boeing 707, the largest commercial passenger plane in service at that time. Morgan Stanley Dean Witter was the single largest tenant in the South Tower, with employees occupying offices between floors forty-three and seventy-four. As employees began assembling to evacuate the building, an announcement was heard that this building was not threatened and everyone should stay in their offices.[34]

Rick, thinking that the North Tower might collapse into the South Tower, ignored the announcement and directed all employees to evacuate the building using stairwells, not elevators. Rick, whose office was located on the forty-fourth floor, was using that floor as an assembly point for people working above that level. He directed workers to proceed to the stairwell as he had planned and the company had rehearsed. All but a few employees did as instructed, pairing up, assisting those that needed help and starting down the narrow stairwells. Rick used his megaphone to urge people to keep moving but to pace themselves. Eighteen minutes after the first tower was struck, the second hijacked aircraft struck the South Tower at 9:03 a.m. Rick was knocked off his feet. He got up and as the building shook and panic ensued, Rick encouraged frightened employees to stay calm. His staff quickly located a stairwell clear of smoke, and Rick directed everyone to use it.

Rick started upstairs to ensure people were evacuating properly. He was seen by one employee around the fiftieth floor. Helping each other, the Morgan Stanley employees made their way down with Rick encouraging them with his megaphone. Finally, they reached the ground floor and safety. After Morgan Stanley employees were outside in relative safety, Rick returned to assist other occupants of the Tower, many of whom had initially

34   While evacuation orders had been issued by Port Authority Police, communications problems resulted in the order not being disseminated throughout the WTC. Orders to remain in offices were most likely issued by civilian fire safety directors appointed by various tenants.

followed directives to remain in their offices. His deputy, Wesley Mercer, a veteran of the Korean and Vietnam wars, went with him.

Later Rick was seen on the tenth floor by his friend John Olson, a Morgan Stanley regional director.[35] Olson urged Rick to leave the building, and Rick said that first he had to get everyone out. Rick, using his cell phone, called Dan Hill and the two briefly talked. Dan also urged Rick to leave the building. Dan told him that the South Tower had been hit in a more vulnerable spot and would probably collapse before the North Tower. Rick replied that he had to make one more sweep and didn't have time to talk further. Rick called his wife, Susan. She was in tears. She said Rick was in his "military mode" and asked her to quit crying.

He told her, "I have to get people out of the building but I want you to know that whatever happens, you have made my life!"

She replied, "And you have made my life!"

That was the last time they talked, and Susan realized that this was probably their last conversation.

Rick called Dan Hill and asked him to phone Susan and try to calm her down. As Susan and Dan were talking, they watched the scene unfold on television. In horror, they saw the South Tower collapse.

Of the 2,700 Morgan Stanley employees, thirteen—including Rick, his deputy, Wesley Mercer, and four security guards that reported to Rick—died when the tower collapsed. At least one executive chose to ignore Rick's direction and decided that he would use an elevator since some elevators were still working. This executive had adamantly refused to leave during the 1993 bombing, claiming he had important work to do. At that time, he required his secretary to stay. This time she refused and left the building. The executive was never seen again. His secretary made it to safety.

Rick once gave Dan Hill his definition of a friend: "A friend—if he needs money, you give him all you have or can beg, borrow, or steal. A friend—if he is trapped and under fire, you tell him to hold on; you will join him and die fighting by his side. A friend will do the same for you."

Susan Rescorla, Dan Hill, and Fred McBee formed a foundation and raised money for a statue of Rick Rescorla to be placed at Fort Benning, Georgia. This statue was based on the photograph of Rick during the Ia Drang battle and that appeared on the cover of the book We Were Soldiers

---

35   Heart of a Soldier, p.261.

Once, and Young. Susan, Dan, and Fred unveiled the statue at the dedication. The statue was later moved to the Fort Benning Walk of Heroes and rededicated in a ceremony in which a ceremonial fire truck (number 343—the number of FDNY firefighters that perished on 9/11) that brought two I beams salvaged from the residue of the World Trade Center. These I-beams were implanted behind the statue of Rick Rescorla. Retired firefighter Danny Prince helped organize the trip and accompanied the convoy from Floyd Bennett Field in Brooklyn to Fort Benning, Georgia. As the convoy consisting of the ceremonial fire truck and fifteen to twenty motorcycles proceeded along the route, radio stations announced the progress of the group and it was met and escorted by police cars as they entered each state. One lane of the highway was closed as they passed with fire trucks, police cars, and cheering people lined up along the way on the overpasses and alongside the road.

Dan Hill, Rick's lifelong friend, said, "God, how I miss him! A part of me died with Rescorla. I am now half the man I was when I was with him during all of our time together."

Susan and Rick had visited Cornwall together and climbed over boulders and hills to the highest point in Cornwall, the home town of Rick's youth. He was so captivated by this place and its beauty, where one could see for miles over Cornwall, that he told her that when he passed on he wanted to be cremated and his remains spread in that area. Twice in the month before 9/11, however, they visited the Raptor Trust, a New Jersey haven for injured or orphaned birds. Rick told her he had changed his mind and wanted his remains scattered at the bird sanctuary. She made light of his comment and said that she didn't think that was going to happen anytime soon. Rick insisted, "I'm serious. Listen to me. I want my remains scattered here!" He said, "Are you listening?" Startled by the intensity of this conversation, she said, "I am listening!" Susan feels that he was expressing a premonition of his death. Soon after she wrote a note saying:

"In loving memory of my sweetheart, my soul mate forever, my Celtic hero in life and our hero in death. Just like the eagle, you have spread your wings and have soared into eternity."

Rick's remains were never found. Susan does not attend ceremonies at the site of the World Trade Center as she feels that Rick is not at the site but has flown into space. In her mind, Rick lives on in her heart. Instead, she has dedicated an eagle sanctuary at the Raptor Trust. Susan commissioned a life-sized statue of an eagle which stands watch over the eagle's home to assure that Rick Rescorla will not be forgotten. The note that she had written earlier is inscribed on the plaque in front of the eagle.

Susan, Mervyn Sullivan (Rick's friend from Cornwall), and Mervyn's wife, Jan, again climbed over the steep trail and boulders to Trencrom, the highest point in Cornwall. There, Mervyn held up a Cornish flag and, with a galelike wind blowing wildly, he bid goodbye to Rick in Cornish, then released the flag into the wind. The flag soared and sailed out over the land that Rick Rescorla so loved. Many more have memorialized this courageous man. The Cornish Parliament paid tribute to Rick by referring to him as "our King Arthur." Hayle, his home town in Cornwall, has erected a monument with a carved eagle on top dedicated to its native son. A special meditation garden has been constructed at the Pentol grammar school, which he attended in Hayle. Susan Rescorla was a guest of Prince Charles at his home in Highgrove, England, where Rick was honored. Princess Anne hosted a ceremony in Grosvenor Square, London, honoring him and the eighty people who were born in the United Kingdom and were murdered on 9/11.

There was a military tribute in Holmdel, New Jersey, where the first Vietnam Memorial was constructed. The FBI, CIA, international banking community, private security firms, firefighters, policemen, NASA, the California Assembly, the New York Giants, and the Tribute Center across from the WTC site all have paid tribute to Rick's heroic, lifesaving actions. He has been the subject of many newspaper and magazine articles. His bravery and foresight have been shown on TV and documented in the Congressional Record. A base in Afghanistan has been named "Forward Operating Base Rescorla." Susan is frequently asked to make presentations in Rick's memory in the United States and England. A foundation has been established by Dan Hill and others in St. Augustine, Florida, in the names of Rick Rescorla and Private First Class Leo Chase, a Vietnam War casualty, providing scholarship funds to qualified, needy students as they complete high school.

After a couple of years, Susan moved to a small nearby town where everyone knows one another and many homes were built in the 1700s. The tiny post office, one of the oldest in the country, posts newspaper clippings of local people's doings. Most importantly, there is less stress in this small community. Susan Rescorla, in referring to the 9/11 Task Force Report, asks that people not try to pass the blame for what happened on September 11, 2001, but rather that they take responsibility and correct mistakes that were made.

When Usama Bin Laden was killed on May 1st, 2011, Susan Rescorla said, "This was truly a moment for saying "Today is a day to be proud to be an American!"

South Tower falling-NYPD 911 photo

Chapter Four
Stairwell B

"Am I dead? Am I going to heaven?"

Lieutenant Jim McGlynn

Captain Jay Jonas

Captain Jay Jonas was the first firefighter in his family, having joined the FDNY in November 1979.[36] During the 1993 World Trade Center bombing, he was a lieutenant in Ladder 11. Later that year he was promoted to captain and transferred to Ladder Company 6 in Chinatown, not far from the Twin Towers.

He consciously thought, "The trade center is still around. It could become a target again. Oh well. I'll be all right." It turns out he was wrong.

At 8:47 a.m. on September 11, Captain Jonas was in his firehouse when one of his men saw a large, low-flying plane glide across the sky. Someone in the firehouse shouted into the intercom that a large plane had hit the North Tower of the World Trade Center. He knew that as the second alarm company, they would be immediately dispatched, so he and his five-man crew "geared up" to anticipate the call. They pulled out of the firehouse when the call came in moments later, and in about five minutes were at the site. As they were driving toward the towers, the scene was chaos, with

---

36   Except as otherwise noted this Chapter is based on interviews by the author with Chiefs Jonas and McGlynn, Captain Rohan and Lieutenant Kross.

thousands of pedestrians running from the site. Captain Jonas reflected that it was sad to have such a terrible accident on such a bright, sunny day, where the sky was so blue that it looked artificial. They parked near the North Tower and began pulling equipment off the truck when pieces of the building began falling all around them. They quickly sought shelter under a pedestrian bridge. Jonas rushed to the lobby command post, where he met both Battalion Chief Joe Pfeiffer, who saw the plane hit, and Deputy Chief Pete Hayden, the first chiefs on the scene. Jonas was working for Chief Hayden, who later became the chief of the department, and knew he was a very capable and confident man.

"You hope that you can live up to his standards," he said. "He is an excellent leader, a guy you want to emulate."

Despite the chaos, Chiefs Hayden and Pfeiffer remained calm. "They knew what they were doing and they instilled a sense of confidence in me."

Lieutenant Jim McGlynn

Jim McGlynn is a native New Yorker, born in the Bronx. On that day, Lieutenant McGlynn had been in the New York Fire Department for sixteen years, assigned to Engine Company 39. When his fire station learned that a plane had hit one of the towers, they turned on the television and saw the gaping hole in the North Tower. They immediately realized that on this beautiful, clear day, a large commercial aircraft hitting a major New York City landmark was not an accident, but a terrorist act. Engine 39 was dispatched almost immediately on the third alarm,[37] with McGlynn leading his crew of five people and a High-Rise Unit—a specially equipped truck with extra equipment and massive fans to vent fires in high-rise buildings.

Surprisingly there was almost no traffic as Engine 39, with sirens blaring, rushed towards the World Trade Center during rush hour just minutes later. As they approached the two buildings, he saw what he thought was another explosion in the North Tower, but quickly realized that a second plane had struck the South Tower.

---

37   A third alarm will normally result in four additional engine companies and one additional ladder company for a total of twelve engines and six ladders committed. In this catastrophe many more were committed.

Lieutenant Mickey Kross

Lieutenant Mickey Kross, of Engine 16, first heard an official report over the department radio that a plane had crashed into the World Trade Center. Kross did not even consider that it might have been a large commercial aircraft. Moments later his friend, Christine Gonga, who lived three blocks north of the Twin Towers, called to tell him that she'd heard a very loud noise and the windows in her building were rattling. He told her not to worry, that a small plane had hit one of the Twin Towers and that he would meet her for dinner that evening. At 8:50 a.m., his unit was dispatched to the site, also responding with six men.

Lieutenant Glenn Rohan

Lieutenant Glenn Rohan, Ladder 43, was watching the early reports of a plane hitting the North Tower, and his first thought was that it was a small plane. Minutes later Rohan was doing a roll call of his firehouse when they heard that a second plane had hit the World Trade Center. His wife called, and he told her that it was going to be a long day, that he didn't think this was an accident. He promised to call her later.

Glenn's father had been a police officer with the New York Police Department for thirty-four years. One of his seven sisters was the first female police officer in the Bronx and served for twenty-seven years. But Glenn had always wanted to be a firefighter. While he'd had a good job with Xerox, he wanted to do something more rewarding and meaningful. He liked people, and the New York Fire Department had always seemed to be a place where he would have rewarding work with people that he liked.

Engine 53, collocated with Rohan's company, was dispatched within five minutes of the second plane hitting. Rohan ordered his company to get ready and they loaded on the truck, anticipating an immediate call. One man who had finished his tour asked if he could stay, as they were expecting a "total recall," requiring all available personnel to report for duty. Within five minutes the shrill "tone alarm," which alerts firefighters that they are being dispatched, sounded. Rohan said, "OK, let's go!" and the truck, with one extra man, pulled out of the firehouse.

Rohan was astounded when he read his dispatch instructions—his company was ordered to Madison Avenue and Forty-First Street to free a pedestrian who was stuck in a subway turnstile!

He thought to himself, "You have to be kidding! The WTC has been hit by two airplanes and you are sending us to free someone stuck in a turnstile!"

But orders are orders and Ladder 43 headed to Madison and Forty-First Street.

They freed the man and Lieutenant Rohan called the dispatcher, asking, "Do you want us to respond downtown?"

The reply was, "No. Ladder 43, return to quarters." Here was the biggest fire in the history of the department and they weren't going to be allowed to go.

The chauffeur (fire engine driver) asked him, "What do you want to do?"

Lieutenant Rohan replied, "I can't just go, we're not assigned. Just start heading back, I'll get us there."

Reluctantly the crew started back up Third Avenue. Before travelling more than a couple of blocks, frantic messages started coming in on the department radio. Someone was on the radio calling for help and the crew heard "collapse" and "trapped"! They heard the dispatcher trying to find out what was happening in the confusion, then, suddenly, the calls for help stopped and the only voice heard was the dispatcher trying to contact first the caller, then other units that had been dispatched to the WTC. When the dispatcher didn't get a response, he asked for "any unit operating downtown."

Lieutenant Rohan responded, "Ladder 43, I'm in Manhattan at Forty-Eighth Street and Third Avenue. Let me go to the box (an automatic reporting station where assigned firefighters sign in) and I'll let you know what's happening."

The dispatcher approved and Ladder 43, meeting no traffic, arrived in the area in about six minutes.

Captain Jonas

While Rohan was heading downtown, Jonas's crew waited outside the North Tower while he went to get orders. As he was waiting at the command post in the lobby of the North Tower, he saw a large black shadow out of the corner of his eye and then heard a loud explosion and saw debris showering down from the South Tower. At first he thought it was something that had happened in the North Tower. Then a man came running up shouting that a second plane had hit the South Tower. What had been a noisy lobby now was silent. No one said a word. Suddenly, there was no doubt that this was a terrorist act. Jonas stood among a group of firefighters from Rescue Squad One, located on Forty-Third Street four miles away, also waiting for orders from Chief Hayden. In the near silence, one of the Squad One men said, "We may not live through today!" The men agreed, shook hands all around, and said to each other, "I hope to see you later."

Jay Jonas was next in line to receive orders, and he said to Chief Hayden, "You know that a second plane just hit the South Tower?"

Chief Hayden closed his eyes and said, "I know; just take your men and go upstairs and do the best that you can for search and rescue."

Captain Jonas saluted Chief Hayden and walked over to his crew.

He told them, "Here's what we have to do. We are going up into this building; our mission is search and rescue. We have to do it on foot because the elevators have been exposed to fire."

Each man carried about one hundred pounds of equipment on a warm, late summer day, and he was asking them to climb countless flights of stairs in the humid heat.

He said, "OK, guys. They are trying to kill us. Let's go!"

He heard a voice say, "OK, Cap. We're with you."

Lieutenant Kross

As Lieutenant Kross's crew approached the World Trade Center thirteen minutes after being dispatched, he saw that seven or eight floors of the North Tower were on fire. As they parked their fire engine, the second plane slammed into the South Tower. Kross saw a huge ball of fire as the plane hit, but thought it was another explosion in the North Tower, as he could not see the South Tower. Steel and debris rained down like a meteor shower. In the lobby, Kross reported to Chief Joe Pfeiffer, the first chief on the scene, for orders. He saw badly burned people there, which he later learned was because flaming jet fuel had poured down through the elevator shafts. His unit, Engine 16, was instructed to team up with Engine

Company 1, Kross's old unit, and ascend the B Stairwell to a command post on the twenty-third floor. They decided to ascend with one officer in front and one in back. Kross took the rear and they trudged the long climb to the twenty-third floor. When they reached the twenty-second floor, Kross ordered his men to take a break while he went up to the next level to find the chief at the Command Post.

Lieutenant Rohan

When Ladder 43 arrived downtown, Lieutenant Rohan hadn't heard any reports of the South Tower having fallen, but he could only see one tower. Seeing the huge cloud that had formed, he thought that the South Tower had collapsed, but not being familiar with the area, he thought it might be possible that the North Tower was blocking the other one from his view. The area was congested with fire trucks, ambulances, and police cars, and they were forced to park their rig about ten blocks away. Rohan instructed his men to take extra oxygen cylinders, but only essential tools and ropes.

They also shed some of their heavier protective clothing. "We're going to do a lot of walking. This is going to be bad! We have to find Engine 53 (their companion company) and we are going to be here all day."

As Ladder 43 was two blocks away from the North Tower, the crew initially heard a muffled noise as the giant structure started to fall. This was followed seconds later by a massive explosion as the building collapsed to ground level and below. The men turned and started to run, realizing that if the tower fell to the north, they were doomed. The crew ducked into a school yard and put on their masks as they watched the cloud approach. Although the building fell in the opposite direction, the men were still enveloped in the thick gray cloud of pulverized Sheetrock, concrete, and other materials now rushing through the streets of downtown Manhattan.

Lieutenant Rohan said, "It was so thick it was like living in oatmeal!"

The firefighters had two-hundred-foot-long "search ropes" to be used in fires so that firefighters could find their way out of dangerous situations in low visibility. They tied one of the ropes to a pole and started moving through the "oatmeal" cloud. When they reached the end of the first rope, they tied on a second. Lieutenant Rohan looked back and saw fifteen additional firefighters and policemen, who obviously thought that this was a good idea, lined up on the rope behind his crew.

Lieutenant McGlynn

Meanwhile, Lieutenant McGlynn and his company reported to Peter Ganci, chief of the New York City Fire Department, who had arrived and was in the street near the Twin Towers. Chief Ganci ordered McGlynn and his men to the base of the North Tower to "hook up" with Engine Company 65 and proceed up the B Stairwell. The scene was chaotic, with civilians escaping and firefighters organizing and starting up the stairwells. McGlynn understood that with no clear orders, he must decide what his crew needed to do as they went up into the conflagration. As they left, Peter Ganci's aide warned them to be careful entering the building because they were in danger of being hit by people jumping from the Towers. (The first firefighter killed that day was hit by the ricochet of a shattered bone from a person who had jumped to his or her death.) As they cautiously approached the tower, they could hear a loud "thud, like a drum" and when they looked for the source of the noise, they would see in horror what looked like a pile of clothing, as the bodies of "jumpers" disintegrated upon impact with the concrete below. With the North Tower elevators disabled, the crews of Ladder 6 (Jonas's company) and Engine 39, although not together, started the long climb up the B Stairwell as directed. To conserve energy for the climb and to check the condition of their men carrying heavy loads of tools, masks, and oxygen containers while wearing heavy firefighting clothing, both Jonas and McGlynn would stop about every ten floors to give the men a short break, take a head count, and make sure everyone was all right.

The stairwells were only wide enough for two people to walk side by side. While a column of firefighters was going up, a column of civilians was coming down.

Jonas said, "The people coming down were very orderly. They were happy to see us, and I later heard comments from people that when they saw us coming up, they knew that there was a way out of the building. I want to give those people a pat on the back. We're used to calamity—they are not. Some people were injured, some were burned, and others were helping them. If they had been out of control, it would have made our job a lot tougher."

Lieutenant Kross

While on the twenty-third floor, Mickey Kross heard a commotion in the C Stairwell. Among the people that were coming down the long, narrow stairwell was Josephine Harris, being helped by Joe Garcia, her supervisor at the Port Authority. Josephine had been hit by a car a couple of weeks earlier and was still recuperating. The two of them had slowly proceeded down fifty flights of stairs from the seventy-third floor. But she now seemed unable to proceed. Kross told them to go to Stairwell B, where he knew there were firefighters who would be able to assist them. They were reluctant to leave the stairwell, so he shouted at them, "Get over to Stairwell B!" They quickly departed as ordered, a move that probably saved their lives.

Captain Jonas

Near the twenty-seventh floor, Jonas turned around to take a head count of his men. Two men were missing, so he told the others to wait while he went back to check on them. He went back and found them two or three floors below. When they returned to the twenty-seventh floor they experienced something that they had never felt at any fire before. The building began to shake and sway back and forth, the lights went out for about thirty seconds, and they heard a very loud noise outside. Captain Billy Burke from Engine 21 was also on that floor, and Jonas asked him to check the windows on the south side of the building while he checked those on the north. All Captain Jonas could see on the north side was a white cloud of dust right up against the glass, and he thought that part of their building had collapsed. Billy Burke came back and, with a troubled face, said, "The South Tower just collapsed!"

Lieutenant McGlynn

At the same time, Jim McGlynn was taking a head count and crew check on the thirty-first floor when the building began to shake so violently that the men couldn't stand up. "We hit the floor! We thought that it was part of the North Tower we were in that had collapsed," he said. The building, suffering the effects of the collapse of the neighboring South Tower, continued to shake for about ten seconds.

When it stopped, McGlynn stood up and, finding Battalion Chief John Paolillo of Special Operations Command Battalion 11 nearby, asked, "Chief, what are we going to do?"

Paolillo replied, "Time to go!" and gave them the order to evacuate the building.

The Engine 39 firefighters left behind most of their gear, keeping only the most essential items, to expedite their evacuation, and then started down the long, narrow staircase. As they continued, Jim's crew helped people escape and told other firefighters that the evacuation order had been given.

Lieutenant Kross

Lieutenant Mickey Kross was on the twenty-third floor when the building suddenly shook so violently that he fell over. He initially thought that it might have been an elevator falling. Not able to find the chief at the command post, he headed back down to join his men on the twenty-second floor. Fortunately, firefighter Tim Marmion, Kross's second in command, had already received the evacuation order from FDNY Chief Picciotto and had started to lead the rest of the Engine 16 crew safely out of the tower. Kross then also started back down the stairwell.

Captain Jonas

Captain Jonas was aware they were in danger and that they would be lucky to get out. He told his men, "It's time for us to get out of here."

His crew surprised him, as they were reluctant to leave. It wasn't until later that he realized they didn't know the South Tower had fallen. In the days following 9/11, many of them came to him almost in tears, wondering how he had managed to stay calm. He said that he may have appeared calm on the outside but he was "screaming" on the inside.

While it was a terrifying situation, Jonas had developed the trait of speaking a bit more slowly and dropping his voice during emergency situations. "I didn't want to add to the stress."

Captain Jonas's crew immediately started down the narrow stairs. Other firefighters and civilians were on the stairs but they were moving quickly until they arrived near the twentieth floor. Jonas and his men found Josephine Harris standing in a doorway crying. With Joe Garcia's help, she had descended a few more flights of stairs after they met Lieutenant Mickey Kross. Jonas saw that both of them were exhausted.

One of Jonas' men, Thomas Falco, said, "Hey, Cap! What do we do with her?"

"I looked at Josephine, with every part of my being screaming at me in this situation," Jonas said. "We have to get out of this building," he thought. "Every second that we spend is one second closer to dying!"

Jonas knew there was no choice and said, "Bring her with us!"

He then signaled Billy Butler, one of his crew, to take her arm around his shoulder. Other men grabbed Butler's tools.

Jonas then shouted, "Stay together! We can't come back here looking for anyone."

They started down the stairs again and along the way passed Lieutenant Warchola of Ladder 5, also going down. Michael Warchola, fifty-one years old, had his retirement papers posted on the wall of his firehouse in Greenwich Village. He had become a firefighter in 1977 after being on the waiting list for five years.[38] Captain Jay Jonas, who in his younger days carpooled with Lieutenant Warchola, saw him assisting a man who was experiencing chest pains. Captain Jonas told him that it was time to go, but Lieutenant Warchola replied that he was working on the man and would be coming down shortly.

Their pace slowed now that they were assisting Josephine, literally step by step.

Captain Jonas was the last one of his crew, and he kept encouraging Billy Butler, "Can we move a little faster?"

---

38   Portraits, p. 526.

Butler would reply, "OK, Captain!" and do his best to pick up the pace.

The other men still were not aware that the other tower had collapsed. Twice, the Ladder 6 men stepped aside to let people behind them pass. Later, Jay Jonas was gratified to find that among those that they let pass were the men of Engine 28, who got out of the building only minutes before it fell. All survived.

Lieutenant McGlynn

McGlynn's Engine 39 crew also passed the men of Ladder 6 and descended to the lobby. Looking outside, they saw piles of rubble and twisted metal covered with powdery dust everywhere. Jim passed a chief standing in the lobby, directing people to safety. McGlynn describes it as one of the bravest things he had ever seen, the chief, standing in the darkness of the lobby, using his flashlight to quickly but calmly guide people to safety. Everyone knew the North Tower, in which he was standing, had been the first one hit and that the South Tower had already fallen.

"He knew that the clock was ticking on the North Tower," McGlynn said. He later learned that the man was Battalion Chief Richard Prunty.

Before leaving the building, Lieutenant McGlynn said to his men, "Let's do a roll call. You go in together and you come out together."

A roll call is standard procedure to make sure that everyone is accounted for. John Drum, one of his crew, was missing, so they went back into the stairwell to look for him, as they thought he might have gone back to help Captain Jay Jonas's company. They climbed two flights of stairs and didn't find Drum. They then concluded that he had gone ahead of them and left the building, which in fact he had done.

Captain Jonas

On the fourth floor, Josephine Harris fell to the floor and said she just couldn't go any further. She begged the men to leave her. The firefighters refused. Captain Jonas left the stairwell and broke into a room to search for a suitable chair to carry the woman down. Unfortunately, that floor was a mechanical floor rather than an office floor, and the only seats were a swivel chair and an overstuffed chair, neither of which would work. They would just have to haul her down the stairs, he thought.

Instilled in Jay Jonas throughout his career was never to run in a fire. Never, ever. But today, separated from his men and far from Stairwell B, he ran. About three feet from the stairwell door, the floor under him suddenly shook, forming little waves like ripples on a pond. The building was collapsing, he thought! He reached for the stairwell door and pulled it. It wouldn't budge. On his second attempt he forced it open and dove into the stairwell landing, rolling into a ball while covering his head as best he could. As the building floors pancaked far above him, crashing one on top of the other in quick succession, the deafening roar became progressively louder. Boom! Boom! Boom! The screech of twisting steel and the massive dust storm added to the chaos. As the building collapsed, the air beneath each floor above was compressed and rushed into the space below with hurricane force. Jonas, his crew, and the others in Stairwell B were being pelted with a torrent of airborne debris. Firefighter Matt Komorowski, waiting for Jonas on the fourth-floor landing, was lifted up by the tornado-like wind and thrown down three flights of stairs. Everyone else, including disabled Josephine, crouched down, covering their heads to protect themselves. As the stairwell shook and twisted, they thought, "This is it!" Everyone waited for the big boom and a massive piece of concrete to crush them. But it didn't happen. Instead, after a few seconds, there was only silence and darkness.

Mickey Kross had arrived at the third floor when he suddenly heard the tremendous noise of the collapse. He moved towards the railing to try to make himself as small as possible. Hurricane winds surged down the stairwell and picked him up. Debris hit him from all angles, the lights went out and the stairwell was plunged into total darkness. He prayed that the end would be quick. As suddenly as the chaos began, it ended, and he was covered with debris and engulfed by silence and darkness.

At the same time Jim McGlynn's men were nearby starting back down the stairs. The whole building shook violently. As the shaking worsened they heard a noise like a large, loud oncoming freight train. Then the boom! Boom! Boom! Each noise was louder than the one before as the floors were banging, crashing together, one on top of the other, as the building collapsed.

Like the others, McGlynn and his men couldn't stand up. Jim rolled into a fetal position, and said a couple of prayers.

His life didn't pass before his eyes as many people state when faced with sudden death, but, he thought, "There are too many things left to do in my life!"

As the floors of the building pancaked, one after another almost instantaneously, McGlynn and his men also felt the enormous rush of wind. Ten seconds later the shaking stopped. The building collapse, however, had created a vacuum, and a sudden onrush of wind blew back. To Jim it didn't make sense; it was "beyond reality." He had first felt a tremendous rush of downward air, and now he felt the same rush of air going up! The strange, eerie feeling in the now-total darkness, he thought, was like being in a black hole in outer space.

As Jim felt like he was almost being lifted by the gush of wind in almost total darkness, he asked himself, "Am I dead? Am I going to heaven?"

Aerial View of Ground Zero-photo courtesy of FDNY

Chapter Five
In the Rubble

"I'm coming for you, brother! I'm coming for you!"

Firefighter Cliff Stabner

When that rushing wind finally stopped a few seconds later, Lieutenant Jim McGlynn realized that he was still alive.[39] He found that although he was covered in debris and coated with powdery dust, he was basically all right. Battalion Chief Picciotto was close by. Captain Jonas, on the highest part of the stairwell, did a roll call. In near darkness in the smoke and dust, Jim could hear Captain Jonas as he called out to his group. One by one he could hear their voices as they answered him. Jonas was grateful that all of his men and Josephine had survived.

Once the collapse started, fear seemed to leave the people trapped in Stairwell B.

Many of them later remarked that "what was going to happen was going to happen. It's no longer under my control."

Then, slowly, the noises stopped. The stairwell stopped twisting. The wind stopped. People realized that they were still alive, although they were covered with debris in the darkness. As far as the group knew, the building still existed, although they thought there had been a partial collapse.

---

39   Except as otherwise indicated this chapter is based on interviews with Chiefs Jonas and McGlynn, Captain Rohan and Lieutenant Kross by the author.

51

A portion of Stairwell B was badly bent, with holes in the floor, twisted steel, and covered with wreckage, but it was still there. One wall in the center of the building was intact. As they struggled to get the dirt out of their eyes, noses, and mouths so they could breathe, they still couldn't see.

As Lieutenant Kross uncurled himself, at first he was angry.

He thought, "I could have retired and then I wouldn't be here. He couldn't imagine that he had survived this without injury; but he found he was basically unhurt. He then heard calls from others and realized that he wasn't alone. The wall to his right had collapsed. He was hesitant to jump to a more open part of the stairwell, fearing it might cause a secondary collapse. He took his chances and jumped, however, and landed safely. There he found the other firefighters, Josephine Harris, and Port Authority Police Officer David Lim, all bruised, battered, covered with dust and debris, but not badly injured.

Others nearby weren't as fortunate, and in the silence after the roar and wreckage of the North Tower collapse, the survivors started getting messages from two nearby firefighters. Battalion Chief Richard Prunty, the man that Jim McGlynn had seen in the lobby of the doomed building hurrying people to safety, was trapped below the others. Although still in what had been the lobby area, he was able to talk to the others and tell them that he was pinned down by debris and losing consciousness. Minutes later, as conditions cleared, McGlynn desperately tried to reach him. In the twisted stairwell he and another firefighter were able to wrench a door open and crawl in for about fifteen to twenty feet to try to get to Chief Prunty but then found the way blocked.

"Here was a guy crying out for help and there was nothing I could do. I had always been trained to act, to get to people who were trapped. Here was one of our own firefighters looking for help and I was unable to do anything. I had to ask, 'God, why are you doing this to me?' "

All Jim could do was try to give him some hope by saying, "Chief, hang in there, we're going to get you out!" although he knew that there was nothing he could do.

Then Captain Jonas received a "Mayday!" call on his radio from Lieutenant Mike Warchola, Ladder 5, the man they had passed earlier. He was now trapped above them and badly hurt. He said that he was on the twelfth floor, so Jonas clambered up the twisted stairwell. He pushed aside mounds of debris and shinnied up a banister until he reached the fifth-floor landing. Mike Warchola called again with another "Mayday!" Jay Jonas continued to climb as best he could until, halfway between the fifth and sixth floors, he came to a large pile of rubble that he couldn't move and couldn't pass.

Then he had to call Mike and report, "I'm sorry, Mike. I can't help you."

As he was returning down the stairs, Jonas found Chief Picciotto's bullhorn and returned it to him. He also located a freight elevator on the fifth floor and considered rappelling down the shaft, hoping to find a way out through the underground passageways. This thought was discarded because Tom Falco said that they might not be able to climb back up.

The group still thought that there was some sort of structure above them. Although they had masks to furnish oxygen, they hesitated to use them, even though the air was badly contaminated, as oxygen might later become critical to their survival. They heard fires crackling, some of which were getting closer to their location. Since they had no way to deal with the fires, they started to climb down the stairs. After going only a few steps, Matt Komorowski, shouting from below, told them that they could not exit that way.

The fifteen survivors—Captain Jonas and his men, Lieutenant McGlynn and his crew, Chief Picciotto, Officer David Lim, and Josephine Harris—then began a waiting game. They were amazed that they were still alive. With no communication with the outside world and in almost total darkness, they understood that there had been a major collapse in both buildings, but they didn't know how much of their building was left standing. Thinking that there were still thirty, forty, or fifty floors above them still standing, they were sitting on eggshells wondering if the rest of the building would come down. They tried in vain to establish communications with someone outside, making "Mayday!" calls on their radios. Although they didn't know how long they might be trapped or, indeed, if they would ever be rescued, there was no panic. Instead, intense planning began on how to survive. Smoke from nearby fires and those below blew through their crowded space. Sometimes the men were forced to put on their masks until the smoke cleared. At this point, unsure how long they might be trapped, the Stairwell B survivors went into survival mode, conserving flashlight and radio batteries as well as oxygen supplies.

As Jim McGlynn explained, "You want to do something, force your way out, but at the same time you're wondering if any kind of movement will result in the collapse of the rest of the building. We were trying to figure out what we could do, because we were getting no acknowledgment to our mayday calls."

Not knowing how long they might be there, Jim McGlynn realized that they could go for as long as a couple of weeks without food, but water was a different matter. They did have a two-and-a-half gallon, water-filled fire extinguisher, which might not taste very good but would help out for a short time. It wouldn't go far for fifteen people, he thought.

About that time they again heard Chief Prunty of the Second Battalion calling them for help. Every time Captain Jonas called a "Mayday!" on his radio, Chief Prunty would say, "Don't forget about Battalion 2." While they could talk to Chief Prunty, they were not able to see him or get to him. Chief Richard Prunty's last words were, "Tell my wife and my kids that I love them!"

Meanwhile, the Ladder 6 crew was taking care of Josephine. They talked to her, comforted her, and promised that they would shield her with their own bodies if there was any further collapse or danger. One man took off his fireman's coat to cover her. She became the reason that they were there. Captain Jonas said, "Come hell or high water, she was going to survive!"

Chief Picciotto told everyone to turn off their radios, while he continued to make "Mayday!" calls. Initially, Jay Jonas complied, but since his radio was on a different frequency, he also continued to make "Mayday!" calls, realizing that by using the other frequency he could improve their chances of making contact with someone outside.

Somehow, firefighter Bill Butler got a call through to his wife in Middleton, New York, more than seventy miles away, on Port Authority Police Officer David Lim's cell phone. He asked her, "Do me a favor? Call the fire department and tell them where we are!" After about forty minutes, both Chief Picciotto and Captain Jonas were able to establish contact with people outside. Deputy Chief Tom Haring, who Jonas knew, heard the "Mayday" and replied, "All right, we have you recorded, Ladder 6. You are trapped in the B Stairwell of the North Tower." Then Jonas started getting replies from others, some of them good friends, including his neighbor, Cliff Stabner, who said, "This is Cliff, where are you? How are you doing?" Cliff would end each of his transmissions by saying, "I'm coming for you, brother! I'm coming for you!" These transmissions gave the trapped firefighters a strange feeling. They were accustomed to being the ones doing the rescues, the ones in control of the most dangerous situations, and now they needed rescue themselves.

Captain Jonas said, "I had twenty-two years in the fire department, and it took a giant mental leap to realize that I was no longer in control of my own destiny. While it was an emotional feeling, it was also comforting to know that those guys were coming for me."

Lieutenant Glenn Rohan's group made it to the site at 11:00 a.m., about thirty minutes after the second tower collapsed. He met Chief Mark Ferran, commander of Battalion 12, who told him, "Richie (Chief Picciotto) is trapped," and asked Rohan to find him. First though, they had to find Stairwell B.

In this seventeen-story pile of rubble and fire, the Stairwell B survivors' call was the only "Mayday!" so all attention was focused on getting to them. Deputy Chief Nick Visconti, a friend and mentor of Jonas, took over the rescue effort. Captain Jonas couldn't understand the reasoning behind some unusual questions that Nick was asking. "What fire trucks were you parked near?" Later he learned that searchers had located some of the fire trucks and were trying to get a focal point since the building no longer existed. Nick Visconti didn't know how much Jay Jonas knew and didn't want to cause him more anxiety, so he said, "All right, but I'm not that familiar with the World Trade Center. Can you tell me how you got in?" Jonas replied, "We came in through the glass doors off West Street. We made a right turn then a left. The B Stairwell is the first stairwell on your left. You can't miss it!" Outside, surrounded by firefighters, Nick Visconti heard a collective groan from the entire group when they heard Jonas' response.

Jim McGlynn thought, "Why can't they understand? There's only one Stairwell B." The response to their calls was, "Uh, uh. Yeah. OK. We kinda have an idea where you are," but it was clear that there was confusion. The men inside were thinking, "What do you mean, you don't know where we are? There's only one Stairwell B in the North Tower and we're on the second or third floor."

Lieutenant Rohan, who was not familiar with the WTC, got a general idea of where the North Tower and Stairwell B had been located. He was told that if they went into the U.S. Customs building, part of the complex, they could find the North Tower—or where it had stood. They put up a thirty-five-foot ladder and started their trek, trying to find a way up and over an enormous pile of rubble. Finding the direct route towards the tower impassable, they spent thirty minutes exploring and finally took a circuitous route, through the Verizon Building, then to West Broadway, then through the endangered Building Seven, leading them through an almost complete circle from their starting point. They met some other men from Ladder 43, their company, who had been off duty. These men joined the crew. Even though World Trade Center Five was on fire, they went through the delivery ramp, then across the mezzanine, where they found some escalators. After a two-and-a-half hours, they arrived in the general area of the North Tower, where they found piles of concrete and steel but, strangely, no file cabinets, no desks, no computers, only fires and paper everywhere. Rohan, now with his crew numbering ten men instead of the seven that he had started with, thought that in this desolate landscape they might as well have been on the moon. Strangely, a giant earth globe set in the ground nearby was untouched, not a mark on it.

Back inside Stairwell B, Lieutenant McGlynn still had two of his men trapped below the rest who hadn't been able to join the group. They were in a lower part of the staircase, their way blocked by tons of debris from the collapse. Jim shined his light through a crack in the floor, and the two men shouted that they could see the light. McGlynn asked them if he were able to open the crack up some more would they be able to climb through the widened gap. The first firefighter said that he thought he could. The second, a heavier man, said, "There is no way the fattest man in the New York City Fire Department can get through that crack!" Up until that point, Jim had worried about the mental state of his men, but he thought that if they could still crack jokes, they were probably all right.

Meanwhile, the survivors in Stairwell B had been told by people unaware that Rohan's crew was already looking for them, "There's a forty-story building, World Trade Center Seven, now fully involved and we have to deal with that. It'll be a while. We're not sure how long we're going to have to work on this."

This meant that evacuation of World Trade Center Seven had to take priority as they expected it would also collapse, as it did hours later. McGlynn's later assessment was that this was a very difficult, but necessary and proper decision for the man making it. The man making it had to weigh the risk of sending additional firefighters, without proper heavy equipment, into an extremely volatile and dangerous area. There was a good possibility that WTC Seven would collapse before rescuers could reach the trapped survivors in the North Tower. These men would be risking their lives in an effort, which might not be successful, to save those who were trapped. They did not know where they were, or if the rescue effort would result in further disaster if either Building Seven or the remainder of Stairwell B should collapse.

Chief Billy Blaich told Captain Jonas that it would take hours for them to get to the group, saying, "It's really bad out here!" Billy Blaich didn't know the status of his own son, Peter, a firefighter in Engine 9 at that point, yet he was coming to help the survivors. (A few hours later Chief Charlie Blaich, Billy's brother, was informed that Peter got out of the tower before it collapsed and was uninjured.)[40]

Captain Jonas also resigned himself to the thought that they might be trapped there for a couple of days. About fifteen minutes later, however, the smoke and dust cleared enough that a ray of sunshine suddenly hit the stairwell. Jonas thought, "We're in the middle of the fourth floor in a stairwell with no windows and I see blue sky!"

As small beams of light slowly penetrated the darkness, thirty or forty feet above the trapped group, the smoke and dust started to clear. Jim McGlynn, thinking he was in an enclosed staircase, thought, "How am I seeing light? We're in the middle of the building." Then, for the first time, McGlynn, Jonas, and the others realized that the North Tower was gone. They were above the remains of the World Trade Center with only a couple of badly damaged floors above them.

They now understood the confusion among the other firefighters about their location. At the same time, they were relieved to learn that there weren't fifty stories precariously perched above them ready to fall at any time.

Chief Picciotto was anxious and wanted to leave immediately, but Captain Jonas convinced him that they should wait until the smoke and dust cleared as they still didn't have good visibility. He emphasized that it would be better to plan their exit and leave as a team. About ten to fifteen minutes later, when the visibility improved, Chief Picciotto climbed up the stairway to the opening, where he could see a firefighter, probably Lieutenant Glenn Rohan, in the distance. Captain Jonas told Picciotto, "All right, you can go, but we'll do this as a group." They tied a rope to the banister in the stairwell and lowered Picciotto to a position where he could get free.

---

40   Chief Charles Blaich, interview with author.

With the siren on the air horn that Captain Jonas had returned to him, Picciotto was able to signal the firefighter outside. Working his way through the pile of rubble outside, Rohan was finally able to zero in on the sound. Chief Picciotto, Rohan said, in his thirty years of service with the FDNY, had never carried a bullhorn before. However, after having been involved in the 1993 bombing of the Trade Center, he thought that it might come in handy and had brought it with him. It sounded like the siren was on the other side of the Tower, and without it, "We would never have found them." Using the rope that they had tied off, Chief Picciotto climbed down from the opening and made contact with Glenn Rohan, then he went to the command post and said, "Ladder 6 is trapped, you have to get them out!"

Rohan and his men then started to make the extremely dangerous climb to the opening in the destroyed stairwell, easing past forty-foot-deep crevices that they could have easily fallen into with a single misstep.

Chief Pete Ferran called him on his radio and said, "You have to come back!"

Rohan replied, "Hold on, Chief! They are right here. They are on the other side of this pile. This is the last section we have to go over."

He then silently asked for help from God, thinking, "Someone has to help me here!" Then, as they cleared the last obstacle, he reported, "Chief, we're there!" then lost contact.

As he arrived, Captain Jonas had started sending people out, climbing down a piece of steel using the rope that had been tied earlier. As they exited they were awed by the desolation around them, saying, "Oh, my God!" and "I can't believe what I'm seeing!"

Rohan ordered one of his men, firefighter Jerry Suden, "a super fireman, "Jerry, you have to take them out of here!" Reluctantly, because he didn't want to leave the area where others might still need help, Suden started leading the survivors back down the steep, dangerous climb through the rubble. Rohan entered the stairwell and started to help the survivors out. Captain Jonas told Rohan that Jim McGlynn and some of his men and others were still in the stairwell. Then he told him about Chief Prunty and that Lieutenant Mike Warchola was badly hurt on the twelfth floor. Rohan looked at Jonas with a curious expression and said, "Twelfth floor?" Captain Jonas replied, "What?" to which Rohan said, "Never mind. You'll see."

Tommy Falco, one of Jonas' crew, left the stairwell, then returned saying, "Cap! Wait until you see this!" Captain Jonas poked his head out and said, "Oh, my God! I can't believe it!" The building didn't exist. The twelfth floor didn't exist. Mike Warchola's "Mayday" calls were coming from somewhere in the rubble!

One by one, the remaining men climbed to the top of the destroyed staircase and through the opening. Captain Jonas left the stairwell after all of his men and Josephine were out. Lieutenant Mickey Kross also got out, climbing and crawling across the devastation.

"What can I do for you?" Lieutenant Glenn Rohan asked Jim McGlynn. Jim, who at this point was totally exhausted, replied, "I have two guys below me here and I don't know how I'm going to get them out." Rohan and Jim Lanza walked into the stairwell that was covered with rubble, then slid down the debris to a landing where they found a hole in the floor near a standpipe. Lanza dug out the hole as much as he could, then Lieutenant Rohan cut out the drywall between two metal studs to gain an extra four inches. They passed a rope down two stories to the two firefighters, and the first, James Estianidis, climbed out. The second, Jeffery Coniglio, supposedly "the fattest man in the fire department," also climbed out "scraping all four sides of the opening," according to Lt. Rohan. The two men then made their way to the exit hole and joined the rest of their crew outside of the remnants of Stairwell B.

McGlynn told Lieutenant Rohan, "There's a chief down there! We were talking to him through the walls—I haven't talked to him in awhile. There's a door down there a little bit open, we heard him on the other side of the door." As other firefighters were arriving at the stairwell, Lieutenant Glenn Rohan told firefighter Tom Corrigan, an imposing man at six foot six inches, "Don't let anyone else go down into the stairwell!" Rohan said, "This was the second time that day that I asked God for help," as he and Mark Carpenella climbed down into the dark abyss using the same rope that the others had used to climb out. Rohan found a hole, "so deep that I couldn't see the bottom of it with my light." Lieutenant Rohan found the door the two men had described and forced it open a bit. He realized that the door had saved the men's lives as it was packed with debris behind it. He called Chief Prunty on his radio and could hear the chief's radio but didn't get a reply. Carpenella was able to make his way in and then said, "I got him! He's over here! I see his shoulders and head." Rohan was able to get through the door and joined Carpenella. Chief Prunty was buried in debris up to his chest. Later, asked if the chief was still alive when they found him, Lieutenant Rohan almost broke into tears, "No! I would never have left him. We worked for hours to try to get him out."

Jerry Suden, the firefighter who had led the group of survivors out, had turned them over to other firefighters and made the arduous journey back to the stairwell. He and David Ryan went into the cavern and the four men worked to free Chief Prunty. After two hours one of the men said, "I smell airplane fuel and I'm getting dizzy!" Recognizing the symptoms of carbon monoxide poisoning, Lieutenant Rohan said, "OK, we have to go. The men said a prayer for Chief Prunty and, with heavy hearts, climbed back up the rope and left the stairwell.

As Jonas's Ladder 6 crew exited, they came on a scene of jagged steel, broken concrete, and rubble, with fires everywhere. Everything was covered with the now-universal thick coating of powdery gray dust that made their descent dangerously slippery. The fires intensified. They were surprised to find that there were no recognizable items. No desks, chairs, or computers. Nothing but nondescript rubble and twisted steel. Everything was pulverized. There was, however, a lot of paper—paper fluttered through the air everywhere like a bizarre September snowstorm.

Jonas's group picked their way across the rubble through the smoke, realizing that they could get lost amidst the poor visibility and the mountains of wreckage. They were all bruised and banged up and "beat up a little," with Mike Meldrum, who had suffered a concussion, the most seriously injured.

As they passed near World Trade Center Buildings Five and Six, it sounded like a gunfight as fire reached a Secret Service ammunition storage area where boxes of cartridges were "cooking off." They scrambled across rubble, sometimes tightrope walking across iron beams stretching over twenty-foot-deep holes. After about a half hour, deep below ground level, they arrived at West Street, where they were faced with a sheer cliff about thirty feet high. Men above dropped ropes to the survivors and yelled down to them to climb up. Captain Jonas watched the exhausted men climb out of the hole, hand over hand, with their feet against the wall of rubble, then make it over the top.

Finally, only Mike Meldrum and Jay Jonas were left. Mike said, "I can't do it." Jonas replied, "Yes, you can! Your wife and children are on the other side of that hill. You can do it! I'm not leaving until you climb out of here." Mike Meldrum, despite his injuries, climbed up the rope, and Jay Jonas followed. When they arrived at ground level on West Street, the men were hurried toward the ambulances. Captain Jonas resisted, however, and insisted that he be allowed to report to the command post, telling the authorities, "You don't understand. There are hundreds of people looking for us and I have to tell them that we're OK. I don't want anyone to get hurt going through the fire and rubble trying to rescue us." He made his way to the command post, which was a fire department truck still connected to a fire hydrant. Chief Hayden, now in charge, was on top of the truck where he had better visibility. Pete Hayden looked down at Jay Jonas and said, "It's good to see you!" Jay Jonas replied, "It's good to be here!" Then the longtime friends both broke into tears.

As he peered down on the scene below, the impact of the devastation first hit Jim McGlynn. "It looked like Hiroshima, like World War II. City blocks upon blocks of nothing but rubble." McGlynn's Engine 39 men still had to step gingerly through the mountains of broken concrete, piles of shattered glass, the electrical debris. Then they had to walk alongside Seven World Trade Center, the building in imminent danger of collapse.

Jim said, "It was a miracle that all of my men got out alive." They had minor injuries, cuts, and bruises, but no serious wounds. Both Chief Pao-lillo, who gave the evacuation order, and Captain Ill were killed when the North Tower collapsed. Of the group of men that shook hands and wished each other "good luck!" in the lobby of the North Tower earlier that day, Captain Jay Jonas was the only one who survived.

At 5:20 p.m., thirty minutes after the group of survivors passed by Seven World Trade Center, the forty-seven-story-high building collapsed, and those in the area again experienced the cloud of dust and the rushing wind. The collapse of Building Seven had been expected and precautions had been taken to clear people from the building and avoid further casualties.

Mickey Kross found a desk set up on West and Vesey streets with a list of about four hundred firefighters who were presumed dead, including himself. He still is amazed that he was able to cross his own name off that list. Many of his longtime personal friends, six firefighters from Ladder 7, the unit he shared the firehouse with, and the officer from Engine 1 who he had been with going up the stairs, also would, sadly, never be crossed off that list. Kross was checked out by a doctor at the site and was released to return to duty. He worked at the site until later that evening and then got a ride back to his fire station. Arriving there, he found his friend, Christine, waiting for him. Her apartment building had been evacuated as there was no electricity, no lights, and the elevators were not working. Mickey doesn't remember if they ate their scheduled dinner together that night.

Jim McGlynn, Jay Jonas, Mickey Kross, Josephine Harris, and the other survivors escaped from their tomb at around 3:30 or 4:00 p.m. after having been trapped in the rubble for almost six hours. Joe Garcia, the man that helped Josephine down from the seventy-third floor, made it safely out of the building before it collapsed. Captain Billy Burke, the firefighter who was with Captain Jonas and first reported that the South Tower had collapsed, died when the North Tower fell.

Matt Komorowski was taken out in an ambulance. The other men were treated and released. Their fire truck, which they thought was parked safely under the pedestrian bridge, was crushed, so they walked back to their firehouse. As Jonas walked slowly back to the firehouse, a group of people followed him. One of the group came up and asked if he was all right. He replied, "If I keep walking, I'm OK. If I stop, I'm not going to want to start again." He just kept on walking. After checking in at the firehouse, he finally drove his car home, which he later realized wasn't a good idea as his eyes were very bad. Arriving home, he found that his wife had been kept informed of his situation by his firefighter nephew and a neighbor. In addition, his neighbor, Cliff Stabner, had called her as soon as Jay was out of the "pit" and told her that he had just seen him and that he was walking.

Captain Jay Jonas couldn't sleep well for several days. He would lie down and relive the experiences of the day. Then he would awaken with the bed shaking.

While he felt confident they would rescue other trapped people, the only ones that were later rescued were Will Jimeno, rescued later that day, and John McLoughlin from the PAPD and a Port Authority civilian employee, Genelle Guzman McMillan, who were rescued the following day.

After rescuing the survivors of Stairwell B, Lieutenant Rohan and his men came out of the stairwell where they slid down a piece of steel. By then Rohan was totally exhausted- more exhausted than he had ever been before in his life. They finally left the site at about 12:30 a.m. and got a ride with about forty other firefighters on a fire truck which dropped the men off near their firehouses along the way. Rohan said, "It was an amazing thing that my men did that day!" He also thought there would be other survivors waiting to be rescued in the following days, but this turned out to be an empty hope.

Lieutenant Glenn Rohan wanted to go back to help retrieve the remains of Chief Prunty, but he couldn't convince authorities to allow him to do that. "It drove me crazy. For the next couple of days I tried to convince them to let me go get him. I told them that I knew exactly where he was and that his family would want to know." Chief Prunty's remains were recovered three days later when a recovery team broke into the side of the stairwell wall.

Philosophically, Captain Jonas said, "Josephine Harris is alive today because of us. We could also make the argument that we are alive because of her. If she hadn't been there, there would be no telling where we would have been. We might have made it and we might not. Once out of the building, you had to be a distance away or you wouldn't make it. Our fire truck was right near the building and it was crushed. We probably wouldn't have made it." [41]

Offered the opportunity to take retirement, Jonas declined, saying, "If I retire I'll spend the rest of my life seeing a psychiatrist." Captain Jonas was placed on medical leave for a month after which he returned to duty. The weekend after 9/11, he was promoted to battalion chief and has since become deputy chief of the department, where he is one of the senior officials in the FDNY.

Chief Peter Hayden later became the chief of the New York City Fire Department. Chief Picciotto retired from the FDNY. Josephine Harris, who had a broken leg, was carried out in a "Stokes basket."

Mickey Kross worked on the "pile" for nine months. He retired after more than twenty-eight years of service, then became a volunteer at the Tribute Center honoring the victims and heroes of September 11.

Jim McGlynn has been promoted twice since September 11 and is now a battalion chief in the FDNY. Two of his uncles (both deceased) were retired New York City firefighters.

Lieutenant Glenn Rohan went back to work at Ground Zero whenever he could, working there the entire month of February. While he found the work very difficult, it was also very rewarding. Glenn Rohan has since been promoted to captain.

---

41   Josephine Harris passed away on January 12, 2011 more than nine years after 9/11; Al Barker, "Mourning a Woman who Shared a 9/11 Miracle," New York Times, January 17, 2011.

Lt. David Lim
Port Authority Police of NY & NJ.

2001

September the 11th

In Loving Memory
K-9
Badge
#17

Yellow Lab "Sirius"
Died in Tower 2

Police Officer David Lim and Sirius-photo courtesy of David Lim

Chapter Six
Partners: David Lim and Sirius

"He was the best partner I ever had."

David Lim, Lieutenant, Port Authority Police Department,
speaking of his police dog, Sirius

As a young boy in the early 1960s, David Lim, a first-generation American, often met policemen who were customers in his parents' Chinese restaurant on Beach Twentieth Street in Far Rockaway, New York.[42] He was impressed with the work they did. Although law enforcement was important, he learned that their main job was helping people. After he finished college he followed the advice of a retired policeman neighbor (Archie Bauer) and took tests for the Port Authority Police Department. David passed the examination, and in April 1980 he was sworn in.

David Lim's first experience with terrorism occurred after the February 26, 1993, terrorist attack on the World Trade Center. David and some of his fellow police officers were at the airport in Myrtle Beach, South Carolina, returning from a golf vacation where they learned of the attack through the television news. When he returned and called in, Port Authority Police officials, wanting fresh officers the following day, asked Lim not to report there until the next morning. When he arrived he helped secure the crime scene until the investigation was complete.

---

42   Lieutenant David Lim interview with the author.

"Everyone wanted to sneak in and take a rock or a photo for a souvenir," he said.

When TWA Flight 800 crashed into Long Island Sound on July 17, 1996, killing 230 people after taking off from John F. Kennedy airport in New York City, there was speculation it may have been a terrorist act. Although it was later determined the explosion was likely caused by faulty wiring that exploded a fuel tank in the wing, the Federal Aviation Administration initiated a program to use canines to assist in screening passengers and their baggage. Police Officer David Lim was one of the first Port Authority Police officers selected to become a dog handler. Lim was sent to Lackland Air Force Base, near San Antonio, Texas, to attend the three-month military dog handler's course, where he and his dog were trained in patrol and explosive detection.

Explosive detection dogs are trained to be passive when an explosive is detected—they will lie down or sit to inform their handlers that they have detected an explosive material. Small amounts of explosives are routinely used to maintain their proficiency. Large amounts such as those used in truck bombings are much easier to find. These dogs would be able to detect this much explosive material one hundred feet away. The only explosives that Lim and his second dog, a four-and-a-half–year-old yellow Labrador named Sirius (named after the "Dog Star"), found were in training. Lim said that his primary job was to provide peace of mind. In a bomb threat situation at a school or airplane, for example, he and Sirius would survey the suspected area and then confirm that it contained no explosive material.

On September 11, 2001, Police Officer David Lim patrolled the entry point to the underground levels of the World Trade Center complex. Both Twin Towers as well as Buildings Four and Five were connected by underground passageways. Trucks entering the parking area had to pass the checkpoint. Officer Colon with his dog, Jagger, had taken the day off. Officer Lim was checking vehicles as they entered the complex. While Lim was on a break eating breakfast in the first basement level of the South Tower at 8:47 a.m., the first plane hit the North Tower. Although he was in the other tower, Lieutenant Lim felt the vibration resulting from the blast and realized instantly that an explosion had occurred. A radio report confirmed a detonation on an upper level of the North Tower. Sirius looked at David with a puzzled look.

David, thinking they had missed an explosive device, said, "Uh-oh! We're in trouble now! You stay here—I'll be back!"

Since Sirius was trained to detect explosives and not to find bodies, Lim thought it better to leave his partner in the kennel, where he thought he would be safe.

Officer Lim immediately ran into the North Tower to the second-floor plaza level. There he found confused, upset, and frightened people rushing down the stairwell. He saw no apparent injuries. Lim lowered the volume on his radio as he didn't want to alarm passersby and started directing people to safety through the lobby. He ordered a Port Authority Police officer to turn off the "up" escalator so both lifts could be used to evacuate the building. He noticed a woman carrying a pair of shoes. Lim looked up as someone screamed when she saw the body of a "jumper" in the passageway outside the lobby. The scene was surreal. Lim got on his radio and reported that they had found a body.

The person receiving the report asked, "Are you sure the person is dead?"

Then another person crashed into the concrete below.

Realizing that things were getting worse by the minute, Police Officer Lim pushed forward into Stairwell C. People he passed coming down couldn't understand why he was going up.

He told them to keep going down saying, "Down is good!"

Although with sporadic radio transmission he had not received the evacuation order. As he climbed he found burned or injured people. He assigned uninjured people to assist them to a triage point that he assumed would be set up in the lobby. He climbed to about the twentieth floor, where he found a man in a wheelchair accompanied by a friend. The two of them wanted to go down, but were waiting for other people to pass so they wouldn't slow them down.

As he was thinking about how to get the man down, some firefighters came over from Stairwell B and a lieutenant said, "We'll take care of him!"

Although they were wearing all of their heavy clothing and carrying all their gear, the firefighters carried the man in the wheelchair and started down the stairs. Lieutenant Lim, now in Stairwell B, again started up the stairs. He encouraged people to continue down directing them not to use elevators. Everything was going well until he approached the forty-fourth floor, where express elevators took people to the top. Then, at 9:03 a.m., the second plane hit the South Tower. The North Tower shook. Now, it was clear the city was under attack.

Fifty-six minutes later Officer Lim was directing the fleeing people on the forty-fourth floor when suddenly the South Tower crashed into the street. Now the situation became desperate, and he urged people to move quickly. The number of people had lessened significantly, and many of those still in the stairwells were handicapped or physically challenged, many elderly or overweight.

David started down the stairs, clearing each level as he went, yelling out, "Go down! Go down!"

When he reached the thirtieth floor, he met Chief James A. Romito, chief of the Port Authority Police Department, Captain Kathy Mazza, commander of the Port Authority Police Academy, and Lieutenant Robert Cirri, an instructor at the Police Academy. The three officers were using a piece of fire hose to tie together a makeshift stretcher from a hand truck to carry an injured woman down the stairs.

Lim told Chief Romito, "I don't know if you know it, but the other building is gone!"

Chief Romito glanced at his pager. He looked up somberly at Captain Mazza and Lieutenant Cirri and said, "Oh! Oh! We have to go now!"

He and Cirri had also been assisting a tall man, and now they put one of the man's arms around each of their shoulders and started down the stairwell. Captain Mazza and some firefighters picked up the woman, and the group started down the stairs.

When David Lim reached the fifth floor, he found Josephine Harris sitting on the steps while FDNY Captain Jay Jonas looked for a chair to use to carry her down. Lim and firefighter Billy Butler started to help Josephine down the stairs.

Captain Mazza called out to Officer Lim, "Leave her with the firefighters and come with us!"

David replied, "I'm right behind boss, go ahead!"

David Lim and Billy Butler slowly worked their way down to the fourth floor as they assisted Josephine Harris. Suddenly the tower started to shake, then fall. The building collapsing around them sounded like an oncoming locomotive. Butler and Lim shoved Josephine to the floor and covered her with their bodies. (Police and firefighters are taught to cover endangered people with their bodies to protect them. As a result, piles of entangled bodies were often found in the wreckage of the World Trade Center.) The hurricane force wind created by the floors collapsing picked up firefighter Matt Komorowski, who was thrown over the huddled group of Lim, Butler, and Harris. Then everything went black.

Expecting a piece of the North Tower to fall and crush him any second, David Lim thought of his family. He hoped that they would think well of him. He worried about Sirius and if people would find him. He hoped that he wouldn't be lying in a pile of rubble for a week, slowly starving to death. He just wanted to die quickly. Then, suffering a concussion, he passed out briefly. When he awoke in the darkness and quiet after the turmoil stopped, he thought he was dead. He opened his eyes but was engulfed in total darkness. Then he started to cough. He thought, "Wait a minute... dead people don't cough!" He spat the grit and dirt out of his mouth. He heard someone call out and realized that he wasn't alone. At first he was just happy to be alive, but then reality hit him. He was buried in 110 stories of rubble, and he and the people with him would likely be together for the rest of their shortened lives.

As the dust began to settle and they could see with their flashlights, they crawled around seeking ways out. They looked into elevator shafts and the stairway below. When they couldn't find a way out by going down, they started digging their way up. They searched for sources of water. They smelled jet fuel and saw fires burning all around them. Several hours later, as the dust cleared, they saw some light. David thought the light was coming from the floor above them and that somehow a light was still working. He soon realized that he was looking at sunlight. The survivors understood they were on top of what was left of a 110-story building. As the radios started working better, Captain Jonas, one of those in the stairwell, was trying to direct rescuers to their position.

Officer Lim, more familiar with the layout of the World Trade Center, said, "I can help you with that. Tell them to go to the giant globe in the middle of the plaza and work their way about one hundred yards west and we'll be there."

The firefighter that he was talking to responded, "What globe?"

The globe had been shattered and covered with rubble.

Meanwhile, David's wife had called his K-9 unit in New Jersey and had been told that he was missing and probably dead. His co-workers thought that from the location he had been when he had called them earlier, there was little chance he could have survived. His two children, Debra, age fourteen, and Michael, age twelve, along with the children of other people thought to be in the World Trade Center, were called out of class and brought to the guidance counselor's office. Lim's wife decided to leave the children in school because she wasn't mentally prepared to take care of them. A neighbor friend came over to be with her. She telephoned her father, a Presbyterian minister, and told him tearfully that she thought she was a widow.

He replied, "No! No! We'll pray for him!"

He got a group of people together and started an informal prayer service.

David's radio only worked sporadically, but he had two cell phones. He contacted his base in New Jersey by radio and then was able to call his family on his cell phone. It was difficult to talk to his wife at first. He didn't want to upset her, but she was elated to hear that he was alive, even though buried in rubble and waiting to be rescued. David's wife called her father again, just thirty minutes after their first conversation, and relayed the news to him.

He said, "Boy, those prayers worked fast!"

Some survivors climbed up to the opening where sunlight was pouring through. They saw Lieutenant Glen Rohan and his Ladder 43 crew being guided to their location in the distance.

Lim said, "I was never so happy to see a fireman in all my life!"

Firefighters from Ladder 43 climbed up to the opening and, using the ropes provided by these men, the survivors helped each other down through the rubble and devastation. One of Lim's vivid memories as they made their way across the rubble was seeing women's shoes. Many women working in the World Trade Center wore sneakers or comfortable shoes to work. They would keep dress shoes in their offices and would change when they arrived. When the towers collapsed, those shoes were strewn around in the rubble. He later admitted that his focus on these "shoes" made him less aware of some of the more gruesome sights.

The survivors trudged north through mountains of shattered concrete, twisted rebar, and fine grayish powder towards Building Six, the U.S. Customs House and planned to escape through that building. As they approached they saw it in flames and heard what sounded like gunshots. Initially David Lim thought that they were under attack. Then he realized

PARTNERS: DAVID LIM AND SIRIUS

that it was confiscated ammunition exploding in the fire. The group quickly diverted toward West Street, walking through the broken concrete and rebar and avoiding flames. They passed under the skeleton of a wall that was still standing.

The wall was teetering and Lim thought, "Great! We survived in the tower and now this wall is going to fall and crush us!"

But they pushed on past it and came to a deep hole blocking their way to West Street. They gingerly climbed down into the abyss, then climbed back out using ropes tossed down by firefighters above. After he reached the safety of West Street, a firefighter offered David a bottle of water. He didn't know whether to use it to try to rinse out his eyes or to drink it, so he did both.

David sat on the front bumper of an ambulance while medics checked him over. He had leg and back injuries and had suffered a minor concussion, but he wanted to go to his command post, which had been set up at nearby Manhattan Community College. First he wanted to get his partner, Sirius. Now, at 3:30 p.m., he was surprised to see that everyone was so clean. Then he realized that those who had escaped had already left the area or been evacuated in the seven hours that had passed since the first plane hit. He went to the ramp on Barclay Street that led to his office under Building Seven, which was fully engulfed in flames.

A firefighter stationed there said, "No! You can't go there!"

Lim replied, "You're not stopping me! I'm going to get my dog! He's my partner." The firefighter asked, "Why would you go in there to get a dog?"

Lim answered, "Because he's my partner, that's why!"

He started down the ramp and the firefighter flagged down a passing Port Authority Police car.

The firefighter told the officers, "One of your guys is trying to get back into the building!"

Lieutenant Dubrowski and Officers Breensteen and Greff grabbed Lim and forced him into the car, then drove to the Port Authority Police command post at the community college.

Lim, who has since been promoted to Lieutenant, says, "In hindsight, I would not have been able to get back into the area where I left Sirius."

Medical people at the command post examined David and sent him to St. Vincent's Hospital. In the meantime, K-9 officers Petriello and Steve Montgomery brought the Lim family to the hospital.

His injuries were minor, considering, as David said, "that a building had fallen on me."

They put him in a patient's room but David told the doctors he wanted to go home.

One of the doctors said, "Well, you have some injuries."

David replied, "There are a lot of people hurt much worse than I am."

His ten-year-old son, looking out the window, interjected, "Daddy—there's nobody here!"

Although many people suffered from smoke inhalation or were injured by flying debris, for the most part, people in the World Trade Center had either been killed or were able to walk away. The doctors decided to release David, but warned him not to fall asleep due to his concussion.

Chief Romito, Captain Mazza, who had urged Officer Lim to leave Josephine Harris with the firefighters and come with them, and Lieutenant Cirri were killed. Matt Komoroski had a separated shoulder from his brief flight through the air. Mickey Nelson, the chauffeur of Ladder 6, suffered a concussion. The men from Ladder 43 carried Josephine Harris out separately on a Stokes basket.

David Lim had no trouble staying awake that night. Like other survivors, he had difficulty sleeping for days. He stayed up all that night watching television, his wife by his side. The following day, the only people rescued were Port Authority Police Officer John McLoughlin, Lim's classmate at the Police Academy, and Genelle Guzman McMillan, a Port Authority employee. No other people were found alive.

In the Port Authority K-9 program, the dogs become part of their handler's family and live at their homes.

In the days that followed, David's son kept asking, "When is Sirius coming home?"

At first his parents, who feared the worst, explained to him that searchers had to find people first, and then they would find the dogs. After a few days, they knew that Lt. Lim's partner would not be coming home, and they had to break the news to the children. The children cried inconsolably. The parents, heartbroken themselves, explained that Sirius was also a police officer and had died in the line of duty with thirty-seven other Port Authority Police officers.

In February 2002, Lim was at Port Newark training his new dog when he received a phone call from Police Sergeant Devlin.

Devlin asked, "Did you ever loan a shirt with your name on it to anyone?"

When Lim replied that he had not loaned a shirt to anyone, Sergeant Devlin said, "We found some guy with blond hair with your shirt."

Lim and the dog trainer, Joe Martusi, then went to Ground Zero to investigate. When they arrived, they determined that a shirt belonging to David Lim had fallen on top of the remains of Sirius when the building collapsed.

David was asked if he wanted to see Sirius, but he declined. He wanted to remember his partner as he was when he was alive. Sirius received the same honors as the other Port Authority Police officers. They drove his remains around the Port Authority Police headquarters in Jersey City, New Jersey, then to the Holland and Lincoln Tunnels and the PATH station. The police officers at each of these locations lined up and saluted their fallen comrade. Then they brought him to the morgue at Bellevue Hospital, and at that point David Lim broke into tears. The seasoned medical officer at Bellevue also cried when the animal was brought in. It was a small measure of comfort for David to learn that Sirius had died instantly when the building collapsed on his kennel. David knew that Sirius had been lying in his kennel waiting for him to return when the building fell.

A memorial service was planned, but Police Officer Lim asked that it be delayed until all of the memorial services for the thirty-seven fallen police officers of the Port Authority had been conducted. In April 2002, a fitting memorial service was held. A hundred K-9s and their handlers came from all over the country, including California, Florida, Massachusetts, New Jersey, and New York. Each of the dogs with their handlers passed by the urn containing Sirius's remains and saluted. More than four hundred people attended.

While Lieutenant Lim still has some sadness about things that happened, he has come to terms with it. He had urged Chief Romito, Captain Mazza, and Lieutenant Cirri to help the injured civilians leave the tower while he stayed behind. They were all killed.

He sums up his feeling by saying, "Nobody would have said anything if I had just taken my dog and left the area, but I didn't want to leave anyone behind. People have said that once the first building fell, I should have gotten out as quickly as I could, but I couldn't have done that." I swore an oath to protect life and property"

While he still sometimes finds it difficult to talk about that terrible day and his partner, Sirius, David Lim started getting over the pain of losing the "best partner I ever had" when he finally acknowledged that he missed him as much as his other thirty-seven fellow police officers

In the wake of the news on the death of Usama Bin Laden, now Lieutenant David W. Lim stated, "My only regret was that I was not the one to put that bullet in his head! Back in 2001, when I had more than twenty years service, I was asked if I would retire from my job because of 9/11. I stated then 'I'm not gonna let some knucklehead in a cave in Afghanistan dictate when I'm going to retire'.

Here I am still working and he's dead."

Searching for survivors-photo courtesy of FDNY

Chapter Seven
Lieutenant Joe Torrillo and Welles Crowther

"The nearby screams slowly turned to whimpers. Then the whimpers turned to silence as people died."

Lieutenant Joe Torrillo

Lieutenant Joe Torrillo was temporarily working at Engine Company 310 on Snyder Avenue in Brooklyn.[43] Two minutes after the ball dropped in Times Square on New Year's Day 1997, his company was dispatched to a fire where a woman was reported to be trapped on the second floor in the rear of her home. Joe's was the first company on the scene. As they pulled up, fire poured out of every window of the dwelling. People who had been celebrating the year's end screamed in horror outside the burning home.

Torrillo dashed into the blazing house to rescue the woman as other firefighters scrambled up a ladder to the roof. Firefighters are trained to let smoke, gases, and heat out by opening a hole in the roof to vent a fire. The easiest way to do that is to break a skylight. As the men on the roof did that, Joe was rushing upstairs inside. As he came to the top floor of the two-story home and was under the skylight, broken glass and steel suddenly

---

43   Lieutenant Joe Torillo interview with the author.

crashed down, slashing his hand and almost ripping his thumb off. (The woman had left before the fire started and was at a neighbor's house.)

Joe was hospitalized with what came close to being a career-ending injury. During his year-long recuperation, he and other firefighters recuperating from injuries or illness, were assigned to the FDNY Office of Fire Safety and Education. These experienced men visited schools, senior citizens' centers, and civic organizations to teach fire prevention and survival. Eight months later, Torrillo, to his surprise, was named director of the office—a program he hadn't known existed prior to his injury.

Fire Commissioner Thomas Von Essen asked Torrillo to build a learning center in New York City where school children could go on a field trip to learn about fire safety in a Disney-like setting with hands-on interaction. The men, with the assistance of Media Works in Manhattan, developed a multisensory learning program. In October 2000, FDNY opened the new learning center, named "the Fire Zone," in Rockefeller Center next to Radio City Music Hall. Their ingenuity won them an award.

In January of 2001, Fisher-Price Toys called Torrillo with a proposal to develop an FDNY action figure named Billy Blazes to add to their Rescue Heroes line, which included a police officer, a lifeguard, and an EMT. Fisher-Price offered to donate one dollar to the FDNY education program for each doll sold. With approval from Mayor Giuliani and Commissioner Von Essen, Joe eagerly accepted. He could use the money to purchase smoke detectors for needy New York families. By the end of July, a final product had been developed and was ready to go into production.

Fisher-Price, very excited about their new product, asked Torrillo to recommend a place for a press conference. He suggested they hold it at the new learning center—which would help him publicize his education effort. He also suggested that this be done in October, Fire Prevention Month, but Fisher-Price executives wanted more time to market the new action figure before the holidays. Joe countered with September 11, since the date would be 911, the telephonic emergency number, and the Fisher-Price executives agreed that it was a great idea.

On the morning of September 11, Joe Torrillo arrived in his office at FDNY headquarters near the Brooklyn Bridge at 6:00 a.m. Three City University college students, known as cadets, interested in becoming firefighters, worked two days each week with the FDNY and assisted him with coordinating the press conference. Suddenly he realized time had slipped away from him.

He said to himself, "Oh, my God! It's twenty-five minutes to nine! I have to get over to Manhattan by nine o'clock."

He had shut down his computer and closed his desk when one of the cadets came rushing into his office with a frightened look on his face and breathlessly said, "Lieu,[44] Lieu, a plane just hit the World Trade Center! It's on TV in the conference room!"

Joe ran to the TV, where he saw a plume of smoke pouring from the top of the tower.

He said, "Hurry up, guys! We have to get moving! Once the World Trade Center and a plane are involved, every police car, fire engine, and ambulance in the city will be rushing to the scene and the Brooklyn Bridge is going to be backed up."

He thought to himself, "I'll never get to that press conference, and my boss, a deputy commissioner,[45] will kill me because she's going to say, 'You should have gotten there early!' "

Torrillo, like many others in New York that morning, thought a small plane had hit one of the towers and there would be limited damage but much excitement and a predictable traffic nightmare.

He ran with the cadets to the parking garage and raced to the Brooklyn Bridge, arriving there two minutes later. Ladder Company 110, located on Tillary Street, blocks away from the bridge, was ahead of them, and the chief of Battalion 31 followed.

As he looked up at the North Tower, Joe Torrillo was shocked to see that eight to ten floors were burning.

One of the cadets asked, "What do you think, Lieu?"

Joe replied, "Everyone on the top of that building is going to die! That building is going to collapse! Today will be like no other day anyone ever remembered about New York City! To hell with the press conference!"

Joe drove directly to his old firehouse, "Ten House,"[46] directly across the street from the World Trade Center, where he had spent sixteen years before being promoted. He arrived at 9:00 a.m., fourteen minutes after the first

---

44   "Lieu" is short for lieutenant.

45   Lynn Tierney.

46   This station was commonly called "Ten House" because Engine Company 10 and Ladder Company 10 were collocated in this station.

plane hit the North Tower. He parked his official car behind the firehouse. Torrillo and the three cadets ran to the front of the building and went in to find firefighting gear. The doors were open as both the engine and truck companies had already responded. Entering, they found about twenty-five frightened people seeking shelter inside. Some had been injured by the flaming jet fuel that had spilled down the elevators and others by falling debris from the stricken tower. Some were bleeding, some were crying, a few screaming in pain, others in shock. Joe saw that none were missing limbs or appeared to have life-threatening injuries. He ordered the cadets, who had received emergency medical training, to treat the injured as best they could, call ambulances, and remain in the firehouse.

Torrillo then found the firefighting clothing of Lt. Thomas McNamara, an off-duty officer he knew. He donned his coat, pants, boots, and gloves and, missing only an air mask, ran towards the South Tower. At 9:03 a.m. he heard a deafening roar, looked up, and watched in horror as United Airlines Flight 175 passed above him and exploded into the South Tower. Only twenty-five feet from the firehouse, he instantly turned and ran back inside as a huge fireball fell from the tower and landed on Liberty Street, where he had been standing.

He told the cadets that a second jet had just hit the South Tower, then said, "I'll be back later, or I may never be back again, but whatever happens, don't leave this firehouse!"

Torrillo ran down Liberty Street, then to West Street towards the North Tower. Needing a mask to go into the tower (he knew that OSHA, the Occupational Safety and Health Administration, required fire engines to carry an extra one), he went to find his old engine company, which he knew from emergency plans would be near that tower. He found the engine and Danny Peritore, the chauffeur and an old friend, who remained with his engine to pump water. Joe asked to borrow the extra mask from his friend, but another firefighter had already taken it. He sought out masks at other fire engines, but they also had been taken. As he passed the various fire engines, he made sure that the chauffeurs knew how to get water on the fires, as Torrillo was an expert at that.

He heard someone calling his name. Looking up, he saw Lieutenant Tony Mancuso, a friend that he hadn't seen in five years.

Mancuso, having just pulled up, knew only that two planes had hit the buildings, and he asked, "Joe, Joe—what's going on?"

"Tony, look!" he replied. "Those buildings are going to collapse! We're going to lose all of the water around the Trade Center. Take your engine and go about six blocks north, connect to a hydrant there and bring the hoses back so we'll have water if we lose it here!"

Tony and Joe had been promoted to lieutenant on the same day. Tony was at first reluctant to leave the disaster scene, not knowing why Joe would have such insight. Joe, while studying structural engineering, had often gone to the WTC to learn about the novel design. Frequently, when a tenant moved out, the entire floor would be gutted, so he and the other students could see the detailed construction close up. While impressed by the design, it was apparent that the buildings did not have the same traditional construction that had been required previously in high-rise buildings. No high-rise building had ever fallen before, so Tony was obviously hesitant to take the advice of a contemporary.

Pete Brown, his chauffeur, asked, "Hey! Lieu, what are we going to do?"

Joe said, "Tony! Listen to me! These buildings are going to collapse!"

Mancuso took the advice and moved his unit six blocks north to connect their hoses. All of his crew survived.

Minutes after the second plane hit, many more police cars, ambulances, and fire trucks were rushing to the scene. (One of the lessons learned from the 1993 WTC bombing was that streets had to be kept open so emergency vehicles could pass. In the February 1993 bombing, more than one hundred emergency vehicles parked around the WTC. As a result, ambulances with injured patients couldn't get out because drivers were in the towers.) Concerned that streets would be blocked as they were in February 1993, Torrillo ran to the corner of Liberty and West streets and stopped ambulances coming up from the Brooklyn Battery Tunnel. He told the first two ambulance drivers that the buildings would fall and that they should make a U-turn, go back towards the tunnel, and park the ambulances at the curb. The drivers then passed the word back to the others. An Emergency Service Unit police car pulled up and Torrillo went through a similar exchange to convince reluctant policemen to turn around and park out of the way. He explained there would be many injured people, and that emergency vehicles would need both access and a way out. It worked. Once the first police car turned around, the others followed.

Ladder Company 113 from Brooklyn pulled up.

Lieutenant Ray Brown asked, "Joe, what's going on?"

Torrillo explained the situation and said, "Hey, Ray, go back! Go back now!"

Then Torrillo saw one of the ambulances racing toward the South Tower. Angry, he ran to the South Tower. As he did that, Lieutenant Brown pulled his ladder company up about one hundred feet and parked in front of the Hotel Marriott, adjacent to the towers. (He and his crew survived.) But Torrillo's immediate concern was the ambulance that hadn't followed his instructions.

He confronted the man in charge, who demanded, "Who are you? You don't have any authority! We don't work for you. We're going to set up a triage center in the lobby of the South Tower!"

"No you're not! That building is going to fall!" Torrillo answered. "Get out of this building right now!"

The EMT retorted, "No! Who the hell are you?" Torrillo angrily replied, "Either you get out of here or I will drag you out of here!"

The ambulance crew members looked at each other, got into their ambulance, turned around, and drove to Liberty Street as they had been instructed—saving their lives!

Suddenly Torrillo heard a gigantic rumble and a roar.

Looking up he thought to himself, "You idiot! You're the one who knew this building was going to collapse and you put yourself right underneath it!"

While he expected it to collapse, he had estimated that it would be five or six hours later.

He thought to himself, "Joe, you ain't outrunning a 110-story building; you got about 10 seconds left to live. I want my body to be identified because my family ain't going to accept this. If they get my body, they at least get a piece of me."

Joe started running as fast as he could down Liberty Street towards a footbridge, hoping to make it under the bridge, where his body could be found and identified. As the South Tower fell, it compressed the air and, like a gigantic bellows, blew it out with tornado force, winds were later estimated at two hundred miles per hour. Joe's helmet flew into the air much faster than he was running and lofted it out of sight. The wind lifted him off his feet and he flew like Superman for about twenty-five feet. Joe never made it to the footbridge. He landed face first at the side of the twenty-two story Marriott Hotel. The tower came crashing down on the hotel, which collapsed and buried Joe in its rubble.

He could see nothing in the total darkness; he was barely conscious and was in pain in every part of his body.

"So now I was buried under the South Tower and it's completely dark, black; I can see nothing and I'm in a lot of pain. The first thing I remember was getting hit over the head with a piece of steel. My scalp was split open and chunks of concrete were hitting my body, one after another. I didn't know the extent of my injuries, but I had a fractured skull, my ribs are broken, my arm is broken, I'm bleeding internally, and I'm suffocating. I can't breathe, there's no air, and I can't see. It's darker than midnight, and I'm pinned under steel and concrete. People were screaming and crying all around me. We can't see each other. I could only move my neck a little bit."

Then fires started burning all around him. In the darkness he had a flashback to the day that he was standing in front of the fire commissioner and the mayor of New York City with 124 other young guys with short haircuts, suits, and ties as they took the oath of office that one day they would be willing to lay down their lives so that someone else might live.

He thought to himself, "I never thought I'd have to live up to this vow."

Then he thought, "You know, this was the life you wanted; this is the life you loved, and you would never have run from this. I always thought I would retire with a pension. I never thought that instead of walking out of headquarters, I'd be carried by six guys into a cemetery."

He was, however, angry at himself, thinking of the impact that his death would have on the lives of his wife, children, two brothers, and four sisters. He prayed to God, asking forgiveness for what he had done to his family. He asked for a quick death and thanked God for the life that had been given to him. Then he put his head down in the dirt. The nearby screams slowly turned to whimpers. Then the whimpers turned to silence as people died.

But Lieutenant Joe Torrillo was still alive. Dirt clogged his eyes, his nose, mouth, and throat. The fires raged all around him and he was suffocating on smoke and dust. He was pinned down amidst tons of rubble. As the dust and smoke outside began to clear, people who had sought shelter inside the World Financial Center came to help victims. They were digging and lifting debris, entirely by hand, when they found him. Joe couldn't see, didn't know what was happening, but he felt people pulling him out of the wreckage and then carrying him. They brought him to the lobby of the World Financial Center, laid him on the cold marble floor. He still couldn't see but he heard voices tell him that they would take him somewhere.

In great pain, bleeding, his head split open, he said, "Please don't touch me. Just go! I'm going to die."

Remembering that he had heard some policemen say that two more planes had been hijacked and rumored to be headed to New York City, he said, "Run! Get out of here! Don't waste your time, because I'm not going to make it."

He told them his name and begged them to leave.

Someone that he couldn't see, replied, "No, we're going to put you on a boat and get you out of here."

The EMTs, thinking he might have a broken neck, gingerly strapped him to a "spine board." They carried him to a marina behind the World Financial Center near the North Tower and laid him on the deck of a boat. (All types of boats had come, many from New Jersey, to help evacuate injured people.) As they held his scalp together, Joe heard them say that he wouldn't make it if they didn't get him to a hospital.

Suddenly, he heard the same rumble and roar he'd heard when the South Tower fell.

He heard someone say, "My God! Here comes the other building!"

Everyone jumped off the boat running for their lives, leaving Torrillo lying on the deck. He couldn't move, could barely see with dirt and smoke still in his eyes. Shards of glass started hitting the deck. Glass, debris, and dust were, again, burying him. In a panic, he moved his index finger to try to find a release to the strap that held down his arms. He found the release, tripped it, and was able to free his hands. He ripped the tape off his neck, reached around and felt a doorway. In spite of his injuries and intense pain, he leaned over and fell head first into the engine room.

Half an hour later, he heard stomping as people were jumping back onto the deck of the boat.

He heard someone say, "Start the engines."

A crewman came down the long, steep flight of stairs in the darkness, and stepped on Torrillo's chest. Screaming in pain, Joe says he "scared the daylights" out of the man.

The crewman shined his flashlight down and yelled to the people on the deck, "Oh, my God! There's a fireman down here and he's not going to make it!"

The captain came down and said, "We've got to get this guy out of here!"

The mate replied, "We can't! We're tied to the dock, we can't even move!"

"Cut the lines! Get a knife and cut the lines!" said the captain, who went up on the deck to supervise.

A few minutes later, the mate said, "I think the lines are cut."

The captain replied, "OK, back her out."

"We can't!" said the mate. "We're surrounded by boats. We can't see and we'll have an accident."

"I don't care who you hit! Back this boat out now!" ordered the captain. The engines started revving in reverse.

Still in the engine room, tended to by a mate, Joe could feel the vibration and shaking of the boat as it slowly started backing down into the Hudson River channel.

Then he heard someone say, "I think we're clear! Turn the boat around."

The boat turned around and picked up speed, skipping towards the New Jersey shore. Torrillo, lying on his back, could see a faint brown light from the doorway. The brown light became increasingly lighter as the craft moved out of the cloud of dust. Soon he finally saw sunlight.

Ten minutes later the boat pulled up to a pier in Hoboken on the other side of the river. He heard the sound of people jumping on the deck.

A voice shouted, "He's in the engine room."

Paramedics put him on another spine board, gingerly lifted him, feet first, up the steep ladder and carried him to a waiting ambulance. Joe lost consciousness. When he woke up he was in the hospital operating room, surrounded by doctors and nurses. They cut off his clothing, shaved his head and "put needles and tubes in every part of my body that needles and tubes can go." He was moaning with pain, wondering why they were wasting their time. He remained sure that he was going to die. Then he was sedated. Joe awakened about eight hours later, all alone, with his hands tied to the side of the bed. He had been given morphine and could feel nothing. He couldn't see. He didn't know if he was dead or alive.

In his euphoric drug-induced state, he thought to himself, "If I'm alive, how come I can't see? If I'm dead—well, it's peaceful. Nothing could be better than this."

Pleasant thoughts were followed by more somber ones. "Wait a second, if I'm alive then doctors will come in and tell me that my feet are gone or that I only have one leg. Maybe they will tell me that my eyes are missing, my ears are gone, I don't have fingers or that I don't have hands."

Minutes later, five doctors came in. Joe started to cry, afraid of what they were going to tell him. He still couldn't see and thought he was blind. He didn't know what other parts of his body were affected, or even if they were missing. He was hoping that God would take him, thinking that it would be better just to die.

One doctor, trying to find the extent of his injuries, started asking questions. "What is your name?"

He replied, "My name is Joe Torrillo." The doctors looked at the hospital chart and started whispering.

One of them said, "This man has a brain injury. He doesn't even know his own name."

Again they asked his name, and again he replied, "Joe Torrillo."

"Are you sure?"

"I'm positive!"

"Joe, do you have any family?"

"Yeah."

"What do you do for a living?"

"I'm a New York City firefighter"

"Joe, do you know that you got hurt?"

"Yeah."

"Do you know where you got hurt?"

"Yeah, at the World Trade Center."

"Do you know what happened down there?"

"No. I just remember being buried."

"OK, so your name really is Joe Torrillo. Can you spell it for us?" Joe spelled it.

"Do you have any family members?"

"I have a wife, four children, and two brothers."

"What is one of your brother's name?"

Joe replied, "Michael."

"Do you know his telephone number?"

Joe gave them the number and they called Michael from the phone in Joe's hospital room. "This is the Jersey City Trauma Center."

Michael asked, "Do you have my brother there? Is he alive? What does he look like?"

"Yes, he's in critical condition. He's going to be OK." With that, Michael broke into tears and asked to speak with his brother.

Torrillo said, "This is Joe. I'm in the hospital. Calm down. Tell everybody that I'm alive. Call Vicky (his wife, Victoria) and the kids."

Joe tried to figure out the brain injury comment by the doctors. Then it hit him. All fire fighters write their name inside their fire-fighting clothing. When they cut off Torrillo's clothing, they found the name Lt. Thomas McNamara. The cadets, who were shaken up but unhurt, told authorities that Lt. Joe Torrillo had last been seen going towards the South Tower. They found his FDNY car, but since he did not return, he was reported dead.

Joe later learned that the hospital authorities called the FDNY and reported that they were treating Lt. Thomas McNamara, who was in critical condition.

When the FDNY called McNamara's wife with that information, she responded, "What are you talking about? He's sitting here having a cup of coffee with me."

A firefighter from the firehouse had called Victoria and informed her that Joe was missing. She never believed he had been killed. She said she knew he was injured. She knew working at the FDNY headquarters so close to the World Trade Center he would have gone there, but she also knew he was not dead.

When his family came to see him, they could hardly recognize him. His eyes were shut and he had so much bleeding and bruising that his skin was black as though he had been badly burned. Three days later, when he was allowed to go into a bathroom, he looked at a mirror and thought someone else was standing in front of him.

Lieutenant Joe Torrillo spent a week in the hospital and then was released to recuperate at home. A month later he was able to walk around. He started attending funerals for firefighters who had been killed. He went back to Ground Zero and Ten House, hoping to go back to work there. The FDNY doctors, however, informed him that this time, he would be medically retired. Joe has recuperated well from his massive injuries. His eyes, which were scratched, have never been the same, and now he has to wear glasses and must squint to work at his computer. He travels internationally as a public speaker, teaching fire safety and survival as well as leadership and training management.

Six fire fighters from Ten House were killed. Two of the cadets, Joe Broadbent and Eddie Gonzalez, became firefighters. The third cadet did not join the New York Fire Department.

Welles Crowther
"Follow me! I know the way!"
Welles Crowther, September 11, 2011

Six-year-old Welles Crowther, the oldest of three children, liked to emulate his father. Getting ready for church one morning, he asked his dad if he could also wear a handkerchief in his lapel pocket.[47] Jefferson, his father, folded a handkerchief neatly and placed it in the little boy's pocket. Then, while Jefferson carried a blue bandanna, he gave Welles a red bandanna, explaining that the white handkerchief was for show and the red one was to use if he needed a handkerchief for any reason.

Welles always carried a red bandanna, and, years later, used it under his lacrosse or hockey helmet to keep perspiration from his eyes. When he was in high school and old enough, he again emulated his father, joining volunteer firefighter Upper Nyack Emerald Hook and Ladder Company No. 1.

On September 11, 2001, twenty-four-year-old Welles was an equities trader working for Sandler O'Neill and Partners on the 104th floor of the South Tower in the World Trade Center.

After United Airlines Flight 175 struck the building between the seventy-seventh and eighty-fifth floors at 9:03 a.m., Welles called both his parents and left voice-mail messages saying that he was all right. His message to his mother, Allison, said, "Mom, this is Welles. I just want you to know I'm OK!"

There was tension in his voice and disturbing noises could be heard in the background, but Welles was obviously very much in control.

Lights were out. The stairwell was full of smoke and dust. He covered his face and headed downstairs, feeling his way as he went. He arrived at the seventy-eighth floor sky lobby, where people can change from express to local elevators. He found a group of people, many injured, afraid that if

---

47   Jefferson Crowther, father of Welles, interviews with the author.

they moved in the darkness, they might fall into a hole in the floor. Welles's firefighting training kicked in immediately.

He ordered, "If you can get up and walk, come with me now! Help someone else if you can. There are some people here that we can't help, but we have to go down now! Follow me! I know the way!"

Some of the people started to follow to the only stairwell that was not blocked. Welles picked up a young black woman who was in shock and put her over his shoulder. Ling Young, a woman in the group, had a big gash in her forehead with blood gushing into her glasses. She was burned over 40 percent of her body. Welles asked her if she could carry a fire extinguisher that he took off a wall.

She said, "I'll carry it."

They started down the stairs, and when they made it down to the sixty-first floor, the lights were on and the air was clear.

Welles uncovered his face and said, "Everyone keep going!"

Ling Young asked if she still had to carry the fire extinguisher.

He said, "No, we probably won't need it."

Young set it down in a corner of the stairwell. As the rest of the group continued downstairs, Welles headed back up.

Back at the seventy-eighth floor, some people who had been reluctant to follow him earlier now lined up and the second group started down the stairs. When they reached the sixty-first floor, he again instructed the people to continue down. Judy Wein, a senior vice president for Aon Insurance, was in this group. She recalls seeing a fire extinguisher in the corner of a stairwell and thought that this was an odd place for it.

Welles went back and brought a third group of people down. This time he accompanied them to the fortieth floor, where they found a working freight elevator and took it to the lobby. There he met FDNY Assistant Chief of Department Donald J. Burns and an FDNY lieutenant. The men had obtained a "Jaws of Life" machine, and Welles and the lieutenant were preparing to take it upstairs to lift slabs of concrete and debris to free victims.

Meanwhile, Ling Young and Judy Wein, coincidentally, had been placed in an ambulance with a third woman who Welles had also led to safety. This woman was suffering an asthma attack and was obviously in great distress. Ling Young yelled at the ambulance driver, "She's going to die of an asthma attack! Go now! Get her to the hospital!"

The ambulance started out.

Suddenly Welles and those at the fire command desk in the South Tower heard a roar as the building started to fall. Within eight seconds the men had been blown out of the South Tower and up against a wall of nearby World Trade Center Building Four. The men were killed instantly by a wind estimated to be as high as 180 miles per hour. The ambulance had just pulled away from the building or it would have been buried.

Nineteen was Welles Crowther's number. He wore it on his lacrosse and hockey uniforms for four years in high school and four more years at Boston College. When he found an apartment in New York City, he chose apartment number nineteen. His body was found on March 19, 2002. His right hand and part of his jaw had been sliced off in a manner consistent with flying glass, according to the medical examiner's office. Police came to the Crowther home on March 22 to bring them the news. Jefferson and Allison Crowther were concerned their two daughters would be upset. Instead, they were relieved that his body had been found and that he "had been brought home." Welles's body was cremated and the remains placed in a columbarium in his church.

Jefferson Crowther could not bring himself to read anything about 9/11, but Allison wanted badly to find out more about how their son was killed. On Memorial Day 2002, Jefferson saw an article titled "Trying to Stay Alive when the Building Dies," about 9/11 in the New York Times. He gave it to his wife, as he thought she might want to read it. The article described two women named Ling Young and Judy Wein who had been saved by a man wearing a red bandanna. Allison immediately knew that this was Welles. The Crowthers contacted Judy Wein's employer, who gave Judy the Crowthers' telephone number. Within twenty minutes, the Crowthers, Judy, and Ling had the answers to their questions. Later, the Crowther family invited Judy and Ling and their families over for a barbeque, and they remain friends today.

When a big storm destroyed the baptismal font in their church, the Crowther family had it replaced with a new one constructed from Texas granite and dedicated to Welles' memory. Using money donated to surviving family members of 9/11 victims, they formed a foundation, wellescrowthertrust.org, in Welles's honor. In honor of their son, the foundation awards two scholarships each year to deserving scholar athletes who have done volunteer service. The volunteer work can be of various types, including volunteer firefighting, ambulance attendances, Meals on Wheels, etc. The students are selected by a committee consisting of the school principal, guidance department, coaches, and teachers.

Additional donations are received from people including former Upper Nyack High School and Boston College classmates of Welles's. An annual fundraiser, "Raise a Cup," has become an impromptu reunion for graduates of his high school. Another fundraiser, "Red Bandanna Skate," is organized by John, who was Welles's high school hockey teammate. John, shorter than his teammates and not quite as good a skater as some, perhaps because he was younger, nevertheless showed the enthusiasm and guts needed to earn a place on the team. He had, however, never scored a goal.

One day Welles asked the coach to let John play center when he was on the line. The coach agreed. John was really excited to be playing center on the first line!

Welles, who played right wing, told him, "Listen, John! If I get the puck, I'm going down the right side along the board. I want you to skate right down the middle toward the goal. Keep your stick on the ice!"

Welles, who had an excellent wrist shot, got the puck and skated down the side. As he neared the goal, the opposing goalie, very much aware of Welles reputation, shifted a bit to his left to block the expected shot. Instead Welles passed the puck to John who put it right in the middle of the net! He was elated. He had scored his first goal!

Welles skated over to the goal, picked up the puck, and handed it to John.

One of Welles's younger sisters, named Honor, is married and has three children. Honor, who was very close to Welles, had decided her first child would be named after her brother, regardless of gender. Welles's niece, now in elementary school, is very proud of her uncle and will relate his story to anyone who will listen.

Welles's parents both work as volunteers at the Tribute Center, located across the street from Ground Zero. While they grieve for their loss, Welles's parents, siblings, classmates, and friends are very proud of the brave young man who gave his life to save others.

Searchers at Ground Zero-photo courtesy of FDNY

Chapter Eight
Survivors

"We're at war!"

Al Fuentes

Al Fuentes

Al Fuentes came to the United States from Ecuador with his parents in 1959, when he was eight years old, looking for a better life.[48]

On 9/11, fifty-year-old Al Fuentes was the acting battalion chief of the Marine Division of the FDNY. After the first plane hit the North Tower, he was responding on one of the fireboats. As they approached the Twin Towers along the Hudson River, he saw a plane flying very low. The plane made a U-turn, then, as it neared the South Tower, it dipped its wing and as it passed overhead, he heard the engine rev up to full speed and he watched as it crashed into the South Tower. He saw an "incredible fireball."

Al put his hand on one of his firefighter's shoulders and said, "We're at war!"

They docked the boat and Al went with his aide to the command post on West Street. He was shocked as he saw people jumping to their deaths from the towers. He kept hearing explosions and looked up to see where

---

48   Al Fuentes interviews with the author.

they were coming from. Then he realized that the sounds that he heard were bodies hitting the pavement.

He reported to Ray Downey, battalion chief in charge of special operations, who was directing the FDNY response, and said, "Give me two companies. I gotta get up there!"

Ray responded, "No, Al. Stay here. You're in charge of the Marine Division."

That was the first time that day that Ray Downey saved Al's life.

Minutes later Al heard an "unbelievable sound" as the South Tower started to fall. He and dozens of others ran to the ramp of an underground parking garage to seek shelter. They huddled against one of the walls; Al got on his knees up against the wall and said a "Hail Mary." As the cloud of drywall dust, dirt, and debris enveloped him, he couldn't see. He couldn't breathe. Then the noise stopped and he knew he had survived. People around him started to talk, and through the rubble, smoke, and dust, they made their way out to Vesey Street. There Al met William Feehan, the FDNY deputy fire commissioner. Al had lost his helmet, but he found another one and he put it on as tight as he could. He couldn't believe that the South Tower was down.

Ray Downey, with a concerned look, said to Al, "We lost a lot of good people!"

Again, Al told Ray that he wanted to go into the remaining tower to help rescue people. For the second time that day, Ray saved Al's life. Ray told him instead to help direct people to safety, and Ray and Al went to the Marriott, which had been badly damaged but was still standing. There they directed people escaping from the building to come towards the hotel. People were still jumping from the North Tower, so he and others used hand and arm signals to warn people not to try to go through to safety whenever someone was jumping. When the way was clear they would wave wildly and yell at them to run to safety.

Then Al Fuentes heard that horrible roaring noise again as the North Tower started to collapse. As he tried to run on West Street, he would partially sink in the piles of debris and powder. Realizing he could not escape the falling building, he knelt down in the middle of the street and curled up and put his hands over his head. He started reciting the Hail Mary again and prepared to meet his maker, as he believed his time on earth was coming to an end.

He was completely buried by rubble. Badly hurt, unable to see, unable to move, he was semiconscious with a piece of iron pinning him down. He struggled to reach a radio that he called his "super radio" because it could reach a dispatcher. He had picked it up at the last minute because he knew he could talk to dispatchers on it. Although buried, he inched the radio up near his right ear, cradling it partly in his hand and partly with the debris that covered his head. Despite difficulties with radio communications that day, he was able to contact a dispatcher as he slipped in and out of consciousness and tell them generally where he was. Finally, some firefighters got a glimpse of his yellow firefighter coat through an opening in the rubble, and dug him out. Al Fuentes was injured. Badly injured. Very badly injured. He had suffered a skull fracture, nine broken ribs, a broken arm, and a collapsed lung. Doctors later told him that he had about twenty minutes to live when he was rescued. He doesn't know exactly how long he was buried because he wasn't conscious the whole time, but it was well over an hour. They put him in a Stokes basket, used to move injured people, and he was evacuated by one of the fireboats that he commanded across the river to New Jersey.

Al Fuentes's friend, Ray Downey, battalion chief in charge of special operations, the man that had twice saved his life that day, the man that had said, "We lost a lot of good people!" became another of those good people lost on September 11, 2001. He was killed saving others when the second tower fell.

An ambulance was waiting on the New Jersey shore, as was a priest, who gave Al Fuentes, then unconscious, the last rites. The EMTs put tubes in his lungs and he was moved to the New Jersey Medical Center, where doctors performed a tracheotomy, started ventilation, and put him in a drug-induced coma. A portion of his skull was temporarily removed due to brain swelling. He remained in this coma for two weeks, during which time he was transferred to the pulmonary intensive care unit in the Bronx. When they first brought him out of the coma, he had a nightmare in which he saw people jumping from the Twin Towers.

He called out to his wife, "Get Father Judge! We need Father Judge!" (Father Judge was the renowned fire department chaplain.)

When she gently told him that Father Judge had been killed, he broke out into tears and the doctors then put him back into the coma. Al was in the hospital for another week, then went home where his wife,

Eileen, tended to him. It was eight months before he could walk on his own again, and he couldn't drive. He has since had eight operations. Now, years later, he still gets flashbacks of people jumping to their deaths from the fiery hell of the falling buildings.

The doctors told him that he would not be able to go back to work again. He kept saying, "Let's wait and see what happens." Eventually, though, it became clear that he would not be able to work as a firefighter again, and he was medically retired from the New York Fire Department. Posttraumatic stress counseling was available for firefighters for a couple of years after 9/11 but Al wasn't initially capable of traveling or participating in this program. Later, however, he joined a similar program.

Al Fuentes' health has continued to improve. His short-term memory has also improved, but he does have to make a lot of notes and takes precautions to avoid missed appointments, and he relies on his wife to help him in this regard. He also suffers from "survivor's guilt," in which survivors of traumatic experiences often feel guilty because their friends and associates died. His therapist suggested that he write about his experiences. He has since written a book, *American by Choice,* describing his experiences.

Al received many awards, which he awkwardly and modestly feels were not deserved. Among these was the City Spirit Award presented to him at the New York Knicks arena in front of twenty thousand cheering fans. He donated the $5,000 check that came with the award to the Wellness Center of Cornell University. Al also formed a foundation, the Patriot Group (www.the_patriot_group.org) to honor the 343 N.Y. firefighters that died on September 11.

He is now a consultant for the Department of Homeland Security, has testified before the 9/11 Commission, and participated in an eight-month Homeland Security study which included the city of Memphis, Tennessee. One of the findings was that this Mississippi River port did not have a marine firefighting capability. Knowing that the FDNY had just upgraded its fleet, he asked if he could get one of the old boats donated to the city of Memphis. This request was approved. FedEx, whose headquarters is located in Memphis, arranged transportation of the boat from New York to Tennessee. After the boat was refurbished, Al Fuentes and two firefighters went to Memphis at their own expense and spent three days training eighty Memphis firefighters on their new boat. At the dedication ceremony, the Memphis Fire Department surprised Al by naming the boat,

"Al Fuentes 343", the 343 being the number of New York firefighters who were killed on September 11, 2001.

Al completed a course of study at the University of Connecticut and was awarded a master's degree in homeland security leadership. Al's father still lives in New York City, but his mother passed away in 2007.

Will Jimeno and John McLoughlin, PAPD

Port Authority Police Department (PAPD) Sergeant John McLoughlin had worked in the WTC for most of his career.[49] He was very familiar with the complex layout of buildings and subgrade levels and was the expert for the area's elevator evacuations. After his promotion to sergeant, he had been transferred to the bus terminal command.

John was a trained emergency services officer and remained the lead trainer for elevator evacuations and weapons of mass destruction response. He would routinely practice rappelling down elevator shafts of the Twin Towers and in 1999 had rappelled down 110 stories in an elevator shaft.

On 9/11 he was working at the bus terminal. When he heard of the planes hitting the WTC, he and his supervisor, Inspector Lawrence Fields, assembled a team of twenty-two officers and gathered necessary equipment to go to the site and start a rescue effort. The men went in a commandeered bus led by a police car with lights flashing and sirens blaring.

As they approached, debris was falling and people were jumping to their deaths from the towers. Inspector Fields and Sergeant McLoughlin agreed that McLoughlin should gather equipment and lead a team of men into the North Tower. McLoughlin located some oxygen masks and, with three other volunteers—Officers William Jimeno, Antonio Rodriguez, and Dominic Pezzulo—headed through the concourse to the South Tower to get more equipment. While on the concourse they suddenly heard a loud noise and saw the ceiling start to collapse. They started to run to the freight elevator but saw that this area was also about to fall and, not realizing it was collapsing, they tried to get to the South Tower.

---

49   This account is based on interviews by the author with PAPD Chiefs (retired) Joseph Morris and Christopher Trucillo.

As the tower fell, large pieces of concrete and steel piled up over them, knocking them down and trapping them under tons of rubble. Officer Jimeno was wearing a safety helmet which was ripped off his head by the crushing wave of debris. Officer Antonio Rodriguez was killed instantly. The three surviving officers were all trapped in the rubble. Sergeant McLoughlin's legs were pinned down by concrete and steel, but he was able to do a roll call, receiving answers only from Pezzulo and Jimeno, who told McLoughlin they were also trapped.

The three men were having difficulty breathing due to the pulverized debris that formed a fine powdery dust, and smoke from the fires that permeated the air. After several minutes, Officer Pezzulo worked his way free. Will Jimeno urged Pezzulo to dig his way out through one of two openings where the men could see light. Instead, he made his way over to Jimeno and was working to free him when they heard a roar caused by the collapse of the North Tower. Officer Dominic Pezzulo was struck and killed by a piece of debris, and the two remaining officers were buried deeper in the mountain of rubble.

Sergeant McLoughlin urgently tried to contact rescuers with his radio until the battery died. The men were now running out of time when, ten hours later, they heard a voice calling out. "United States Marines—is anyone there?" Sergeant McLoughlin and Officer Jimeno responded and were able to direct Marine Sergeants Karnes and Thomas to their location. Rescuers were able to pull Jimeno from the wreckage after about two hours but were unable to free McLoughlin until around 7:30 a.m. the following morning, twenty-two hours after the building fell.

John and Will sustained massive tissue injuries to their entire bodies, spending lengthy stays in the hospital undergoing numerous surgeries, medical treatments, and hours of physical therapy. Will, during a visit by Chief Morris on October 8, despite all his injuries, expressed most of his concern toward his fellow department officers for their long hours of work and inability to spend much time with their families. The two survivors proved an important inspiration to their fellow police officers during the difficult weeks that followed 9/11.

Men would inquire about families of their fellow officers who had been killed, then would ask, "How are John and Will?"

Tim Brown
"The New York firefighter is the greatest job in the world!"

Tim Brown

On September 11, 2001 thirty-eight-year-old Tim Brown was an aide to Mayor Rudy Giuliani and was working in the New York City Office of Emergency Management.[50] Although his office was in the city's Emergency Operations Center (EOC) in World Trade Center Building Seven, his job was to work in the field. Accordingly, when the first plane hit the North Tower of the WTC, he immediately ran from his office to the lobby of that building. Ten minutes after he arrived, the second plane hit the South Tower. He and Assistant Chief Donald Burns, a thirty-nine-year veteran of the FDNY, hurried to that building.

As they ran toward the building, Brown, a fifteen-year veteran of the FDNY, asked Burns, "Chief, what do you want me to do?"

Chief Burns looked over to Brown and replied, "Tim, there's nothing that you or I can do! I've called for a fifth alarm but it'll take some time for them to get here. Do the best you can!"

Burns then added, "You know we're at war, right?"

Brown replied, "Yes, Chief, I know!"

Shortly after they arrived in the South Tower, Chief Burns approved six Port Authority Police officers going up into the building. A civilian rushed up to Tim Brown, grabbed his arm, and told him there were people trapped in an elevator in the lobby. They ran to the elevator, where he found the elevator doors open but the elevator had stopped well above floor level. They could see men's and women's feet through a small opening. The people inside were screaming for help. There was fire burning in the pit below the elevator and they were being roasted alive. Brown could see arms and legs as the people tried to pull the elevator down so they could get out. He had no tools, so he ordered a Port Authority employee to gather up as many fire extinguishers as he could. The man replied that he had already done that, but Brown found that most of them were empty or not charged. Tim was desperate when he turned and bumped into Michael Lynch, from

---

50   Tim Brown interviews with the author.

Ladder Company 4,[51] a fireman friend. Brown had been his mentor during Lynch's probationary year with 4 Truck. He describes Lynch as "a big guy, very confident, one of the best firefighters in the department."

Lynch put his hand on Brown's shoulder and said, "Timmy, don't worry! I got it!"

Brown said, "He might as well have had wings, because he was the angel that was going to save those people."

With that Brown started back to the command post in the South Tower to find Chief Burns. The lobby was packed with burned, bloody, or otherwise injured people. These people had made it down to the lobby and just collapsed, thinking that they were now safe. They were wrong. Soon the stairwells were backed up with people who couldn't move because of all the people in the lobby.

Brown told Chief Burns, "I'm going to get some paramedics with stretchers to get these people out of here."

He ran out of the building, where he saw the body of firefighter Danny Suhr, who had been killed on Liberty Street by a "jumper." With people jumping and debris and rubble crashing to the ground, it was a dangerous way to go, but Brown had no choice because that was where the ambulances were. As he left the entranceway of the South Tower, he saw firefighter Michael Lynch wrestling with a "Jaws of Life" machine.

The motor of this device is very heavy, and Mike called, "Hey, Timmy! Give me a hand!"

Tim started running over, but a "probie"[52] got there first and started helping, so Brown went on to find some paramedics. Tim Brown continued running toward the paramedics, where he found his friend, Chief Charlie Wells, a medic from FDNY Special Operations who he had worked with in Oklahoma City after the bombing there, and in Atlanta after the bombing at the Olympics.

Charlie said, "Give me a minute—let me get my guys and gear together!"

A minute or two later the four men started back to the South Tower. They were about twenty-five feet away from the entrance when they heard

---

51   Ladder companies are often referred to as "trucks." Ladder Company 4 would be called "4 Truck."

52   A firefighter trainee on probation until he or she has successfully completed initial training and a supervised first assignment with a firefighting company.

an ominous crunching noise and looked up to see the tower collapsing. They could hear the floors slamming against each other in rapid succession. The noise became closer and grew louder. They ran, but realized immediately that they could not outrun the crashing building. The men ducked into World Trade Center Building Three, housing the Marriott Hotel, which was attached to the South Tower. They dashed inside the hotel restaurant. Everything was clear, then in an instant it turned pitch black. The front of the building, including the windows and doors, was blown out. The powerful wind created a deafening noise as the tower crashed down on the Marriott Hotel. Tim Brown wrapped his arms around a massive column, four feet in diameter, knowing that he had a chance of survival if the column created what is known as a "tent collapse," leaving some space around him where he might be spared. Even knowing this, he realized that his likelihood of escape was slim. He thought he was a dead man. In addition to being scared, he thought how sad it was that he would never be able to see his brother again. The wind and noise roared even louder. He describes it as being surrounded by a dozen 747s with engines at full throttle. Even though partly sheltered by the column, his legs were swept out from under him and his helmet flew off, but he held on. A scientist later estimated the wind velocity at 180 miles per hour.

As suddenly as it started, the wind and the noise stopped, replaced by an eerie silence. Reality kicked in. Tim Brown knew that, somehow, he was still alive. He wanted desperately to get out and run for his life. He turned to go out the way he came in, but the way out was now a pile of collapsed rubble. He made his way out but in the darkness ran into an indistinguishable truck, probably a fire truck, with its headlights on and the motor running. With the unbelievable happenings, our nation under attack, he convinced himself that it was a truck bomb.[53] He turned around and told the people that lived through the collapse to run the other way. They ran to the other side of the building and came to a roll-down gate. Some of them had reached under it to try to lift it when they were met by fingers from the other side as people there also were trying to raise the gate. Slowly, the two groups lifted the gate, and Brown and his people learned that there was no way out on that side.

---

53   Terrorists frequently set up a bomb near the site of a terrorist attack to kill people that respond to investigate or help survivors.

A firefighter had climbed over the five-story-high pile of rubble with a large emergency flashlight and called to them, "Come this way! Over here!"

They formed a chain and, hand in hand, followed the firefighter out of what was left of the building.

Later Tim Brown was in charge of the field command post for the Office of Emergency Management. Under Spartan conditions, he would climb up on a chair to make announcements and give orders to the assembled group representing a number of city, state, and federal organizations. They also approved passes for people to enter Ground Zero.

As he was issuing instructions at one point, a man tugged on his shirt sleeve and said, "I need to talk to you right now!"

Brown got down from the chair and the man, an FBI agent, showed him his identification and said, "I am an FBI agent. There is a man in here wearing an FBI jacket who is not a FBI agent. I don't know who he is. He has a backpack with him."

With the city under attack, there was immediate concern that the man could be a terrorist plotting to blow up the forward command post. Tim Brown and the FBI agent instructed two undercover NYPD officers to go over near the man. Then they sent a uniformed police officer over, and the group confronted the individual. The confrontation was a strange sight. Two men in civilian clothes had a man wearing an FBI jacket spread-eagled up against a wall! The man adamantly insisted he was an FBI agent.

The real FBI agent said, "You are not! I know everyone here and you are not an FBI agent!"

Finally, as the policemen were starting to handcuff the man to take him away, he pulled out CIA identification papers.

Brown said, "He was there looking out for us, too! He just should have let us know who he was with."

Tim Brown is amazed that he survived. He later learned that the area of the hotel where he survived had been badly damaged in the October 1993 World Trade Center bombing. When it was repaired, architects designed it and the iron workers built it so that it was reinforced to approximately ten times the strength required. Tim Brown has no doubt that this was what saved his and thirty other lives.

Photographs of the area showed that the surroundings were totally destroyed. Brown feels that God did not want him to die and led him away from the elevator to a place where he would survive. He believes there is no other explanation.

Chief Burns died when the South Tower collapsed. The six Port Authority Police officers that went into the tower also perished. Firefighter Michael Lynch's body was found months later with the Jaws of Life tool in his hands near the elevator where the people were trapped. One woman was rescued by Michael Lynch. She later told of the big firefighter with the red "4" (Ladder Company 4) on his helmet who got her out of the elevator. Michael Lynch was posthumously promoted to lieutenant. The rest of those trapped in the elevator died. Chief Charlie Wells and the paramedics survived.

Mark Grillo, NYPD

Mark Grillo, born and raised in the Bronx, had always wanted to be a New York City firefighter.[54] He took the firefighter examination and although he felt confident that he had passed, a friend at the volunteer fire department where they both worked suggested that he also take the test for the New York City Police Department. Since service in the NYPD counts for seniority in either service, he decided to take that advice. He also felt experience with the police department would be good training for a fire department job. He easily passed both examinations and, at twenty one years of age, was almost immediately hired by the New York Police Department.

A year and a half later, on September 11, 2001, he was at his station on Forty-Second Street in Manhattan. He had just finished working the night shift but was still helping out at the desk when the first plane hit the World Trade Center. In the confusion, people, thinking back to when the Empire State Building had been hit by a small plane, thought that this may have been a similar accident, but then a police lieutenant came up and breathlessly announced that a second plane had hit the South Tower. Grillo's precinct immediately dispatched him and seven other policemen to the scene. With traffic already shut down except for emergency vehicles, and with sirens blaring, the men sailed down Second Avenue and were at the site almost four miles away within minutes.

54   Mark Grillo interview with the author.

Upon arrival they were initially assigned to do traffic control and direct pedestrians out of the area. Chief Tom Purtel of the Special Operations Command, a former chief of Grillo's precinct, recognized him and ordered him to come with him. They started looking for the fire department command post, as the FDNY is in charge of coordinating emergency services at fires. They went into the lower level of WTC Building Five or Six near the Twin Towers, where there were shops, then to the Marriott Hotel, because someone told them that the command post was set up there. Not finding the command post, they started out of the concourse level between the buildings and near the Twin Towers.

All at once the building shook as the South Tower fell. Everything went pitch black. Pieces of the ceiling fell and windows were blown out. About thirty or forty people were groping around in the dark, calling out until they found each other. Some of the policemen and firefighters directed the people inside to form a chain and hold hands as they led them to an unblocked exit. Grillo and some others went up a set of stairs and helped firefighters bring an injured woman down on a stretcher. As they approached the bottom of a flight of stairs, they heard a strange, startling noise. Looking up they were amazed to see the North Tower start to collapse.

"You heard it first." Grillo said, "It sounded like you were inches away from an elevated train rushing by. As soon as we heard the roar, we all looked up and people started screaming."

Chief Purtel ran towards the falling tower to find cover behind another building. That building was then completely crushed except for the ten- or fifteen-foot section where he had found shelter.

Grillo's instinct was to try to outrun the falling building, but as he turned around and tried to run, the violent wind from the collapsing tower blew him across the street. The force of the blast tore off his riot helmet and threw him into a building. Picking himself up, still being pelted by debris, he stuck his head inside the wheel well of a van for protection.

Mark said, "I don't know if it saved me or not. I just stayed there with my head in that wheel well and weathered the storm until it got quiet. I had some bruises, bumps, and scratches, but if it wasn't for that van, I probably would have had the crap kicked out of me from all the stuff that was flying around. The other side of the van was totally destroyed."

When the debris quit flying, he checked himself over in the darkness, even though he couldn't see anything, and found that he wasn't seriously injured. To this day he vividly remembers the weird, "gross" taste of the dust in his mouth, the odors, and the eerie, unforgettable quiet that followed the collapse of the buildings.

Grillo stood up and, in the darkness, tried to walk between two parked cars when he bumped into a firefighter. He helped the man up, and the two of them checked each other for injuries. As they stumbled around in the confusion, he didn't know if he was inside or outside of a building.

He saw a newsstand that looked like one he had seen on the inside of one of the buildings and thought, "How in hell did I get back inside the building?"

Then, as visibility improved, he realized that he was still in the street outside. As he was walking up the street a police detective grabbed him and led him into a building where there were some paramedics.

A detective told him, "You're missing your right ear!"

Mark could hear, and it turned out that his ear was almost cut off and was hanging down where the detective couldn't see it. They cleaned him and another police officer and an ambulance took them to a hospital. At the hospital, the doctors were concerned about a cut blood vessel in his arm. While Mark hadn't felt much pain because of nerve damage, he felt it intensely when they clamped off the blood vessel. He spent most of the day there. Despite broken ribs, and other bruises and injuries, he was released.

Grillo was put on medical leave because of his injuries. Eventually he got feeling back in his ear.

He describes getting a haircut: "Getting a haircut was really weird because the vibration of the buzzer was always strange. It was like therapy because after eight or nine haircuts, I started getting the feeling back. I don't know if it was because of that buzzer thing or what. But I always felt good after having to sit there and buzz my head."

Mark Grillo was on medical leave for about two months. He was disappointed because in October he was called up for duty with the FDNY and he had to wait until his ribs healed. On January 22, 2002, after almost two years as a police officer, Mark Grillo fulfilled his lifelong desire and became a member of the New York City Fire Department.

President Bush consoles FDNY firefighter-photo courtesy of FDNY

Chapter Nine
Mayor Giuliani

"This is worse than any war site that I saw in Berlin after the war."

Henry Kissinger, when he visited Ground Zero with Mayor Giuliani

On the morning of September 11, 2001, Mayor Rudy Giuliani was at a breakfast meeting at the Peninsula Hotel in midtown Manhattan.[55] He was meeting with Denny Young, his chief counsel, and Bill Simon, a former assistant U.S. attorney who had previously worked for Giuliani. Simon, a close friend of the mayor, was considering running for governor of California. It was primary election day in New York, so the men were discussing politics, particularly California politics, and the chances of Simon winning the Republican primary, then the general election. Rudy agreed to help Simon raise campaign funds and to help any way he could in the race against Los Angeles Mayor Dick Riordan.

Patti Varrone, one of two detectives on the mayor's security detail, came over to the table just as the conversation there was ending and Giuliani could see her excitedly whispering to Denny.

---

55   Except as otherwise noted this chapter is based on an interview with Mayor Rudolph Giuliani, December 14th, 2010.

She told him, "There's a fire at the World Trade Center! A twin engine plane has hit the North Tower and there is a terrible fire! The mayor will want to know about it and probably will want to go there."

Young quickly came over and relayed the message to the mayor. The men immediately paid the check. Mayor Giuliani knew that this was going to be a long day. He did not know that this would be the first of many very long days. The mayor immediately realized that on a bright, clear, cloudless day, it was unlikely that this could have been an accident.

He thought, "No plane, on a day like this, could get that far off course. It must have been done on purpose."

They got into their van and raced down Fifth Avenue, making their way over to Seventh Avenue, where they saw the flames billowing on the top of the North Tower. The flames looked much worse than those from a twin engine plane hitting the building. He wondered if it had been done by some deranged person or a terrorist.

As they passed St. Vincent's hospital, less than a mile from the World Trade Center, he saw a massive explosion and said, "What the hell was that?"

Immediately, they got another call. Police reported that a second plane had struck the South Tower. Seconds later they arrived at the NYPD command post on Barclay Street one block north of the World Trade Center. The police and fire commissioners and first deputy mayor hurried over to inform him what had happened.

He asked, "Where is the fire department command post?" and was told that it was right below the North Tower.

Mayor Giuliani directed that a separate command post be established for the police to manage citywide security. He had been unable to place calls to the governor's office and the White House using sporadic cell phone service and knew they would need reliable, hard-wire phones not available on the street corner. He had to know if they had air support from the Air Force or the Air National Guard. He had to get in touch with the Stock Exchange and order it to be evacuated, as it might be the next target. He had to call the White House.

He said, "We are going to need hard lines!"

He knew the fire and police departments had to overlap and maintain close coordination but also that they would not function as well in a combined headquarters with their different missions. The FDNY was responsible for fighting the fires, getting people out of the buildings, and rescuing survivors from the World Trade Center. The NYPD had to help evacuate and secure the area around Ground Zero as well as all of lower Manhattan. The majority of its effort would be directed to citywide security as well as keeping order in the rest of the city. Other potential targets had to be evacuated and protected.

Intelligence reports indicated there were Islamic sleeper cells in Union City, New Jersey. Police had to make sure that people weren't coming into the city. Bridges and tunnels had to be closed and secured. The City Hall, Empire State Building, Stock Exchange, St. Patrick's Cathedral, Columbia University, and Statue of Liberty were all potential targets. Every time terrorists were arrested, they had plans indicating that the major targets were the subways, bridges, tunnels, Stock Exchange, Madison Square Garden, and St. Patrick's Cathedral. Police had to inspect these places to make sure there were no bombs placed there. Ironically, the World Trade Center was rarely listed as a target.

The city was in panic. Would there be rioting? Looting? Other crimes? At this point they were anticipating another six or seven attacks, as there were reports of that many airplanes unaccounted for. A police command post located at Ground Zero would not be able to function effectively there.

The police department had already anticipated the need for land-line telephones, and Police Commissioner Bernard Kerik pointed down the street in the direction of an NYPD truck and said, "Don't worry, boss! We're setting it up right there!"

The mayor could see phone lines being strung into a small office.

Giuliani said, "Let's go to the fire department command post. Let's find out what they need, get them what they need, then we'll come back here and decide what has to be done for the rest of the city."

He started to walk the two-and-a-half blocks to the fire department command post. Huge flames were shooting from the top of the World Trade Center buildings. Police were instructing people to look up and watch for debris falling off the buildings and hitting people on the ground below. A later estimate indicated that seventy or eighty people died on the ground before the buildings collapsed. As Mayor Giuliani looked up, he couldn't always tell whether something falling was debris or a person. He would see something falling and think it was piece of an air conditioner duct and then realize that it was a human being jumping from the inferno above, or he

109

would see what he thought was a body, then find it was a piece of debris. As he approached the FDNY command post, he was startled to see someone falling from the tower and hitting the roof of a building below.

He said to Chief Ganci, "Can we get any helicopters up there?"

Chief Ganci said nothing, simply pointed so the mayor could see flames shooting out of a window. That answered Giuliani's question. He instantly understood that it would be too dangerous for a helicopter to get close enough to try to rescue anyone because of the billowing smoke and flames shooting out of the upper floors.

Chief Ganci said, "My guys can save everyone below the fire."

Mayor Giuliani interpreted that to mean, "Don't ask me to send people above the fire because I'll kill them! I can't get above the fire. If the people cooperate and stay calm and don't start trampling one another, we can save those below the fire."

He explained that panic is a concern in a situation like this. Often, when there is a bomb scare, authorities do not evacuate a building for fear that people may be trampled and killed, or injured, during an evacuation.

The mayor asked Ganci, "What do you need?"

Ganci answered, "I have all the firefighters I need. We're OK for the next twelve hours."

Giuliani read that to mean, "I have it all worked out for the next twelve hours. The fire is going to be burning for twelve hours and the buildings will be coming down over a twelve hour period."

Although they did not discuss the probability, he thought that meant the towers would collapse over a ten- to twelve-hour period. First the top would fall, then a wall. Then the rest of the building would collapse in stages.

Chief Ganci went on to say, "Here's what I need. I need all these civilian people out of here!" as he looked around and pointed.

People were coming out of the towers and, even though others were being killed by jumpers and falling debris, some of them would stand around to watch. If twenty people came out of a building, fifteen would move on, but five would stand there and gawk.

Ganci said, "You've got to get rid of these people! You have to get everyone out of here. Go on television; tell them 'Go north! Go north!' Get everyone in midtown Manhattan. The further north I can get them, the easier it will be to get my equipment in and out. I won't have to worry about civilians getting hurt. I'll be able to control these streets and be able to get ambulances in and out."

That made a lot of sense, Giuliani thought. He told Commissioner Kerik and Chief of Police Esposito to carry out those instructions.

Chief Esposito said, "I'll get my men doing that."

Commissioner Kerik said, "I've closed down the bridges and tunnels. No one is coming in. I closed them down about twenty minutes ago. In particular, no one is coming in from New Jersey!"

Getting people across the Brooklyn Bridge and out of Manhattan became a major effort of the FDNY. The goal was to create an environment where the FDNY could concentrate on the fire, on evacuating the towers, and where emergency vehicles could get in and out.

Mayor Giuliani hugged FDNY Chief of Department Peter Ganci, shook his hand for what would be the last time, and said, "God bless you!"[56]

Giuliani and his staff started walking to the temporary NYPD command post, now located at 75 Barclay Street. A retired police officer working for Merrill Lynch had offered his office, with working telephones, for use by the NYPD. Commissioner Kerik had cleared the office.

"When Bernie says, 'Get out!' everyone gets out!" Giuliani said.

By the time the mayor arrived, the office was already a functioning command post. Additional phone lines had been installed. Police officers were manning the desks. His staff was in the process of calling for the National Guard. He had told his staff that he wanted to talk with President Bush, so when he arrived, they led him to a Merrill Lynch office where they had the White House on the line.

He spoke with Chris Henick, Karl Rove's deputy.

He said, "Chris, I need air support! Do we have jets up there? There may be further attacks!"

Henick replied, "You have air support. The jets were sent out about fifteen minutes ago, you should hear them pretty soon. You've got air support from several other places."

The mayor said, "I heard there was an attack on the Pentagon. Is that true?"

Henick replied, "Affirmative!"

---

56   Mayor Giuliani had appointed Peter Ganci as chief of the department in October 1999.

Giuliani asked, "Are there further attacks?"

Henick answered, "Not that we know of so far. There are seven to ten planes unaccounted for, so we can't say for sure."

Mayor Giuliani, wondering whether the unaccounted-for aircraft might be headed toward Washington, D.C., or New York, asked to speak to the president. Henick informed him that President Bush was not there and they were in process of evacuating the White House.

He told Giuliani that Vice President Cheney was in another location and would call back right away. Giuliani, not knowing that the president was in Florida, was left with the impression that he had been evacuated from the White House to some safe underground location along with the White House staff.

Within seconds a White House secretary was on the phone and the deputy mayor informed Giuliani, "The White House is on the phone. Vice President Cheney wants to talk with you."

Mayor Giuliani went into a private office and picked up the phone.

The White House secretary said, "Vice President Cheney will be with you in a minute."

Suddenly, inexplicably, the phone went dead and the desk started to shake! People outside the office were making a lot of noise and were obviously upset. Detective John Huvane, on the mayor's security detail, grabbed him and ordered, "Get under the desk!"

Mayor Giuliani responded, "You're crazy! I'm not getting under the desk!"

He looked into the outer office and saw everyone had gotten under the desks.

"What the hell's going on?" he asked as the building started to shake.

Chief of Police Joe Esposito yelled out, "The tower is coming down!"

Giuliani initially thought he meant the communications antenna structure on the top of one of the towers had fallen and somehow landed on their building causing it to shake. He did not know that the entire South Tower had collapsed, but he felt the building shake as though it was in an earthquake. He looked outside and all he could see was what looked like a cloud of white smoke rushing through the streets. He could see that the building they were in was damaged.

John Huvane insisted, "We have to get out of this building!"

They started toward the front of the building but couldn't go out because of all the debris flying through the street. Mayor Giuliani describes it as like a "nuclear wind"—the wind created after a nuclear explosion. He could see objects flying through the white cloud like the scene from the Wizard of Oz when furniture was flying through the air. The windows were all broken and the street was filled with chunks of concrete and pieces of twisted steel.

The mayor had worked in the building before and remembered that it was connected to a building on nearby Park Row which contained the corporate counsel's offices, so he said, "Let's go downstairs and go out the other way."

The twenty or so members of the hierarchy of the New York City government, including the mayor, his deputies, the police commissioner, chief of police, and head of the Office of Emergency Management, went downstairs to find a way out. When they tried a door, it was locked. A second door was locked, then another.

Mayor Giuliani thought, "Maybe I was wrong. Maybe it doesn't connect to the other building," and the group started back upstairs.

They wondered if it would be safe to go outside now, but when they looked out, the damage, debris, and devastation was even worse than before. Then two janitors who had heard the group downstairs appeared.

"You were looking at the wrong door!" they said. "There is a door that will take you to the other building."

So the officials followed the janitors back downstairs and were led to a door that took them to the building on Park Row. They all were relieved when they came to the lobby, as they thought that they might be trapped in the building at 75 Barclay Street. Looking outside, they were horrified to see that conditions continued to worsen. Debris filled the street and people, some injured, were fleeing the destruction. Mayor Giuliani saw his friend Tibor Kerekes, a deputy police commissioner and a former member of his security detail, who had staggered into the building, badly cut, bleeding, and covered with white dust. He told the mayor that it was terrible outside. With debris and dust everywhere, it was difficult to breathe and even more difficult to see. Everything and everybody outside was covered with dust. Many people had been injured during the collapse. Some were bleeding; all were choking from the massive dust cloud. And these were the lucky ones.

Mayor Giuliani had to decide whether to stay in the building and conduct a news conference or venture outside. He decided that they should take their chances outside because this building might also collapse.

When they were about a block away, they heard a noise that sounded like an earthquake as the North Tower fell. They looked to see the same white cloud forming again. They rushed up the street until they came to a firehouse on Houston Street and Sixth Avenue less than a mile away. The firehouse was locked, as the crews had gone to the WTC. They broke in and set up a temporary citywide command post where Mayor Giuliani was able to telephone Governor George Pataki.

Governor Pataki said, "For a while we thought we had lost you! We were trying to put something together, trying to reach your people. I'm glad you are OK!"

Half an hour after the North Tower collapsed, Mayor Giuliani held a news conference, talking to New York Channel One. He told people to get out of the area. He said that there was an unbearable loss of life, but that they were doing everything they could to save people. He reassured them that New York City would survive this attack and soon be back to normal.

FDNY Chief of Department Peter Ganci, Deputy Fire Commissioner William Feehan, and many of the senior officers of the fire department directing the evacuation were killed when they were directing operations near the North Tower as the two towers fell.

The NYPD headquarters, another possible target, was also damaged and coated inside and out with gray dust and was unusable. The mayor decided to move the citywide command post to the Police Academy, and they arrived there around noon.

After his talk with the governor, the mayor called his administrative assistant, Beth Petrone.

Beth, who in addition to being the mayor's assistant was also the office manager, said, "City Hall is in pretty bad shape. There are a lot of people here and I don't know what to do with them." Those in the City Hall were primarily staff workers with a few visitors and some people who had come in to escape the chaos outside.

He told her that he would arrange for buses or vans to take them to the Police Academy on Twenty-Second Street and that he would meet them there.

Beth Petrone and Terry Hatton

Recommended by a U.S. marshal whom Giuliani respected, Beth Petrone became his assistant soon after he became U.S. attorney in 1983.[57] When he went into private practice, and later as mayor, she was his administrative assistant and supervised the functioning of his office.

Mayor Giuliani met FDNY Lieutenant Terry Hatton shortly after he became mayor. On January 26, 1994, soon after he was sworn in, there was a gas explosion in a diner in Queens. A woman working there was trapped by pieces of concrete and steel in a hole eight feet under ground level. Lieutenant Terry Hatton went into the hole and stayed with the injured and terrified woman for an hour and a half until firefighters could get her out. Giuliani went to the scene where he could see Lieutenant Hatton and talked with him during the ordeal, the first time the two had met. The woman was hospitalized and recovered. Fire Commissioner Thomas Von Essen recommended Hatton for a medal, and Mayor Giuliani awarded it to him.

A year and a half later, the mayor often noticed Lieutenant Terry Hatton hanging around City Hall. By this time he knew Hatton well, as he had presented him with several awards on behalf of the FDNY. When the two passed, he would greet Hatton and the two would exchange small talk. They would discuss Hatton's studies in preparation for taking an examination to be promoted to captain.

Mayor Giuliani would say, "Hi ,Terry. I'm sorry but I don't have any medals to give you today."

He was so busy that he didn't question why Hatton was there so often. Then one day Tony Carbonetti, the mayor's chief of staff, Bruce Teitelbaum, an advisor, and Christine Reneguamo came into his office. When they walked in as a group, the mayor expected bad news.

He said, "Well, what do you want?" The group informed the mayor that Beth Petrone had something to tell him but that she was embarrassed.

---

57   This account is based on interviews with Mayor Giuliani and Tim Brown.

115

Mayor Giuliani said, "Well, what is she embarrassed about? What is she afraid of?"

They answered, "Well, she's going to have to tell you because she won't let us tell you. So she's going to come in now. Just be gentle with her."

The mayor thought, "Gee! I knew I was tough, but I didn't think that I was so bad that a woman that has worked for me for almost eight years is afraid to talk to me."

Beth came in and told Mayor Giuliani she had been dating Lt. Terry Hatton. She didn't know if this was appropriate because she worked for the administration and Hatton was also employed by the City. She was concerned it might be a conflict of interest and that she would have to resign. The mayor clearly understood that she was not going to stop dating Terry.

Mayor Giuliani said, "Beth! You are so serious! Well, let me tell you. I think it's great that you are going out with him. He's the nicest person for you and he is a great guy! I think it is fabulous. Number one, I hope it works out for you. Number two, there is nothing inappropriate with you dating someone in the fire department. You're not his boss or direct supervisor or vice versa. You have a perfect right to date him, and if anybody ever gives you any trouble we'll claim the 'love and marriage exception'! I think this is wonderful. Now I understand why Terry has been hanging around City Hall."

Not long after, Lt. Terry Hatton and Beth Petrone came in to see Mayor Giuliani and asked if he would perform the marriage ceremony for them. He said it was one of the nicest ceremonies he ever performed.

Now, at the Police Academy, Mayor Giuliani suddenly looked at Beth Petrone and saw that her face showed a terrific strain. Immediately an alarming thought hit him.

He said, "Beth! Was Terry working today? Where's Terry?"

Beth burst out crying. Giuliani asked Judith, a nurse, to look after her. Fifteen minutes later Beth, composed, returned.

The mayor asked, "How are you?"

Beth replied, "I just know he was there. I haven't heard from him and it was right near the end of his shift and he's not home and he's not anywhere else. I can't imagine there's any other place he would be. I know he's gone."

Giuliani said, "Well, you know, we don't know that."

At that point there were still some people being rescued and he wanted to give her some hope. He didn't realize that very few people would be rescued after the buildings fell.

Earlier that day Tim Brown, with over fifteen years in the FDNY before he left to work in the Office of Emergency Management, ran into Captain Terry Hatton near the elevator bank in the lobby of the North Tower. He spotted six-foot-four inch Hatton, whose head stood out among a group of about thirty firefighters. Catching his eye, Hatton motioned for Brown to come over. Brown ran over and the men hugged. Captain Terry Hatton, Tim Brown, and Captain Patrick Brown, no relation to Tim, were inseparable best friends.

Terry hugged Tim tightly and whispered, "I love you, brother! I don't know if I'll see you again."

Brown passed off the fatalistic remark, replying, "Yeah, yeah, yeah."

Later he realized that Hatton, while speeding down the West Side Highway in the front seat of his fire truck, not only had a clear view of what was happening at the World Trade Center with his binoculars, but had the foresight to think way ahead of most people. This exceptional ability resulted in his being selected to command Rescue One, the most elite FDNY unit in Manhattan.

As they were trained to do, Capt. Hatton and his men, each lugging some sixty pounds of oxygen tanks and tools, started climbing up the stairs of the North Tower with the mission of going as high as they could to rescue people below the fire. Eyewitnesses and firefighters who heard Hatton on the radio reported what happened.

Rescue One had climbed at least as high as the eighty-third floor of the North Tower when the South Tower collapsed. They were rescuing people, many badly burned. Then Captain Hatton was heard to broadcast a "Mayday" call and said that Rescue One was trapped shortly after the South Tower fell. One injured firefighter was able to start down the stairwell.

He found a group of firefighters and pleaded with them to save his trapped team, saying, "My company is trapped upstairs! Help!" The men had been trapped by an interior collapse within the North Tower. One theory is that a portion of the South Tower landed on part of the North Tower, causing a partial collapse inside the other building.

Captain Patrick Brown was in the building and heard Terry Hatton's "Mayday." He proceeded up the stairs to try to help his friend. Both Captain

Patrick Brown and Captain Terry Hatton died when the North Tower fell a few minutes later.

Some of the firefighters that the injured firefighter had met also proceeded up the stairs. Others went down. Those that went up to rescue their comrades died with them. Those that went down told the story of what happened to Rescue One.

Ten days later, Beth called Mayor Giuliani and said, "I have good news!"

Giuliani thought that she meant they had recovered Terry Hatton's body.

Instead, she said, "I'm pregnant!"

Mayor Giuliani, Tim Brown, and all that knew her were elated to hear such good news following the tragedy in their lives. The widows of all fire fighters and police officers killed were assigned people to help them through the period of grief and mourning. Beth was assigned a family friend and police officer named Keith McLaughlin to help her as needed. Those around her were concerned that with the stress she was under, her pregnancy might be in jeopardy. Keith would pick Beth up and drive her to work. He would take her to medical appointments or wherever she had to go.

On September 28th, Tim Brown, a close friend of Beth, was in upstate New York attending a memorial service. He got an urgent call from Keith McGlaughlin.

McLaughlin said, "I don't know what you're doing or where you are, but you have to come here right now!"

He would not give any details.

Brown was mortified. What was happening with Beth? Was she in the hospital? How about the baby?

He headed back to Manhattan, speeding so fast on the Bronx River Parkway that at times he felt the wheels of his car were barely touching the pavement. He had been told to meet McLaughlin at St. Patrick's Cathedral.

When he arrived, he was totally mystified. There were thousands of people in the street. He could see the cathedral was packed. There was a Jumbotron[58] set up outside where he could see that Mayor Giuliani was among a group of people. A memorial service was being conducted for Marsh and McClennan Corporation. The corporation's offices had been

---

58   A giant television screen normally used at large sporting events or concerts.

located on the eight floors directly in the path of the plane that hit the North Tower of the World Trade Center. Not one person in those offices lived. Marsh and McClennan lost 295 employees and 200 consultants.[59]

Totally confused, Tim Brown went to the residence of the cardinal, where he found a member of the security detail.

He asked, "What is happening? What is wrong with Beth?"

The security officer replied, "Well, I'm not supposed to tell anyone, and you can't tell anyone either, but here..."

The officer pulled out something that belonged to Terry Hatton and they knew he had on him when he was killed.

Brown now understood that they had found Captain Terry Hatton's remains. The secrecy had been imposed because Mayor Giuliani wanted to be the one to tell Beth that her husband's remains had been located, and he wanted Tim Brown to be there.

Tim found a seat next to Beth and listened while Mayor Giuliani finished speaking at the memorial service. When the service ended, the mayor came down and Tim moved over so Giuliani could sit next to Beth.

Mayor Giuliani reached into his pocket and pulled out a set of keys and put them in Beth's hand and said, "Beth, we found him."

Then, according to Tim, "We all had a good cry."

After the Attack

After they relocated the citywide command post to the Police Academy, Mayor Giuliani again called Governor Pataki, and the two decided to put their forces together and run a joint City/State command center. This would expedite decision-making, eliminating the usual bureaucratic process where the City sends in a request, which is then reviewed by the State and forwarded to the federal government. Arrangements were also made to have representation from the U.S. Government to further speed up processing of paperwork.

At the Police Academy they set up a large table manned by city, state and federal officials. They held three meetings a day. A myriad of questions came up. What if additional firefighters or police officers were needed? How many body bags should we order? What actions were needed to

---

59   Wikipedia, http://en.wikipedia.org/wiki/Marsh_%26_McLennan_Companies.

protect suburban communities? What is needed at the newly established Family Assistance Center helping families of victims? Where should it be? Who will staff it? When do we reopen the schools? If approval was needed for death certificates, the approving authority was at the table. Decisions were made on the spot.

This arrangement was crucial to the success of the mission, not only helping families of victims, but also in responding to emergencies. There were hundreds of bomb threats every day for about ten days, many in public places such as Grand Central Station, Columbia University, or Penn Station. They developed a strategy to deal with it and got on television to discourage unnecessary phone calls. Anyone caught making a false, malicious threat was prosecuted publicly to deter others from making similar threats.

They soon realized they didn't need many body bags but, instead, needed DNA testing when body parts were found. They had to find a way to not only get DNA tests performed but also to set up a procedure to get DNA samples both from remains that had been found and from victims' family members.

Concern arose there might be hate crimes against innocent people of Islamic faith. They had to know if abuse was verbal or physical and where was it happening. The police department put together a special force to collect information and protect the Arab community. The Community Assistance Unit monitored the intensity and scope of the problem.

After four or five days, the original room had become too small for the joint Command Center and it was moved to Pier 92 on the Hudson River; the Family Assistance Center was relocated to Pier 94, three hundred yards away, where both organizations had ample space.

President Bush's Visit

The Secret Service had advised President George W. Bush against coming to New York. There was still concern of more attacks. Ground Zero, in particular, was still a very dangerous place, with fires still burning and others starting up in unexpected places. Toxic fumes, hazardous debris, and parts of buildings still falling made for dangerous conditions. Yet, Mayor Giuliani felt, and the president agreed, that his visit would be a terrific morale builder. New York City made tremendous efforts to ensure the safety of the president. Mayor Giuliani and Governor Pataki were up late the night before he arrived, making arrangements with the Secret Service, which was especially concerned about the president visiting Ground Zero, but President Bush insisted on going to the site.

On Friday, September 14, Mayor Giuliani and Governor Pataki flew by helicopter to McGuire Air Force Base, New Jersey, to meet the president. Air Force One arrived at McGuire and the presidential party then went to Fort Dix, adjacent to the air base. President Bush came off Air Force One, shook Governor Pataki's hand, and hugged him. Then he shook Mayor Giuliani's hand and hugged him.

The president asked, "Mayor, what can I do for you?"

Mayor Giuliani replied, "You know what you can do for me, Mr. President? If you catch this Bin Laden, I want to be the one to execute him!"

In some circles his meaning was taken a bit out of context. Giuliani didn't mean that he wanted to necessarily pull the handle, although he probably would have been willing to do that. What he meant was that he had been a very successful prosecutor and throughout his career when he was faced with a difficult, complex case, he would try it himself rather than trust it to a subordinate. If Bin Laden was caught, he would want to be the prosecutor and would make sure that he got the death penalty.

The president then invited them to join him on his helicopter, Marine One, and they flew to New York and over Ground Zero.

The president's first expression flying over the site was, "Oh, my God!"

The mayor asked the president, "What do you think?"

President Bush replied, "It is much worse than I realized!" meaning that the television photos could not realistically show the extent of the devastation.

Later, Mayor Giuliani said he favored making the entire site of Ground Zero a monument. By maximizing the number of office buildings to be constructed, the memorial would be confined to a much smaller space. He felt that the memorial should give people a sense of the enormity of the event. The planning commission, however, did not accommodate his suggestion.

Dignitaries Visiting Ground Zero

Decisions as to which foreign dignitaries should be permitted to visit were made by the State Department or Condoleezza Rice, the national security advisor.

The State Department's guidance to the mayor was, "The job you can do for us when you take these people down there is to get them angry that this happened. We want them to come away with some emotion. We want them to see what was done to our country."

When Henry Kissinger visited the site, he said, "This is worse than any war site that I saw in Berlin after the war. I was all through Berlin; the bombings, of course, were all through the city, not just in one part. But I've never seen anything worse than this. I've never seen more damage than this. It's hard to believe."

During visits by about fifty leaders Mayor Giuliani heard similar expressions which he felt meant, "There is much more destruction than I expected."

Among others, he took Jacques Chirac, president of France; Chancellor **Gerhard** Schroeder of Germany; Vladimir Putin of Russia; the emir of Qatar; and other world and religious leaders. All exhibited a sense of shock. Some cried.

On October 11th Saudi Prince Alwaleed Bin Talal visited Ground Zero. The State Department had asked Mayor Giuliani to show him the site. Prince Alwaleed was one of the wealthiest men in the world and a major shareholder in CitiBank. He was doing business with Sandy Weill, chairman and chief executive officer of Citigroup Inc., who Giuliani knew. He was considered generally friendly to the United States.

This visit was different than that of the other dignitaries that came. The prince had an entourage of about twenty people. He said he felt bad about what happened and went on to say how terrible it was and that he wanted to help the families of the victims. In Mayor Giuliani's words, he "said the right things." But he did not seem to have the same sense of shock and disbelief or show emotion at the scene. Some people accompanying him appeared to be giggling in the background.

The mayor thought the strange reaction of the prince and his people might have just been due to cultural differences. The prince thanked Mayor

Giuliani for his leadership and gave him a check for $10 million for the Twin Towers Fund.

This fund was initially established for the families of first responders killed at the World Trade Center after the chairman and CEO of General Electric, Jeff Immelt, presented the City with a check for $10 million. After that a number of corporations and individuals donated to the fund, some giving millions of dollars. The parameters of the fund were that the money would go to the families of firefighters, police officers, and rescue workers, no one else. The administrative expenses of handling the fund would be handled separately so all the money would go to the families.

Mayor Giuliani gave the check to Larry Levy, one of his lawyers, and got into a helicopter and rushed off to a funeral, where he met Fire Commissioner Von Essen. He told Von Essen of the gift, what a wonderful thing it was for the families, and that this was exactly the momentum they needed for the Twin Towers Fund. [60]

After the funeral and on the way to his next event, Giuliani got a phone call from Sunny Mindel, his communications specialist. She told him there was a problem with the check.

He chuckled a bit and said, "It bounced? A $10 million check bounced? What's the problem?"

Mindel replied, "It isn't the check. After you left, you know Prince Alwaleed held a press conference. Do you know what he said?"

Giuliani asked, "No. What did he say?

Mindel answered, "He said in a prepared statement, and I'm going to fax you the statement, in part that this attack was caused by American foreign policy and America's friendship with Israel. He also said that America is taking advantage of the Islamic world."

Mayor Giuliani at first thought that the prince didn't seem to be that kind of person, but then he reflected on the strange behavior of the group when they were at Ground Zero.

Sunny said, "What do you want us to do? I think Larry has already deposited the check."

Mayor Giuliani answered, "We can always send it back. If Larry has deposited the check, tell him to put a hold on it. If he hasn't deposited it

---

60   Mayor Giuliani had hoped to raise $20 million-$30 million for this fund, but over $220 million was raised.

tell him to hold it. I'm not sure what I want to do with it yet. Just give me a little time."

He started thinking. He wanted to return the check, but it wasn't his money. The money belonged to the families of the first responders who were killed. It had been specifically intended for families of those killed. Yet $10 million was a significant amount of money.

He thought, "I want to give the money back. This guy is saying exactly the wrong thing. He is part of the problem rather than the solution. We shouldn't be taking money from people who believed in attacking and killing three thousand innocent people."

He called Fire Commissioner Von Essen and asked his advice. Von Essen thought the firefighter families would want to return the money. He talked to Beth Petrone, who had been not only his assistant but also his friend for many years before her husband, Terry, was killed on 9/11.

The mayor asked, "How would you feel about it?"

She replied, "We wouldn't want blood money!"

He asked Richard Sheirer, director of the New York City Office of Emergency Management, to get some firefighter families together so he could talk to them before he made his decision. He discussed it with seven or eight firefighter widows. He asked for an opinion from Jimmy Boyle, former president of the Uniformed Fire Fighters' Union, whose son, Michael, had been killed on 9/11.

The response from everyone he talked to was the same: "We don't need his money!"

The most common answer was, "We don't want blood money!"

Some were more explicit as to what the prince should do with his money. All were adamant.

Mayor Giuliani called Larry Levy, who told him that he had not deposited the check.

Then he held a news conference and said, "We're going to give the money back. We don't want to insult him, but we don't want him to insult us either. We can't take the money on the theory that it was an attack that was in any way justified by anything the United States did. This was a totally unjustified attack!"

Captain Timothy Stackpole

Mayor Giuliani first met then-Lieutenant Timothy Stackpole at the burn unit of the Cornell Medical Center. Stackpole was fighting a fire in east New York on June 5, 1998, when the floor collapsed. Two firefighters were killed and he was burned over 30 percent of his body.

When Mayor Giuliani walked into his hospital room, it looked like an Irish wake. The room was crowded with people and Stackpole was cracking jokes. He was kidding Fire Commissioner Von Essen. Giuliani says that it was the happiest hospital room he has ever seen, except that recurring memories of Stackpole's colleagues who had been killed would put a cloud on the festivities.

Offered the opportunity to take a medical retirement, Lieutenant Stackpole said, "I want to get out of here. I want to go back to work!"

Mayor Giuliani visited him several times during the months that he was hospitalized. Following his hospitalization, he went through a difficult period of rehabilitation. When he had recuperated sufficiently, the commissioner gave him a desk job while he was on "light duty." For the next few months Stackpole drove Von Essen crazy with his requests to be restored to full duty.

Finally, Commissioner Von Essen let him go back to full duty. Three years after he was injured Lieutenant Stackpole was restored to full duty and was promoted to captain five days before 9/11. Captain Timothy Stackpole, survivor of severe burns at the earlier fire, newly promoted, recently restored to full duty, off duty at the time the towers were struck, was killed on September 11, 2001, when the South Tower collapsed.

When the mayor and the commissioner went to talk with Stackpole's wife after he died, it was obvious to her that Von Essen felt guilty for letting Stackpole go back to work on a full time basis.

Even though the commissioner didn't say anything she understood his feeling and said, "I was with him. I love him. Don't feel bad. He had no choice. Even if you didn't put him back to work, you know what he would have done. He would have gone and done what a bunch of others did, right? He'd have gone there. You didn't put him in that situation. He would have seen the flames from Brooklyn and would have been there right away. Never think of it as you put him there ever again!"

The World Series

Mayor Giuliani can't remember how many wakes he went to, probably more than one hundred. At many of these he saw Yankee caps, New York Jets uniforms, Ranger memorabilia, New York Mets shirts, or a combination of these items displayed. Widows would tell him that their husbands were out-of-control Giants fans, or children would say that their father took them to every Rangers hockey game or that he hated to watch a Mets game because he was a Yankee fan.

As the city started to get back to normal, and realizing how important these sporting events were in the lives of the people killed and their families, Mayor Giuliani seized an opportunity. Both the Yankees and the Mets had donated millions of dollars to the Twin Tower Fund. The Mets had also donated office space. He thought it would be nice if they could take some of the children of deceased first responders to the World Series where the Yankees were playing the Diamondbacks in Phoenix in the final two games.

Donald Trump offered the use of his private plane, but soon there were too many people, so Trump arranged for a larger plane which was donated by Continental Airlines. Major League Baseball donated tickets and hotels donated rooms. Approximately twenty people, not including the mayor and his two children, flew to Phoenix for the final two games.

In the eighth inning of the first game in Phoenix, the sixth game of the series, when the Yankees were being slaughtered by a score of 15-2, Giuliani got a phone call from his chief of staff, Tony Carbonetti, who wanted to talk on a secure line. He went into a Diamondback office for a phone and was told that anthrax had been found in the office next to the mayor's in the City Hall.

Carbonetti said, "The news is going to break tomorrow. I think I know how it happened. NBC sent me a videotape and NBC had been infected. We think the tape was contaminated. We don't think it is all over. We still have to do some checking, but some people are going to panic."

Giuliani said, "Well, I better come back."

Carbonetti replied, "You don't have to come back."

The mayor had made up his mind and answered, "I have to come back!"

He had his twelve-year-old daughter and fifteen-year-old son with him.

126

He left the children with John McCain and his family, telling the children, "I will either come back and get you tomorrow night or you'll come back on the plane Monday morning. Mr. McCain will take care of you and put you on the plane."

He got on an airplane about midnight, flew back to New York. He showered and went to City Hall, where he got briefed, decided what action to take, and held a press conference at seven o'clock the following morning.

The New York City Marathon happened to be scheduled that morning, so he went to the Verrazano Bridge and drove along in front of the racers. Then he flew back to Arizona for the final game of the World Series, which, he regretted to say, the Yankees lost.

North Tower after plane hit-NYPD 911 photo

Chapter Ten
The Vigiano Family

"They were good boys and I miss them."

FDNY Captain (Retired) John Vigiano Sr.

The Vigiano family has a tradition of serving with the New York Fire Department. John Vigiano Sr.'s father, also named John, began his service with the FDNY in 1938 and served continuously for thirty-five years as a chief's aide and in the Marine Division of the fire department.[61] When he retired, it was discovered that his badge number, 3436, was broken, and it was put away in a drawer, but never repaired and thus never reissued.

John Vigiano Sr. is a one of those rare individuals who in the organization in which they serve. A former National Guard soldier and United States Marine with more than eight years' military experience, he served in various positions in the New York Fire Department, including in ladder companies, elite rescue companies, and special operations. Additionally, he was one of the first firefighters to serve in a position specially created by former New York City Mayor Ed Koch, as rescue liaison officer between the New York Fire Department and the NYPD rescue teams at a time when there was a great deal of competition, friction, and animosity between those departments. A captain when he retired, he has been awarded ten unit

---

61   FDNY Captain (retired) John Vigiano interviews with the author.

citations and fifteen other FDNY awards, along with a City of New York Public Service Award.

John Sr. and Jan Vigiano's oldest son, John Jr., thirty-six years old on 9/11, joined the FDNY soon after graduating from Stony Brook College. He loved sports, but the first time he walked onto the high school football field, the coach hoped that he would keep right on going because he was so small. Five feet, nine inches in height and solidly built, he became the Most Valuable Player as a lineman! He made up for his size with intensity and speed. His favorite sports, though, were hockey and lacrosse, where his speed, concentration, and passion were his most valuable assets.

At age seventeen, John's brother, Joseph, while still in high school, announced that he wanted to take the police academy test. His father warned him that this was a very difficult test and that many experienced people with college-level education often flunked it on their first try. Joseph insisted, saying that he had read a book about police work, and his parents reluctantly relented, driving him to the test site early one morning. While he took the test, they went to a local restaurant for breakfast. After an hour or so, Joseph came in and asked if he could get something to eat. When asked how he did on the exam, he replied that he "got a hundred." His father informed him that sometimes people don't do as well as they think they did when they are under that type of pressure. Weeks later, when the exam results were published, they found that he had actually scored 110 points. Joe had tremendous energy and focus. After he finished high school, while waiting for his name to come up on the Police Academy list, he got a job driving a Pepsi-Cola truck even before he could drive a car. In a year and a half he made enough money to purchase a new car. In less than two years he went from being a high school student to becoming a police officer in Precinct 75.

Early in his new career, while his team of policemen was facing some criminals, a more experienced officer said to him, "Do you hear those pings? Those are bullets bouncing off of that mailbox—get behind it!"

Joseph learned quickly. In a face-to-face confrontation, an assailant pulled a gun and started shooting at him from close range. Joe threw his hand up and was able to partially deflect the gunman's hand; the first bullet parted his hair in a superficial head wound and the other rounds ricocheted off a wall, striking him in the arm and leg. He returned fire, killing his attacker.

When asked why he shot the man six times, he replied, "Because I ran out of bullets!"

Joseph had been wounded three times while on duty. He killed the first assailant and captured the second. The third was captured by his partner. A member of the NYPD's elite Emergency Services Unit (ESU), he had been awarded the department's two highest commendations, the Medal of Honor (posthumously after 9/11), Combat Cross, two Medals of Valor, and a Purple Heart.

John Sr, was diagnosed with cancer at the time that his oldest son, John Jr., was in his senior year of college. John, not wanting to have his sons disrupt their lives, especially his oldest son's final year in college, decided not to inform them of his illness until he had successfully completed the treatment—a decision he later felt was a mistake, as John Jr. was very upset that he wasn't able to help his parents in this time of great need. During his period of treatment, members of the FDNY, during their own time, voluntarily drove John and his wife back and forth to Sloan-Kettering for his frequent treatments. The surgery and treatment were successful, and almost exactly a year later, John Sr. was back at his job in his rescue company. Upon graduating from college, John Jr. announced that he wanted to become a firefighter.

His father was surprised. "Why do you want to be a firefighter?"

John Jr. answered, "When I saw how the fire department took care of you and mom when you were sick, I decided that I wanted to be part of that team."

John Jr. had to wait his turn, but he used that time to prepare himself for his future job. Every day he would don a weighted vest and run up and down, up and down the stairs at the local train station. When his name finally came up, John Jr. joined the department, and with the same intensity, courage, concentration, and passion he quickly became an outstanding firefighter. The FDNY "fit him like a glove." When John Jr. joined the FDNY in 1990, he asked that his father's badge be assigned to him. The badge, however, had been issued to another firefighter, so he asked for his grandfather's badge. The badge was located, repaired, and issued to John Jr.

On 9/11 John Jr. had arranged to "do a mutual" with one of the other firefighters in his company so that the other man could be off to take care of a problem that he had. His brother, Joseph, was working a double shift so that he could be off that evening to finalize preparation for taking charge of a new Cub Scout pack that his sons had joined.

John Sr. was home shaving when Joseph called him and shouted, "Turn on the TV!" John said, "I'm watching it. They're not sure if it is a Piper Cub or what."

Joe, driving with one other policeman with him, replied, "No, Dad! It's a big plane. We're on the West Side Highway, and just looking at the smoke, I can see that it's not a Piper Cub."

John told him, "Be careful!"

"OK, Dad. I love you!" was the reply.

John Sr. immediately called Ladder Company 132, his other son's company in Brooklyn near the Manhattan Bridge, as he knew he was on duty and was sure that he would be going to the site. John Sr. had to run a quick errand. On his way back he heard the radio announcer, who he described as "really shook up," say, "I can't believe that the building fell!"

John, an experienced firefighter with thirty-six years' experience, thought, "Wait a minute. This guy's a nut. These buildings don't collapse. He doesn't know what he's talking about. They have partial collapses. Walls break down. Sometimes a floor may give way, but these high-rise buildings don't just collapse."

John headed directly home and saw the reality of the situation on TV. High-rise buildings, at least these high-rise buildings, did collapse. He didn't know which of the towers his sons might be in. He knew that Joe was a first responder and was coming from the north and the North Tower was the first one hit, so he figured that was probably where Joe went. Later he found out that as Joe was coming down the West Side Highway in an Emergency Services Unit vehicle with another officer, NYPD Chief of Department Joseph Esposito hitched a ride with him to the WTC by riding on the running board of the truck. Joe felt the Chief should have something protecting his head while riding outside the rig as they were speeding to the site, so he gave the Chief his military style Kevlar helmet.

When they arrived at the North Tower, Joe said "I'm going to need that helmet" and switched helmets, giving the Chief a hard hat ESU helmet.

John and the other officer riding with him gathered their tools and breathing apparatus (Scott Air Paks) and headed into the North Tower.

Chief of Department Esposito years later said, "The composure and the professionalism of your son will always be with me."

A rescue dog located Joe's body far down in rubble of the North Tower, but John Jr.'s remains were never found.

The FDNY arranged hasty accommodations for the relatives of missing fire fighters at One Police Plaza, the NYPD headquarters close to the site of the WTC. John and Jan Vigiano spent their nights there waiting for word from the site. After a few days, First Deputy Commissioner Joseph Dunne came to John and asked him if he would consider moving to a hotel, explaining that if he would do so, others would follow his example.

When he suggested this to Jan, she angrily responded, "You want to sleep in a bed in a hotel while your sons are lying on concrete?"

Chastised, John and Jan spent another few nights sleeping on the cot on the arena floor, then, finally, they did move to a nearby hotel.

John Senior would probably also have been at the World Trade Center the day that his two sons were murdered by terrorists, as he would have been in a ladder company if he had not retired in 1998.

After 9/11 he spent six months at the World Trade Center site helping out. He heard many stories from people working there who knew his two boys. At the wake held for the two Vigiano brothers, people came up and told him stories that he had never heard about his sons. John asked people to e-mail the stories to him so that he could have them made up in a book for his two sons' children. As a result, he received over seven hundred stories.

John Sr. says of his sons, "They were very much alike. They were cut-ups. They had devious minds. They would have made great CIA agents. The practical jokes that they would play on their bosses, their fellow fire-fighters and policemen, were horrible."

Joseph, the policeman, once spent hours perfecting a practical joke on a policeman friend. He set up a CO_2 fire extinguisher so that it would be discharged when his compatriot opened his locker. Time after time it didn't quite work out right. Several times as he tested the booby-trapped fire extinguisher, it didn't discharge the way that he wanted. Patiently, he cleaned up the mess each time until he finally had it set up right. Finally he was satisfied with the setup and, to the surprise of his police officer friend, the fire extinguisher discharged when he opened his locker.

One day, John Jr. was sitting at a table near the kitchen area of his fire station working a crossword puzzle when a lieutenant came in and asked why there was no coffee. Although the fire station had a regular routine and it wasn't the normal time for the coffee to be prepared, John Jr. suggested that the lieutenant have a new firefighter prepare a fresh pot, which the lieutenant did. When the coffee was finished, John poured it out, leaving only a small amount in the bottom of the pot. Then he hid the can of unused coffee grounds in the commissary locker, which was near a bay that the firefighters occasionally used to work on their automobiles in their spare time.

Shortly afterward the lieutenant returned and was quite upset to find that, again, there was no coffee.

He said, "There's no God-damned coffee! I told that guy I wanted coffee!"

He found the rookie firefighter and demanded to know why he hadn't made a fresh pot. The nervous rookie tried to explain, saying, "But I just made a pot!"

He then started to again make a fresh pot but he couldn't find the coffee grounds. John suggested that he go out to the commissary locker to see if there were more grounds there. Moments later the by-now-frightened rookie came back in covered head to toe in a white, powdery substance with only his eyes showing.

The lieutenant looked at him and said, "What the hell happened to you?"

The rookie stammered to the lieutenant, "I'll wash your car! I'll clean it up!"

The lieutenant said, "What's wrong with my car!" and ran out to find it covered with the same white dust.

John had filled the canister of a power vacuum cleaner with flour, and then reversed it so that it could be used as a blower. Then he tied the hose over the car and rigged it up to the light switch so that it went on when the light was turned on. The lieutenant's newly washed Mercedes was covered with the fine white powder.

The lieutenant came back in and glared at John, saying, "It was you!"

John Jr. looked up and said, "What are you talking about?" One of John's senior firefighters asked him why he had done that.

His reply was, "The kid had been working on his car in the bay because it needed new brakes. The SOB made him move it out so he could wash his Mercedes. This was payback time!"

The SWAT team, of which Joe was a member, and the FDNY Rescue Squad, where his father was assigned, were in competition and were natural adversaries.

John Sr. said, "If Joe, in his SWAT uniform, would see me, I'd get out of the fire truck. He'd come over and kiss me and shake hands with all of my firefighters. He would kiss some of the fire fighters that he had known for twenty years since his birthday parties as a child."

The cops would say, "What's with the kissing?"

Joe would reply, "You got a problem with that?"

"No, no," would be the answer.

John and his two sons had a very strong bond.

John describes his sons as "two good boys. They were boys in the true sense of the word. They were cunning, they were scrappers, they were mischievous. They fought each other and they fought with each other. They were such good men. They were good fathers. They were good husbands. They were good sons."

Joe would regularly call his father every day around 2:00 p.m. when he started work. John Jr. would call a couple of hours later when he started on his shift and would fax his father the fire department orders for the day. If John wasn't home, he'd hear the fax machine later and know that his son was at work, and he would call the firehouse. Every conversation ended with, "I love you."

When he was asked if he would like to have his book of anecdotes about his two sons published, he declined, saying that those were only for his grandchildren. When the FBI learned of the books, they asked if they could borrow them and also asked John if he would like to go to visit the prison at Guantanamo Bay.

John replied that he would be glad to go, "if you let me go down there with a loaded weapon."

The FBI representative replied that wasn't exactly what they had in mind.

John and his wife continue to grieve for their sons, but they are grateful for what they had—"a wonderful relationship with two fine young men."

Their regret is that it should have been longer.

John Sr. said, "A parent should never have to bury his child."

He is not willing to accept the premise that people who profess to be religious could massacre people without apparent reason.

John Jr. had joined the fire department when he was twenty-six years old. He had served for ten years when he was murdered on 9/11. He left his wife, Maria, and two daughters, Nicholette and Ariana. Badge number 3436 was retired, having been worn by only two fire fighters, John Vigiano Jr. and his grandfather. Joseph left a wife, Kathy and three sons, Joe, Jimmy, and John.

After his sons were killed, John became involved in the FDNY Wounded Warrior Project, which supports military personnel who have been wounded in Afghanistan and Iraq.

While making a visit to Walter Reed, John was asked by Paul Wolfowitz, then deputy secretary of defense, if he could arrange for FDNY firefighters to visit these soldiers. Since then John has made numerous visits to Walter Reed with groups of ten FDNY firefighters. These visits are upbeat and well received by the service men and women who they visit. John and the other firefighters know that these military heroes don't want pity, but rather the opportunity to return to normal lives. Often the firefighters are told that the soldiers want to return to their units to continue to serve their country.

The Sons of Italy has established two $1,000 scholarships in the Vigiano sons' name. The Sons of Italy has also started a new lodge, named the Vigiano Brothers Lodge No. 3436—the badge number worn by John Sr.'s father and son. The president of Manhattan College has established two scholarships of $10,000 in their names.

Fire engine destroyed on Sep. 11th-photo courtesy of FDNY

Chapter Eleven

FDNY Chiefs Sal Cassano, Charles Blaich, and Gerard Barbara

"In 102 minutes, less time than it takes to watch a movie, we had two airplane crashes, two high-rise buildings destroyed, and almost three thousand people killed."

FDNY Commissioner Sal Cassano

On September 11, 2001, Sal Cassano, then assistant chief of the New York Fire Department, was the citywide tour commander, a daily rotating position in which he was responsible for overseeing actions at any major fire in New York City.[62] A native-born Brooklyn New Yorker, he was working on a special project at a routine weekly planning meeting at fire department headquarters when the meeting was interrupted by a radio report that there had been an explosion at the World Trade Center. The senior officials of the New York Fire Department had been drinking their morning coffee while coordinating their activities for the week. Peter Ganci, chief of the FDNY, Donald Burns, chief of operations, and Gerard Barbara, also an assistant chief, were there. The group of senior officials initially thought the

---

62   This chapter is based on interviews with New York City Fire Commissioner Sal Cassano, FDNY Chief (retired) Charles Blaich and Mrs. Joanne Barbara, widow of FDNY Chief Gerard Barbara.

explosion might have been caused by something such as a propane cylinder that had blown up. They rushed to Peter Ganci's office, where they had a clear view of the World Trade Center, and saw that a plane had hit Tower Number One. The group, composed of the most experienced firefighters in the city of New York, immediately realized that on this beautiful, clear day, with not a cloud in the sky, this was no accident. Cassano immediately hurried to his official car and, with the siren and lights on, raced to the site. Just as he arrived at the tower and was exiting his car, he heard the massive explosion as the second plane hit Tower Number Two.

"At first" he said, "I thought that it was a secondary explosion, never dreaming that another plane had hit."

Large sheets of glass from the exterior of the tower were falling, and Chief Cassano, along with other people in the area, scurried into a nearby post office garage to escape the falling debris. When the way had cleared a bit, Sal Cassano made his way to West Street to help coordinate the rescue effort.

At the corner of West and Vesey streets, right next to the towers, firefighters were setting up a command post. Because large panes and sheets of glass were still falling, Cassano directed that the command post be moved to a location farther away because "it was way too close to the North Tower."

Sal Cassano worked for FDNY Chief of Department Peter Ganci, and after giving these orders, he went back to find Ganci and immediately became his executive officer for the operation. They knew there were firefighters in the South Tower and in the Marriott Hotel, but they didn't know who, how many, or what companies had gone into those buildings. When fire stations across the city realized the enormity of the situation, officers at many of those firehouses, especially those located near the World Trade Center, readied their units for immediate response. Some of those companies had arrived before the command post was set up and went directly into the buildings, most probably trying to report their locations and personnel participating by radio. Radio networks, however, were jammed with many units responding, trying to report their locations and find out where they were needed. Additionally, the massive structures themselves interfered with good radio reception. Because of this, reporting was a hit-or-miss operation. As a result, in the early stages, senior department officials, who were arriving and just starting to set up a command post, did not know what units were there, what their composition was, or where they were in the buildings, or, for that matter, which buildings they were in. There were also many firefighters who, even though they had just gone off duty, "rode heavy" to accompany their units as volunteers.

Accountability for people in a disaster scene is critical. Lives can be lost when the locations of firefighter and emergency personnel are not known.

Commissioner Cassano said, "We knew we had people in the Marriott Hotel, and we were trying to get a handle on what was going on there. I went into the Marriott to see what units we had there, and I met the chief of training, Chief Galvin. I found out what units we had there and I got a phone number from a phone in the lobby so we could talk. The cell phones were going crazy, the radios were blaring, and I wanted a hardwire line. Three of our most experienced captains—Freddy Ill, Walter Hynes, and Dave Wooley—were there. I looked at them and said, "Boy! Am I glad you guys are here! You have the experience we need! Just make sure to be careful and take care of your firefighters! Good luck to the three of you!'"

Then someone from Eleven Truck (Ladder Company 11) said, "I can't get up here into the Marriott. They're not letting us in."

Chief Cassano told the security people that those firefighters had to get in there, and they were let in. "They were all killed. We lost everyone from Eleven Truck." Captains Freddy Ill, Walter Hynes, and Dave Wooley, the experienced captains, also all died that day.

Chief Cassano saw Captain Dan Brethel from Ladder Company 24 and, knowing that he was off duty, said, "What are you doing?"

Then Cassano assigned him a job. "I need you to write down the names of everyone here that is off duty so we know who is here. Then we will assign jobs to them."

Sal Cassano and the others did not expect the towers to collapse, as it was almost unheard of for high-rise buildings to fall, even when engulfed with flames. Sal made his way back to the command post and then, without warning, there was a tremendous roar as the first tower fell.

Cassano said, "It sounded like another airplane was coming in overhead."

He, William Feehan, the deputy New York City fire commissioner, and Peter Ganci, the chief of the New York City Fire Department, quickly ducked into a garage.

Commissioner Cassano said, "It was terrible—really bad! Debris was flying everywhere. I don't know what would have happened if that garage hadn't been right there. We were completely covered in dust, but we weren't trapped."

After the massive dust cloud started to clear and they made their way back out, Chief Ganci started giving orders to initiate rescue procedures.

He told the firefighters at the command post, "We have to get trucks (ladder companies) and get a task force together. We have people trapped!"

Sal remembers Peter Ganci saying, "Get everybody north! We're too close, get everybody north!" and "I need units. Get me five truck companies! We've got people trapped in there!"

Peter called Sal and said, "Move the command post north. Get them outta here!"

Sal immediately started executing his orders to move the command post north. Peter Ganci, however, stayed where he was to direct the rescue.

Sal found Pete Hayden, first deputy chief, and Joe Pfeifer, the first battalion chief, at the site, and said, "Look! Pete Ganci said move them up north—get them out of here!"

After the South Tower collapsed, they expected the North Tower to also fall and knew that they had to completely evacuate the remaining tower. Not surprisingly for a man that has been cited by the New York Fire Department five times for bravery and who, as a young man, had served a tour in Vietnam, Chief Sal Cassano headed back to the area of most danger to assist Chief Peter Ganci. He said, "I had been working with him the whole time and I wanted to see what else I could do to assist him. I started to work my way south down West Street."

As Chief Cassano was hurrying down West Street at the junction with Vesey Street, near the North Tower, to meet with the chief of the department, he heard the same tremendous roar that he had heard earlier when the South Tower collapsed.

He said, "When I looked up, I saw the tower lean and then start to come down. That's when I started to run. So, I started running along West Street to see if I could outrun the building. I looked up and thought, "I don't know if I can outrun this building."

This time there was no nearby building to provide shelter from the devastation that was just starting to happen.

But, he said, "there was a rig (fire truck) on the corner of Vesey and West streets, and I dove under it to get out of harm's way. It was one of the rigs that, although badly damaged, wasn't destroyed by the collapsing building. The rig I dove under held up. I was lucky—we lost other people."

While a number of firefighters dove under fire engines for shelter as the towers fell, some of these men were killed when the trucks were crushed by the thousands of tons of concrete, steel, and other debris. Captain Dan Brethel, the man that Sal had instructed to account for off-duty firefighters, was among those crushed as he desperately sought shelter under a fire engine.

The North Tower had collapsed into the concourse in a southerly direction, somewhat away from where he had sought refuge. Had he gone a little further, another thirty seconds or so, or if the fire engine hadn't been located at the right spot, Chief Cassano would not have survived. As it was, even under the fire truck, he was still in grave danger and was almost asphyxiated.

He said, "You couldn't see anything. I don't know how much more time I had left. The dust cloud just completely enveloped us. I don't know if I had more than five or ten seconds of breath left before I would have been overcome by the dust—so I was lucky. I got pelted by some material and was injured."

Finally, after the dust and smoke started to clear, he crawled out from under the fire truck and managed to get on his feet. He had trouble walking and, as he stumbled along, an emergency medical technician put him on a stretcher and into one of the first ambulances to leave the site. They took him to the hospital, where many doctors and nurses were waiting outside, obviously expecting to be treating many injured patients. However, there weren't many wounded, as the people that had been in the buildings either escaped relatively unharmed prior to their collapsing or were killed when the towers fell.

Once in the hospital Chief Cassano was checked, x-rayed, and cleaned up quickly, then he called for a ride back to headquarters. Someone came and took him to the fire department headquarters. He found virtually no one there to run the operations center, as all of the top officials had either been killed or were still working at the site of the World Trade Center.

Important work urgently needed to be done. With our nation under attack and not knowing if New York City might be hit again, the New York Fire Department urgently needed to reposition its firefighters and replace the equipment that had been lost or destroyed as quickly as possible. As one of the senior people in the department, and with many of those that were more senior now among those murdered by the 9/11 terrorists, Chief Sal Cassano now knew that he had even more responsibility to help the fire department get back on its feet.

He had just had a narrow escape from death, had just survived a more deadly experience than any that he had seen in Vietnam. Even today, he still feels the pain and sorrow for the 343 firefighters, including Chief Gerard Barbara, his closest friend, who were killed that day of terror. He still feels the remorse that Captain Dan Brethel, Captains Freddy Ill, Walter Hynes, and Dave Wooley, and the firefighters who went into the Marriott all died that day, even though he knows that the orders that he gave were the correct orders at that time.

At that critical moment, he had to put aside his emotions and go to work. There were still other fires to fight, people who needed rescuing, and other emergencies in addition to the terrorist attack. The New York Fire Department had lost many key people and much critical equipment. Deputy Fire Commissioner William Feehan, Chief of Department Peter Ganci, Assistant Chief of Department Gerard Barbara, and Chief of Operations Donald Burns had all been killed, as was renowned FDNY Chaplain Mychal Judge.

Cassano immediately started working to reassign personnel, obtain replacement fire engines, masks, tools, and other apparatus. He repositioned both men and equipment within the New York City Fire Department, borrowing from units that had not suffered the devastating losses of those hit the hardest. Chief Sal Cassano worked all night. He worked all the next day. Finally, dead tired, he arrived home sometime around 10:00 p.m. on September 12.

Sal Cassano joined the New York Fire Department on November 29, 1969. On June 17, 2006, he was appointed the thirty-third FDNY chief of department—the highest-ranking uniformed position in the agency. On January 1, 2010 he became the thirty-second New York City fire commissioner. In this position he oversees all of the firefighting operations, including emergency medical services, safety, training, fire prevention, communications, and many of the rescue operations in the city of New York. He also is responsible for coordinating activities with other city agencies and providing advice to the mayor and government.

Commissioner Cassano feels fortunate that he sustained no serious lasting injuries from his close brush with death on 9/11. Still, it is not known what future health problems might develop for people exposed to the toxic conditions at Ground Zero.

On May 1, 2011, the night that Usama Bin Laden was killed, Commissioner Cassano said, "Usama Bin Laden was responsible for killing 343 members of the FDNY on Sept. 11, 2001. Tonight, in firehouses throughout the city, our members are grateful for the news, and thankful to all the brave members of the U.S. military that had a role in this successful operation."

As in many families, firefighting in New York City has become a tradition in Commissioner Cassano's family. His older brother had talked him into becoming a firefighter. One of his nephews is a New York firefighter, and one of his daughters is married to a firefighter. Commissioner Cassano has a Bachelor of Science degree in fire science from John Jay College of Criminal Justice. He and his wife, Theresa, reside in Staten Island. They have five children.

Charles Blaich

"Whatever you use to light up Yankee Stadium—bring it down!"

Chief Charles Blaich at Ground Zero

FDNY Fifteenth Division Chief Charles Blaich served in Vietnam in 1969–70 and in the first Gulf War in 1991 as an officer in the U.S. Marine Corps. He is a retired Marine Corps Reserve colonel.

Chief Blaich was recuperating at home on Staten Island on the morning of September 11, 2001, from surgery after removal of a tumor from his spinal column. He was about to return to "light duty" with the FDNY in a few days but was suffering from a heavy cough and chest cold. His wife, Mary, had left the house before the Twin Towers were struck.

Chief Charles Blaich's brother, Billy (a year and a half younger) was battalion chief of the FDNY First Battalion, located on Duane Street. Billy called Charles from home and told him that a plane had hit the WTC. "I'm going in," he said. Charles Blaich turned on the TV and saw that the plane that hit the tower was a large one.

When he heard there was a "total recall," Charlie Blaich got his uniform and equipment together and called his aide. Then he and his brother Billy, who lived minutes away, loaded the car and Billy's wife drove them to the Staten Island ferry. The massive boat, carrying only emergency workers, police, firefighters, and EMT personnel, raced across New York's upper harbor toward the Hudson River. As it crossed, the deeply anxious public safety passengers could see the WTC buildings burning and then, as the ferry steamed past Governor's Island, they watched in horror as the first tower collapsed.

Chief Billy Blaich's son, Peter, was a fire fighter in Engine 9 in Chinatown near the World Trade Center. Billy felt with deep concern and desperation that he had probably been killed in the collapse.

The ferry terminal several blocks south of the World Trade Center was still intact, and the ferry, avoiding debris in the water, tied up there about the time that the second tower fell. An emergency worker on the ferry called to see if the subway tunnel was still intact, but decided that he didn't want to be underground under the current circumstances.

As the crowd of rescue workers hurried from the ferry, they were not in the toxic "cloud" that accompanied the building collapses, as the cloud was moving in the opposite direction. In ironic contrast to the scene that people found on the east side, the sky in Battery Park, west of the complex, was blue and birds were singing. Everything was now eerily silent, with none of the noises of traffic and pedestrians that were heard on a normal weekday morning in Manhattan.

Charlie Blaich hurried to West Street with a group of firefighters while Billy headed East on Broadway toward his firehouse on Duane Street. Charlie ran into a group of construction contractors who told his group, "Take whatever tools you need." So the men, who hadn't been to their fire stations, picked up picks and shovels until each man had a tool.

Charlie Blaich found an FDNY mobile command post and asked the men manning the CP, "Where is the next higher headquarters?" Their reply was, "You're it!" Charlie found a radio and the men picked up face masks from a nearby ambulance and went to work.

Peter Ganci, the chief of the FDNY, and other senior FDNY officials had been killed when the towers fell. Chief Blaich began to organize a field command post. They started to get some water from fireboats in the Hudson River. Hydrants on the west side failed when the water mains had been damaged. They were able to get water to Tower Ladder 15. Then Charlie named the various command posts that he had control over, calling one "Liberty Street" another "Church Street," and a third "West Street". The north boundary of his area of responsibility was Vesey Street.

Flaming debris from the towers had started a fire in the building at 110 West Street. Charlie got blueprints of the building and rushed men and equipment to fight the fire.

That night someone came up and asked him if he wanted to order lighting equipment. He replied that he would. When asked how much, he replied, "Whatever you use to light up Yankee Stadium—bring it down!" He signed the necessary papers and says that he is still waiting for the bill, because it lit up the place like it was daylight.

Charlie Blaich remained at Ground Zero until about 11:00 p.m., when he was relieved by a deputy chief. Because of his recent surgery, Blaich was not able to hold his head up straight. Earlier that day, the fire department medical office called his wife to ask why he had missed a follow-up appointment. The following day Charlie, still technically not able to work as he was on medical leave, went to the medical office and demanded to be restored to full duty, which he was. He then picked up some spare radio batteries and returned to Ground Zero. Volunteers started showing up—steelworkers, laborers, firefighters, and, in some cases, people claiming to be steelworkers. While everyone expected to find survivors, none were found after the second day.

On one occasion, a shout went up, "We found survivors!"

Two men who looked like firefighters and were wearing firefighter equipment were "freelancing." They were a father and son who had fallen into a hole about ten minutes before they were rescued.

Chief Blaich took over his brother's firehouse on Duane Street and used it as a command post. He served as the logistics chief for the WTC incident command post for five months after 9/11, then returned to his position as commander of Division 15 in Brooklyn. His men would meet every day between 7:00 and 7:30 a.m. and pass out work assignments for the day. There were some problems initially—masks without filters and filters without masks.

They worked fifteen to sixteen hours a day for five months. Since the fire department was in charge of the operation, he coordinated activities in his sector with OSHA, the American Red Cross, and the Salvation Army.

Blaich tried to get everyone to wear the cumbersome masks, and he even told his boss, Peter Hayden, "Put on your mask!" In spite of his emphasis on wearing masks, in October 2001 Chief Charlie Blaich came down with "World Trade Center cough." At a safety meeting with Mayor Giuliani, he coughed so hard that he ended up in convulsions lying on the floor. A year later the cough came back. He has a physical examination every year and said, "So far, thank God, I have not had any lung problems!"

Gerard Barbara

"I didn't 'lose' my husband. He was murdered!"

Joanne Barbara

On the morning of September 11, 2001, Joanne and Gerard Barbara talked in their home in Staten Island about what they were going to do that evening. They kissed and said good-bye as he left to go to the FDNY headquarters in Brooklyn and she left to go to her job at a radiology clinic in Staten Island.

Chief Barbara was an assistant chief of the FDNY, one of the senior officers in the department. When the first plane struck, he and Chief of Department Peter Ganci, along with other staff members, rushed to the elevator to head to the site.

As they rode down the elevator, Deputy Director of Communications Joe Higgins, noticed that Barbara was straightening his tie and remarked, "You're going to the biggest disaster of our lives and you're straightening your tie!"

Barbara, always a professional, replied, "You always have to look good for the public!"

He was at Ground Zero when the second plane struck the South Tower. Chief Peter Ganci put him, as one of the senior chiefs in the FDNY, in charge of rescuing people from that tower. He organized the command post in the tower and directed fire companies in their duties as he supervised the evacuation of civilians.

As events became busier, Chief Barbara's radio wasn't working properly. His aide said, "Take mine. I'll get another one from the FDNY car."

Joanne saw smoke and flames pouring from the North Tower on a television in the lobby of the building where she worked. At first, she thought the plane that struck the North Tower was a small plane off course.

She thought, "Jerry is going to have a busy day!"

When the second plane hit the South Tower, she understood the cold reality that the city was under attack. She wasn't worried about Gerard—he was an experienced firefighter and knew what he was doing. She was worried about their daughter, Caren, who worked in an office near the World Trade Center.

When Gerard didn't come home that night and she hadn't heard from him, she feared the worst. After thousands of civilians below the floors where the plane had hit were successfully evacuated, he had remained at the command center and was killed when the tower collapsed at 9:59 a.m.

Gerard Barbara's aide survived because he had gone to get a replacement radio.

Two or three months later, an FDNY lieutenant called Joanne Barbara. He told her that he had never met Chief Barbara but knew who he was. He related a story about her husband.

He said, "I spoke with Chief Barbara that day because one of the men in my company had been badly injured. I called in a 'Mayday!'"

Chief Barbara told him help was on the way. The lieutenant responded that the injured man was on the sidewalk and gave the location.

Barbara told him, "Stay fast! Don't go away from the building!"

A few minutes later, the lieutenant called again with another "Mayday."

Barbara asked, "Is this a new 'Mayday,' or the same one that you called earlier?"

The lieutenant answered that it was the same one.

Barbara calmly ordered, "I got it. It'll be all right. Stay with the injured man on the sidewalk."

The lieutenant told Mrs. Barbara, "He saved my life because I stayed there."

The injured firefighter died.

Gerard Barbara was still in the U.S. Navy, serving on board the aircraft carrier *Franklin D. Roosevelt* (CVA-42), when he was informed that he had been selected to join the FDNY. He became a firefighter in 1969. He graduated from the FDNY Fire Academy on Halloween in 1970. The following year he married his sweetheart, Joanne. His new wife was concerned about his assignment in Harlem, but after she met the people he was working with, her fears went away.

In 1977 he was promoted to lieutenant and assigned to Ladder 102 in the Bedford-Stuyvesant section of Brooklyn. He and other firefighters formed a study group to prepare for the examination leading to promotion to captain. These men and their families became close friends. They continued their studies together through the ranks leading to battalion chief and higher.

Lieutenant Barbara received the Pulaski Association Medal in 1980 for heroism after rescuing a woman from a tenement fire. Later, working in Manhattan, he became experienced in high-rise blazes and fire prevention. When promoted to battalion chief, he was reassigned to Staten Island. In 1993 he was promoted to deputy chief and assigned as deputy chief of operations, which directed operations for the entire FDNY and the Emergency Medical Services unit.

He later was assigned to the Bureau of Fire Prevention and two years later was appointed as the chief of the bureau with the rank of assistant chief of the FDNY, the second highest rank in the department. This bureau performs almost two hundred thousand fire inspections a year and is responsible for testing sprinkler and alarm systems throughout New York City. Chief Barbara's realistic attitude towards fire prevention was clear. He often said, "You can't close a business down because the sprinkler system is broken. You just make sure that it gets fixed!"

After a five-hundred-pound piece of concrete fell in Yankee Stadium, Chief Barbara was given the task of inspecting the ballpark. He was an avid Yankee fan and, in his wife's words, "he thought he had died and gone to heaven."

In April 2001 he was appointed as citywide tour commander, a rotating position where he was responsible for supervising at major fires in the city.

Monsignor Delendick, the FDNY chaplain, presided over Chief Gerard Barbara's memorial service on October 1, 2001. Two weeks before 9/11, twenty-seven-year-old firefighter Michael Gorumba, Engine 163, had died of a heart attack while fighting a fire at an auto body shop. Chief Barbara called his wife, Joanne, and told her that he would make the next-of-kin notification to the man's family. He had to wait, however, because he did not want to go to deliver the bad news until Monsignor Delendick could go with him.

The monsignor, who had become a family friend, also conducted the wedding for the Barbaras' son, Paul.

Joanne Barbara goes to Ground Zero three times each year. She visits on Gerard's birthday, which is St. Patrick's Day, the anniversary of 9/11, and Christmas Day. She misses the private trailer which used to be at Ground Zero where families could visit in private to pray, bring birthday cards, flowers, baby pictures, and spend a little quiet time to reflect. It was also a place to cry. There were no media, no photographers, just a peaceful atmosphere, but when new construction was started, the trailer disappeared.

When Caren Barbara was about to be married in September 2008, she said, "I'm walking down the aisle by myself."

Her mother said, "You have me. You have your brother. You have your godfather."

Caren replied, "But no one is Dad!"

Deputy Division Chief (retired) Jimmy Bullock, a family friend said, "That is the most profound statement that she can make! No one can replace her father."

Joanne and Caren Barbara were appointed by Mayor Giuliani to serve on the boards of directors for the Family Assistance Council and the Twin Towers Fund, Joanne representing widows and Caren representing adult children. Both also were in the group of twenty FDNY, NYPD, and PAPD family members accompanying the mayor on his trip to Phoenix to see the final two games of the World Series in 2001.

Families of those killed meet every other month to exchange ideas and discuss things that worry or concern them. Family members also give out awards in memory of their lost ones. At a dinner where several people were giving out one thousand dollar scholarships to deserving high school students, Joanne Barbara was seated with Gerard's uncles and his mother. The customary speeches and announcements were becoming tiresome.

As Joanne rose to go to the podium to present an award she said, "Watch this one!"

"I'm here to talk about my husband," she announced. "I'm giving this award out to honor my husband's memory. But my husband was murdered!"

That got everyone's attention. The room went silent as people put their silverware down.

She said, "People say you 'lost' your husband. I didn't 'lose' my husband. He was murdered! I know where he was. He was taken from me abruptly. He went to the work he loved and never came back." Her statement wasn't meant to be offending but, rather, to remind the audience that the attack on 9/11 was still in the minds of those most affected every day and that no one should ever forget.

Joanne went back to work in November 2001 but she was still consumed by the events of 9/11. The FDNY was especially caring and considerate of the families of those killed and injured on 9/11. Uniformed fire department personnel were assigned to help families, often providing transportation and helping them cut through red tape. The FDNY set up a counseling program for families of those killed. Joanne participated in the program, which was conducted on an anonymous basis in which participants did not know others in the program. Some of these people complained that they wanted to meet others in the same situation. That was arranged around Christmastime of 2001.

Four or five years after 9/11, Joanne Barbara decided to start making a life for herself. She is a confident, self-sufficient woman who rarely asked for help. When it was needed, she asked friends that she and Gerard had known for many years, many of whom are senior people in the FDNY.

In 2009 she met a Jersey City police officer whose wife had died at a young age through natural causes. They found that they had similar backgrounds, their children were of similar ages, and they had similar values and mind-sets. They have helped each other plan weddings for their children. Their children get along well and are happy that the two are together.

Gerard Barbara was not only a die-hard Bronx Bombers fan; he was also a big supporter of the "Baby Bombers," the Staten Island Yankees, an affiliate of the New York ball club. Each year, the Staten Island Yankees host a Gerard Barbara Day, from which a portion of the proceeds raised is donated to charity. Money collected is donated through the FDNY Columbia Association, an Italian-American organization in which Gerard Barbara was named Man of the Year in 1999, and dedicated to college scholarships and to helping firefighters studying for promotion.

Senior Detective John Pesce (left) and unidentified officer help injured man- photo courtesy of John Pesce

Chapter Twelve
New York Police Department

"The people responsible for this have got to pay."
President George W. Bush, as he was driven around Ground Zero

Late one Friday in July 2001, representatives of the FBI came to a meeting held by NYPD Chief of Department Joe Esposito. [63] They revealed there was much more "chatter" [64] going on and that a major terrorist attack was likely to occur. They didn't know when, or where, but indications were that it would be overseas. It was important enough, however, that they called a meeting in New York City late on a Friday afternoon.

John Picciano, police commissioner chief of staff, was on the fourteenth floor of the NYPD headquarters at One Police Plaza in Manhattan when he heard that a plane had hit the North Tower of the World Trade Center. He rushed to the conference room, which had a full view of the towers. After one look, he ran down the hall to Commissioner Bernard Kerik's office and banged on the door. Kerik had just finished his morning workout and was

---

63   This chapter, except as otherwise indicated, is based on interviews by the author with NYPD Chief (retired) Salvatore Carcaterra, NYPD Detective (retired) Ralph Cefarello, NYPD Senior Detective (retired) John Pesce and NYC Police Commissioner Chief of Staff (retired) Mr. John Picciano.
64   "Chatter," or increase in communications among terrorist cells, often occurs before terrorist acts of violence.

getting dressed. He said, "I know. I heard a small plane hit the World Trade Center."

"No!" Picciano replied, "It wasn't a small plane!"

Kerik dressed immediately and, with members of his staff, headed to Ground Zero at top speed. With police headquarters less than a half-mile away, they were there in three minutes.

Thinking that somehow it was a terrible accident, they went to a location across the street from the World Financial Center on West Street, where FDNY Commissioner Von Essen, Deputy Commissioner Feehan, and FDNY Chief of Department Ganci were located when the second plane flew over them and hit the South Tower. As debris rained down around them, the leaders of New York City ran up West Broadway Street. Although it was immediately decided that the operation would be rescue and recovery rather than firefighting, there was no thought among the group at that time that the buildings might collapse.

The men, joined by Mayor Giuliani, hurried to World Trade Center Seven, which housed the City's Emergency Operations Center. They quickly saw that it was on fire and uninhabitable. They then went to a small office at 75 Barclay Street. Mayor Giuliani had heard the Pentagon had been attacked. He called the White House and informed an aide to President Bush of the situation in New York, and he in turn was informed that the Pentagon had, indeed, also been attacked and that the White House was being evacuated.

Commissioner Kerik had ordered the NYPD mobile command post to the site. John Picciano went outside to check, then returned and told Commissioner Kerik it would arrive in about five minutes. Suddenly the glass blew out of the windows and smoke poured into the building. They tried to go out one set of doors but were stopped by a huge plume of smoke. An initial radio report said that the top thirty-five floors of the South Tower had collapsed. Some janitors in the building led the group, including Mayor Giuliani, into the basement and back upstairs to the lobby of 100 Church Street. They went outside and headed north. Coming to a nearby hotel, they went inside, but it was dark. Going back outside, they heard U.S. Air Force F-16s overhead. Two minutes later as they started north again, the North Tower fell.

Mayor Giuliani, Commissioner Kerik, FDNY Commissioner Von Essen, John Picciano, and other officials made it up to a fire station on Sixth

Avenue on foot, about three-quarters of a mile away. When they got there, it was locked, as the fire crews had already responded to the World Trade Center. The group was finally able to get inside, where they saw on television for the first time the full extent of what was happening. Commissioner Kerik, Chief Esposito, and Picciano called for a vehicle to pick them up. Their vehicles were all at Ground Zero, many damaged or destroyed. They moved to the Police Academy on Twentieth Street near Second Avenue to set up a command post. The abandoned and gutted command post at World Trade Center Seven collapsed later that day.

Police Chief Esposito had shut down all access to New York City except for emergency vehicles within thirty minutes after the North Tower collapsed. Knowing only that the nation was under attack, and not knowing the magnitude or possibility of follow-up attacks, the police emergency plan was put into effect. The entire police department was mobilized at Level Four, the highest level, establishing 1,200 posts protecting power plants, synagogues, water treatment facilities, stock exchanges, the Empire State Building, and government buildings throughout the city. A perimeter was set up from Forty-Second Street to the south, effectively shutting down vehicular traffic within that part of the city.

That evening Commissioner Kerik and John Picciano went to the auditorium of the police headquarters, where they met with fourteen families of missing policemen. These families were holding out hope that somehow their son or husband would show up or be rescued, but such was not to be. They also visited injured firefighters and police officers at Bellevue and St. Vincent's hospitals.

During the next twenty-four hours, more than 180 bomb threats were received, some with malicious intent, but most called in by concerned citizens, perhaps overreacting to finding an unattended package or suspicious device. Each of these perceived threats had to be taken seriously and investigated. The Empire State Building was evacuated twice that day.

Mayor Giuliani called President Bush and told him that it would be an uplifting experience for the city if he would come to visit. President Bush, over the objections of the Secret Service and security personnel, came to New York City on September 14.

As he went around Ground Zero he said, "The people responsible for this have got to pay."

He was scheduled to meet with family members of people missing, with the understanding that the visit would at most be one hour and fifteen minutes. President Bush stayed for four hours.

John Picciano said, "He was simply amazing! He didn't just shake hands and express his condolences. He sat for photographs and talked with people and asked about the missing people and those that were killed. He asked to see pictures of the missing people."

The mayor and police commissioner wanted to get the city back to normal, but it was difficult to say that people should go back to work and go about their normal business when they couldn't purchase bread and milk or get fresh vegetables. Access across the George Washington Bridge was opened after a couple of days. Over the next two weeks, the restricted perimeter was decreased to permit needed goods and services to reach the citizens of the city.

NYPD Deputy Chief of Department Salvatore Carcaterra

Sal Carcaterra had wanted to become a police officer since he was five years old. By September 11, 2001, he had served more than twenty years in fourteen different assignments and was the senior deputy to Chief of Department Joe Esposito. On that day, Election Day in New York, he got up early and went to the gym. At 8:47 a.m. he was driving his official Jeep to work when the radio started blaring and his phone started ringing as news of the plane hitting the North Tower was spread. He tried to call Chief Esposito on the radio but didn't know if his message got through.

Still on the way in from Staten Island when the second plane hit the South Tower, he heard a radio message from Chief Esposito saying, "We're under attack! I want an evacuation of City Hall!" Carcaterra found it hard to believe the reports he was hearing. He turned on his flashing lights and headed into the Brooklyn Battery tunnel, mowing down three-foot-high lane markers as he sped through. Then he was stopped by the congested traffic. He tried, without success, to establish radio contact in the tunnel. Finally, after what seemed like hours but was only a few minutes, he made his way out and turned right because fire trucks blocked the way that he would normally have gone, a factor that may have later saved his life when the towers fell. He circled around, going against the traffic on

West Street, and parked his car at the corner of West and Liberty streets. He tried to contact Chief Esposito again. Unsuccessful, he linked up with some other police officers and started to set up a headquarters under one of two overpasses.

Even though both buildings were on fire, he never thought that they would collapse. He started to return to his car because it had a booster for the radio, and he thought he might be able to get through to Chief Esposito. He saw papers floating around, then objects falling from the towers. He was shocked when he realized that what he saw falling were people jumping out of the windows. He said, "I will never forget the sound when they hit. It was horrible! Horrible! Horrible! They exploded when they hit. Other people were screaming and crying! It was like scenes from a horror movie."

Still on his way to his car, he felt someone, he doesn't know who, suddenly grab his arm and say, "Chief! The building is coming down!" They turned into a corner up against a wall, then heard the whooshing sound of the gigantic wind created as the building fell. Rubble and debris were falling and he was being pressed up against the wall. Carcaterra felt himself going down. He couldn't breathe as he was being pelted and covered by debris.

As he was gasping, trying to breathe and trying to cover himself, he was angry, thinking, "How did I put myself in this position?"

Carcaterra knew he was losing consciousness. He thought, "Is this how it feels to die?"

The lower part of the wall that the men were forced up against was solid, but the upper part was of hardened glass near the entrance to the Financial Center. Some police officers were able to get their pistols out and break the glass by firing a number of shots into it. All would have been crushed if the wall had been solid. They went into the building, not sure where they were because everything was dark. They turned to the left and came to an elevator bank, then returned to the lobby. They saw a bit of light and headed out toward the East River near West and Liberty streets. Carcaterra went into a small store, where people gave him some water to rinse his eyes. He felt like his mouth was filled with ground-up Sheetrock, which it probably was.

Officer Glen Pettit, a police videographer who had been standing five feet away from Chief Carcaterra moments before, was killed by falling debris.

As Carcaterra walked along West Street, Police Officer Kenneth McCann , who was handing water out to people, told him not to go back to the World Trade Center because the other tower was going to come down. The men worked their way down to the river, where police boats were ferrying people across to the New Jersey side. Chief Carcaterra and Pat Lynch helped women, some pregnant, onto the boat and took them to the other shore. They heard about the plane hitting the Pentagon, and rumors of other planes headed toward New York. Carcaterra said that he had to go back, so the boat dropped him off at Pier 11 near Water Street. Covered with white powder, he walked to the Police Benevolent Association office and tried to use the phones. The phones were out, so he walked back to Police Headquarters at One Police Plaza. When he got to his office, people hugged him because they thought he had been killed. His car was crushed and buried and not found until later. People searching for him couldn't find him because he was on the boat.

Carcaterra reported to Chief Esposito, then called his home to let his family know he was all right. Commissioner Kerik called a meeting of all the NYPD leaders in the auditorium. Then Chief Carcaterra cleaned up, changed clothes, and they locked down the headquarters. Returning to Ground Zero, they found the body of a Port Authority police officer. That night they found an airplane wheel near the Brooklyn Battery Tunnel.

Around 3:30 a.m., Chief Carcaterra went home to take a shower and change clothes. He was driving through the now-deserted Brooklyn Battery Tunnel in a borrowed, marked police cruiser. He passed a policeman guarding the entrance. Then, totally exhausted after a furious day, with our nation under attack, military aircraft patrolling the skies above the city, his mind started playing tricks. He convinced himself that the policeman wasn't really a policeman but an evil man, part of the plot against the city. He backed up a quarter mile in the tunnel to confront the man, engage him in conversation, and verify that he was, in fact, a police officer doing his job, which he was. He laughs self-consciously about it now, but then it was serious.

"Who would have thought that planes would be used as missiles against New York City?" he said, "No one would have thought that those buildings would collapse. Why couldn't a terrorist with evil intentions be 'stationed' in a major tunnel?"

The NYPD, along with the FDNY and the PAPD, started months of work at the site doing recovery operations, coordinating with the families of survivors, arranging and attending funerals while still running every-day operations of the various departments. Two things stand out in Chief Carcaterra's mind. The first is that people who normally did their jobs in a routine, unnoticed way, came forward in the time of need and performed surprisingly exceptional service. The second was the support of the public. Driving down West Street, people would cheer and wave signs. He would go home to shower and change clothes.

When he stopped for a cup of coffee on the way back to work, people would say, "No! I'll pay for your coffee!"

People came out of retirement to help out at Ground Zero. Retired firefighters came down to look for their sons' remains. VIPs would come to the site to build morale and sign autographs. They would stay as long as you wanted them to.

One cold day in February 2002, they got a call that they thought the body of a police officer had been found. They went down and recovered the body, which, while intact, had been flattened to about an inch thick. Chief Carcaterra hopes that because of the way the body was found that the man never knew what hit him and did not suffer. When the body of a firefighter or police officer was found, everything at the site stopped. The workers would line up and pay their respects as the body was removed. This was a scene repeated many times as 403 police officers and fire fighters were lost that day.

Like all those who were there, Chief Carcaterra will never forget what happened on 9/11. As a grim memento, he keeps the clothes that he wore that day in a bag in his basement. Two of his childhood neighborhood friends, brothers who worked for Cantor Fitzgerald, were killed that day.

Two months after 9/11, an American Airlines plane crashed in the Rockaways, killing all aboard. Chief Carcaterra was in his official car and was one of the first people to arrive.

As he approached, he thought, as many people did, "This is happening again!" At that time, the nation was still on alert. (It was later confirmed that mechanical failure, not terrorism, was responsible for the accident.)

But now Chief Carcaterra is concerned. People, he believes, have for-gotten the impact of 9/11, and with the failures of other terrorist plots such as the shoe bomber and the attempted SUV bombing at Times Square, the nation may have become complacent. Young people also don't realize the impact. His own sons were only a year and nine years old at the time. Carcaterra wants them to understand the continuing threat that we face. Each year on the anniversary of 9/11, he sits down with his family and they watch the documentaries of our nation under attack.

People ask him, "Why do you watch that stuff?"

That worries him.

Detective Ralph Cefarello

On the morning of September 11, NYPD Detective Ralph Cefarello, aide to Chief Esposito, was at home when his wife phoned him from work and told him that a plane had hit the North Tower.

"You better get in!" she said, "The chief is going to need you!"

Cefarello hurriedly dressed, picked up an extra shirt that he might need during what he knew would be a long, hard day, and ran to his official car. Then he fastened his seat belt, something that he rarely did. With lights flashing and siren roaring, he tore into the city from Staten Island. He raced across the Verrazano Bridge. Glancing down at the speedometer as he careened through the now-deserted Brooklyn Battery Tunnel, he noted that it registered 115 miles per hour! Later he felt that he had a guardian angel watching over him, as he was slowed by a vehicle in front of him for a few seconds at one point, an event that may have saved his life.

Coming out of the tunnel, he stopped a half block from the World Trade Center where Police Captain George Duke of the Major Case Squad was gathered with some policemen. He rolled down the window and asked Duke if he had seen Chief Esposito. Duke replied that he had not seen Esposito, although he had seen Deputy Chief Sal Carcaterra. Cefarello drove on about fifty yards, then, when he saw Chief Carcaterra, he stopped and started to release his seat belt.

Suddenly, Cefarello heard a noise, so frequently described by people present at the WTC that day, which sounded like a freight train, and saw debris raining down outside. From inside his automobile, he saw a man running toward him, waving his arms, motioning people to run. The man was caught up in a cloud of grayish-white dust and Cefarello never saw him again. He tore at his seat belt but was unable to release it. Then the car was bombarded with rubble and he was enveloped by a cloud of choking white dust pouring in the open window. He heard the car and the ground outside being pounded by debris. He couldn't breathe. He couldn't see. Cefarello thought he was finished. In desperation, he grabbed the shirt on the seat next to him and held it over his face so he could breathe. Now in total darkness, he wondered if he was buried alive in his automobile. Inside the car he did not know what was happening, or that the South Tower had fallen.

When the pounding on the car stopped, he reached into the back seat and picked up his large flashlight. He put on his chief's department baseball cap and exited the car into the now-grayish-dark, eerily quiet street. He said, "It was like a movie, it was so weird, like walking on new soft snow." He looked into nearby fire trucks, one on its side, to see if anyone was trapped or injured inside. He didn't find anyone in them. Then Cefarello came across a man carrying several cameras, probably a photographer for the *New York Post*. The man had a broken leg, so Cefarello, a former football player, put the man's arm over his shoulder and helped him to a safe spot under an overpass.

He met an NYPD lieutenant and the two walked together among the rubble and debris.

They heard a woman scream, "Help me! Help me!"

He yelled, "Keep yelling so I can find you!"

The two men kept looking, but then the screaming stopped and they were unable to find her.

Cefarello said, "She didn't sound like she was in pain, maybe she was just stuck or scared, but I don't know if she lived or died."

Suddenly, he felt a sharp stinging sensation as shrapnel from a car's exploding gas tank, hit him in the leg. He crawled away on his hands and knees. When he was able to get up, Cefarello ran into Detective Pete Moog, who he had played football with years earlier, and told him that he was looking for Deputy Chief Carcaterra, so the two men went together. They looked for Carcaterra, calling out his name as they looked under piles of debris, but couldn't find him. (As described earlier, Chief Carcaterra had narrowly escaped, then assisted people crossing the Hudson River to the New Jersey shore.)

Then an FBI agent ran up and shouted, "Get out of here! This building is coming down!"

As they started running across the street, Cefarello heard the same rushing train noise that he had heard earlier. Very close to the North Tower, they frantically started to run when Cefarello saw an open garage door. The men ran inside as day instantly turned to night and they were enveloped in the cloud. Again, in the midst of the blinding dust, the men couldn't see or breathe. Cefarello got behind a post and Moog ducked behind a parked car.

When the noise stopped, Cefarello called out, "Pete! Are you all right?"

Moog replied, "Yeah, I'm OK."

Cefarello pointed his large flashlight toward the sound of Moog's voice and said, "Come to the light."

Moog, five feet away, replied, "What light?"

He and two other people came to the sound of Cefarello's voice and they linked up. After conditions started to clear, Moog and Cefarello went outside, leading and directing other people toward the river. People covered their faces as best they could; one woman had her blouse up over her head. They came across a man, carrying an eight- or nine-year-old girl, and his wife heading into the cloud of dust, debris, and rubble.

The man said, "I gotta get out of here! I have to get out of here!"

The two policemen stopped him. Cefarello said, "You're going the wrong way! You're going to kill your child!"

The disoriented man argued, but the policemen wouldn't relent. The man's wife finally took him by the arm, and the family followed them toward the water.

When the group got to the Hudson River, they saw that boats were taking people across the river to safety. Many of the boat owners were civilians who had come to transport people out of danger. Commissioner Kerik's personal assistant, Eddie Aswad, was on one of the launches and called out to Cefarello. They then took him to the First Precinct, where his leg was bandaged. While he was there he heard military jets flying overhead.

His father called him on his cell phone and Cefarello told him, "Dad, we're at war!"

He was then taken to a Manhattan hospital, where he was checked over and released. He got a ride to the police headquarters. Cefarello found Chief Esposito, and the two of them worked the rest of the day at Ground Zero, directing the NYPD effort and making sure that needed supplies got to the policemen who needed them. At one point a rumor had gone around that Chief Esposito had been killed, and the staff was devastated. It turned out that both Chief Ganci of the FDNY and Chief Romito of the Port Authority Police Department were the chiefs of department that had died. Someone had written, "Chief Espo, Rest in Peace" on a window near Ground Zero.

When he went home late that night, he took off his clothes in the backyard and went in to take a shower. The next day, he went to Ground Zero with Detective Tom Nigro to look for bodies. They found body parts, but no bodies. From then on, Cefarello and Chief of Department Joseph Esposito worked fourteen or more hours each day for the next few weeks, spending much of their time at the site. Cefarello's eye bothered him, and a few days later he went to see a doctor, who removed something that looked like a small shard of fiber.

A couple of days later, Cefarello was putting on his boots as he prepared to go back to work. He explained to his nine-year-old son, Michael, who was getting ready to go to a friend's birthday party, that he had important work to do and that something bad had happened. He explained as best he could to a young child that he should be good to his mother because you don't know what might happen next. His son left the room.

Cefarello's wife, Tina, came in and said, "What is Michael doing? He's putting on his boots."

She went back and asked their son what he was doing.

"I'm not going to the birthday party. I'm going to help Daddy!"

Later a police lieutenant said that Cefarello had saved his life. Cefarello doesn't remember that, but the lieutenant said that a big man with dark hair wearing a chief of department shirt had saved his life; there was no one else that could have fit that description, and no one else would have been wearing that shirt.

Chief Esposito, Deputy Chief Carcaterra, and Detective Cefarello went to look at Cefarello's car after it was recovered with a pile of debris on top as well as inside.

They asked, "How did you get out of the car?"

Cefarello believes the nearby Deutsche Bank building partially shielded him and saved his life. His car mechanic showed him something that looked like a badly clogged lint filter from a clothes dryer and told him that was the air filter from his car.

The mechanic said, "That's what you were breathing!"

Cefarello wistfully explains that his Andrea Boccelli tape was melted. The damaged car smelled so bad that it could not be used.

In retrospect, Cefarello feels that the slight delay he experienced going through the Brooklyn Battery tunnel may have saved his life, as if he had arrived a few seconds earlier he would probably have exited his car and been struck by the debris that pounded his vehicle.

Cefarello says that he would wake up at night with a lot of congestion for a long time after, but, although he suffers from diabetes, he feels that he is in good health. Like many of the people that worked at the site, however, he worries about what the future might hold.

Senior Detective John Pesce, NYPD

"The fact that I can have this conversation with you is a significant achievement on my part."

John Pesce, in a tearful interview with the author.

John Pesce, raised in the Greenpoint area of Brooklyn, had spent twenty-five years as a policeman, twenty years of that with the NYPD. At 4:00 a.m. on September 11, 2001, he and his partner, David Cummings, set out as undercover police officers to arrest a woman they had tracked for four months. A few hours later they located her in the Bronx, arrested her, and brought her to the Bronx criminal courthouse.

When they arrived, they met a strange situation. There was no one there. Equipped with weapons, radios, and handcuffs, they walked through metal detectors, setting off alarms. Still, no one challenged them. They called out and finally a uniformed officer showed up and told them the courthouse was closed. The man said there had been a horrible accident, that a plane had hit the World Trade Center.

He asked, "What kind of plane? A Cessna or a Piper Cub?"

The man replied that it was a large commercial passenger plane. Pesce knew immediately that it was not an accident because commercial planes were not permitted to fly over Manhattan.

Detective Pesce told the individual that they had arrested a felon they had tracked for four months and they would have to release her so they could respond to the World Trade Center unless they could turn over

166

custody. The court official reluctantly agreed to accept the prisoner and put her in a cell.

Pesce and Cummings ran to their car and headed down Third Avenue at breakneck speed. They tore past Yankee Stadium, running red lights as they went flying into upper Harlem. The middle lane was clear as all civilian traffic had moved over to let emergency vehicles pass. They saw an unbelievable sight: people stood in the streets halting cross traffic and waving emergency vehicles through as they sped toward Manhattan.

Pesce and his partner reached speeds of seventy to eighty miles per hour as they approached Central Park. As they tore through the park, at one point all four wheels of the car left the pavement when they hit a small rise.

Cummings clocked the trip at eight minutes and fourteen seconds for a trip that mapquest.com estimates at twenty-four minutes. Arriving near the WTC after the second plane hit, they found the area congested with fire trucks, ambulances, and police cars. They parked two blocks north of Vesey Street and ran into the complex, avoiding body parts, burning rubble, and plane parts while dodging falling debris.

They saw hundreds of people falling from the stricken towers, some fully engulfed in flames, clothes on fire. Some held hands as they jumped from the building. They could see others hanging out of the windows, yelling and screaming for help. Some people stripped to their underwear because of the heat. Helicopters hovered helplessly overhead with no way to rescue the doomed victims.

The two men didn't know where to report, so they just started helping people. They went into the underground complex under WTC Building Five and started evacuating people. The two men, together with other police officers, led forty-two people to safety, some who had escaped from the towers, others from the underground complex. Pesce and Cummings continued to dodge falling bodies and debris as they led people to the street and safety. At some point in the chaotic situation, the two got separated.

Suddenly, Pesce heard the sound of buckling concrete and twisting steel, something he knew from previous experience was a building starting to collapse.

He looked up and said, "Do you hear what I hear?" to another police officer.

The man replied, "Yes! I do!"

Pesce and the other officer grabbed an injured man and ran for their lives, pulling the man along. Then they ran toward the massive Federal Building near WTC Seven.

All at once, as they were dragging the injured man two blocks away, they felt a massive downward wind and John screamed, "Run for your life! The tower's coming down on top of us!"

Caught in the enormous cloud of grayish powder, it was fifteen or twenty minutes before they could see. After it cleared up all they could see was death and destruction. They took the injured man and led others seven blocks north near Canal Street, where they located a lone ambulance. The ambulance driver told them the ambulance was full with twenty people in the back. He instructed the two officers to lay the two injured people on the hood and to tell them to hold on. After the two injured people were placed on the hood, the ambulance drove slowly away.

Pesce worked his way back across the rubble into the cloud of dust to search for other people he could help. He found his partner, Cummings, and the two started looking for other survivors to assist. A few minutes later he was on Vesey Street when he heard the same buckling, crunching and twisting of steel and concrete as the North Tower collapsed. As a giant rolling ball of fire came out of the rubble, he again saw his life flash before his eyes. He and Cummings desperately ran for their lives through the piles of debris to seek shelter. Pesce thought he was finished.

Suddenly, someone reached out from an open doorway and pulled him and some other people into a building, then slammed the door just as the ball of fire rolled on by. Pesce found himself face to face with a rabbi who had just saved his life. The rabbi offered them some food and drinks then took them into his basement where he gave the men hard hats, paper dust masks, goggles, picks, shovels, rope, flashlights and lanterns. The rabbi then accompanied them back to the pile to look for victims.

He said, "This is my city too! I'm going with you because people need help!"

The men, covered with gray powder, worked at the "pile" until the rabbi was exhausted. They went back to his building with him then returned to the site. Around midnight, now also totally exhausted, they finally located their car covered in debris and powdery dust. They cleared the car off as best they could and returned to police headquarters where they found they had been on the missing persons list. They went through

HazMat procedures to clean off the toxic residues from the day's work. They safeguarded their weapons and had a medical checkup at the nearby Mother Cabrini Medical Center. After being treated for their injuries and released they were told to take a shower, get an hour's rest, and then report back to work. Pesce left at 3:00 a.m., went home, and returned two hours later.

The following day they set up an emergency operations center at the 69th Regimental Armory on Lexington Avenue and East Twenty-Fifth Street, where they took missing persons reports and made death notifications when remains were found. They continued to assist survivors and their families and friends as best they could. When they had free time and on their days off, they would go back to the "pile" to work on search and rescue teams. They would work on bucket brigades, passing buckets of debris along a line of volunteers to carefully excavate debris in the hopes of finding survivors.

On September 15 Detective Pesce was assigned to work with a twenty-five man search and rescue team searching for injured or trapped people or remains. While going through badly damaged outlying buildings, an emergency evacuation alarm was sounded as there was a rumor that another building was starting to collapse. Pesce and others ran for three blocks to get away. Pesce injured his legs while running and was sent home to recover. It was later determined that the noises that people thought was the start of a building collapse had come from nearby construction equipment.

Pesce could barely walk for a week, but declined being put on the sick list and, three days later, was back at Ground Zero working with a canine search and rescue team that had come down from Massachusetts.

Years later, Pesce still suffers from his leg injuries. He also has lung problems as a result of his work at Ground Zero and suffers from posttraumatic stress. He attended annual 9/11 ceremonies the following two years but had to go into therapy each time. Now he treats September 11 like any other day, avoiding ceremonies and television news.

Later, the rabbi was awarded a certificate of appreciation and detective hat at a police department ceremony.

Recovering a fallen victim-photo courtesy of FDNY

Chapter Thirteen
The Chaplains

"If my choice was between burning to death and dying cleanly by jumping out a window, having been burned severely, I would jump, too! You really have no choice."

Captain Timothy Stackpole

The FDNY has seven chaplains—four Catholic, one Protestant, one rabbi, and one imam. [65] Two chaplains are on twenty-four-hour call at any one time. They respond to three-alarm or larger fires, calls involving fire department deaths, injuries, or hospitalizations. The clergy also perform at various ceremonies, including promotions, graduations, memorial services, blessings of new fire trucks, and an annual blessing of the FDNY Marine Division fleet of fireboats. Each chaplain also has his own civilian congregation.

Monsignor John Delendick, Chaplain, FDNY

Monsignor John Delendick was raised in a parish whose priests were good role models. He decided to become a priest when he was quite young. He attended a seminary prep school in high school.

---

65   This chapter is based on interviews with FDNY Chaplain Monsignor John Delendick and NYPD Chaplain Monsignor David Cassato.

On 9/11, Monsignor Delendick, on call for Brooklyn and Queens, but not Manhattan, had just finished saying Mass at his parish, St. Michael's, in Brooklyn when his pager went off with a message that a plane had crashed into the World Trade Center. Like most people, he thought it was probably a small plane, as he knew commercial aircraft were prohibited from flying over Manhattan. The on-call clergy, however, responds anywhere in the city for major emergencies, and when he saw the magnitude of the disaster on television, he called the operations center and told them he was headed into Manhattan.

Driving in, still on the Brooklyn side of the city, he saw a plane flying very low and very fast.

He thought, "That plane is awfully low!"

He wondered if the pilot had flown down to take a look at the damaged Twin Tower. He lost sight of the plane as buildings obscured it. Then he heard on the radio that a second plane had hit the WTC, and that New York City was under attack. He thought the second plane attack may have been a terrorist strategy. He knew that in such attacks a second bomb was often placed to go off when first responders arrived.

The Monsignor arrived at Ground Zero shortly after the second plane hit and immediately reported to the fire department command post on West Street opposite the Twin Towers near the World Financial Center. A nearby garage was being used as a field command post (CP) with a staging area behind the CP for arriving firefighters.

Looking up, he saw what he thought was debris falling from the Twin Towers. Then he realized that the "debris" had arms and legs and that people were falling from the stricken buildings. Shocked, he gave the falling people a general absolution of their sins.

He was standing next to Captain Timothy Stackpole, who had just gone off duty before the planes struck the towers, but came to the site as soon as he heard of the attack.

Monsignor Delendick said, "This is terrible! People are jumping to their deaths!"

Stackpole replied, "If my choice was between burning to death and dying cleanly by jumping out a window, having been burned severely myself, I would jump, too! You really have no choice."

Stackpole, at the first fire that Monsignor Delendick had attended where firefighters perished, had nearly died when he and two other men fell through a floor that collapsed. After months of recuperation, rather than taking a disability retirement, Stackpole had returned to work after a long period of recuperation.

Monsignor Delendick told Captain Stackpole that he thought they should tell the FDNY officers to watch out for their "probies," as he didn't know how it would affect the young recruits. Then he realized that not even experienced firefighters could calmly watch as people jumped or fell to their deaths.

Standing with Deputy Fire Commissioner William Feehan and Chief of Department Peter Ganci, Delendick heard a strange noise. Looking up, he thought he saw the top of the South Tower exploding, but did not realize the building was collapsing. The group ran down a ramp. When the noise stopped, Feehan and Delendick made their way through the darkness back up the ramp. Unable to see, Delendick carefully inched his way up toward the street through the smoke and dust.

He thought, "Where is the doorway? I didn't think we went down that far."

Then he stumbled on a curb and realized they were already in the street. He still thought there had been a large explosion near the top of the tower. It did not immediately occur to him that the building had collapsed.

A man grabbed his arm and told him that someone was injured down the street. Monsignor Delendick started through the midmorning darkness, wondering where he was going. He not only could not see clearly, but also didn't know where the individual was.

Then Chief Ganci came over to Monsignor Delendick and said, "We were able to get Flaherty out." Ed Henry, chief of Battalion 40 and father of four firefighters, had been trapped with Chief Brian Flaherty in the corner of the Hotel Marriott, located next to the South Tower. Henry and Ganci were able to clear out enough rubble that they were able to pull out Flaherty, who had a broken shoulder.

Chief Ganci told Flaherty to find a radio on a fire truck and pass the order to send every available rescue company and squad, and every available truck, to the World Trade Center. Ganci then ordered the CP to be moved north on Chambers Street.

Delendick said, "I think I should stay here because people may need me here."

Ganci replied, "No! Go north to Chambers Street. If we need you, we'll call you. Pick up any stragglers along the way and take them with you."

The monsignor did as he was ordered and started toward Chambers Street, three blocks away. When he got to the corner he heard the same strange noise of the steel and concrete of a building twisting as it started to collapse. The group of people he was with turned west and started to run toward the river. He thought the top of the building was falling off and still did not comprehend that the buildings had fallen.

As they were running toward the river, a police officer running next to the monsignor asked, "Father! Can I go to confession?"

Delendick said, "You want to go to confession? This is an act of war, isn't it?"

The police officer replied, "Yeah, I would think so."

Delendick, for the second time that day, said, "I am giving everyone general absolution."

Chief Ed Flaherty, the man with the broken shoulder, was again trapped in the rubble of a fallen building. An overhanging piece of a structure came down on top of him and he was pinned down with only three-quarters of an inch of clearance. This time he thought he was finished. Slowly and painfully, however, he inched his way out. An EMS crew found him, lifted him onto a stretcher, and took him to Columbia Hospital.

As the monsignor and the other men made their way along the river, they saw ferry boats pulled up to the bulkhead, taking people to safety in New Jersey. As they passed Stuyvesant High School on the way to Chambers Street, students were rushing out of the school, dismissed to return as best they could to their homes. The students, not completely understanding what was happening, gaped in awe at the eerie-looking figures, ashen gray, looking more like ghostly Halloween characters than firefighters and policemen. They could hear the children say, "Look at that!" as the men passed by in the bright, sunny area west of the cloud of dust, debris, and smoke.

When they arrived at the new CP on Chambers Street, the group, for the first time, could see that the Twin Towers had disappeared. The men started back to Ground Zero to look for people who needed help.

Monsignor Delendick encountered Mayor Rudy Giuliani shortly after the bodies of Chief Ganci and Commissioner Feehan were recovered.

Giuliani said, "I want you to escort Commissioner Feehan and Chief Ganci to the morgue and make sure they are treated respectfully!"

The monsignor went with Henry MacDonald, one of the mayor's aides, in an ambulance with the bodies to the morgue. At 5:21 p.m., as the men were preparing to go in the ambulance, WTC Building Seven started to collapse. Monsignor Delendick shocked the young ambulance driver when he ordered, "Get in the ambulance and close the f*&#?ing door!"

They drove off through the deserted Manhattan streets. No people, no cars, no taxis. Lower Manhattan was a ghost town. All they could see were fire trucks, police cars, and ambulances.

When they arrived at the morgue, it was like an armed camp surrounded by police cars. They backed into an ambulance bay and started to move the bodies to a field gurney.

A medical examiner ran out, saw the dirt-encrusted people, and started yelling, "Who are these? What are you doing?"

They said, "These are two firefighters from the World Trade Center."

The medical examiner said, "We're not ready yet. They have to go to a processing center first and that's not set up yet. They'll have to go to a refrigerated truck until everything is ready."

Henry MacDonald walked up to the man and said, "You don't understand. These are two of the most respected members of the fire department. If the firefighters hear that you are treating them like this, they'll come down here and take this building apart brick by brick."

The medical examiner replied, "You're serious about this?"

MacDonald said, "Yes, we are!"

"OK," the examiner said. "I'll take them and put them in the refrigeration unit here and get to them as soon as I can. But who are they? There are no toe tags, no paperwork."

Delendick and MacDonald gave them the names and replied, "We don't normally do this, but we'll get down here as soon as we can with all of rest of their information."

Another FDNY chaplain, Monsignor Marc Filacchione, in charge of hospital chaplains in addition to his job as an FDNY chaplain, got off the train at Cortlandt Street and was trapped in a subway tunnel near the World Trade Center. A policeman led him and the other passengers through the tunnel and up through an emergency exit. Unable to get to the WTC, he went back uptown to his residence, changed his now-soiled clothes, and started visiting hospitals throughout the city to locate injured firefighters.

Rabbi Joseph Potasnik's synagogue was located near the Brooklyn Bridge. He opened it up as a way station to assist people escaping Ground Zero. He let people make phone calls to loved ones, gave them a place to rest after their trying ordeals, and offered them refreshments.

Father Mychal Judge, a well-known and widely loved FDNY chaplain, arrived at the WTC soon after the planes struck the buildings. Some reports were that he was killed while administering last rites to Danny Suhr, a firefighter killed by a person falling from one of the towers. These reports were later determined to be erroneous. Father Judge died of a heart attack as he and others were leaving the North Tower and crossing the walkway to the World Financial Center. Father Judge collapsed at the bottom of an escalator. Other than a gash where he hit his head when he fell, there were no other visible injuries to his body.

When Monsignor Delendick learned that Judge's body had been taken to St. Peter's Church near the WTC, he went there. The monsignor knelt in front of the body, which had been placed in front of the altar, and said a few prayers.

The monks of Father Judge's Franciscan order came to the FDNY command post and asked for the body.

FDNY Chief Medical Officer Dr. Kerry Kelly said, "You can't do that! He's the victim of a crime. You cannot touch his body until the medical examiner releases it!"

The monks said, "No! We want to take him now!"

Dr. Kelly grabbed an ambulance crew and ordered them to go to St. Peter's Church and to take the body anywhere but the Franciscan monastery. The crew did as directed. They took Father Judge's body to the firehouse across the street from the friary!

The firefighters brought out a bed, and Father Judge's body was placed on the bed. People came from all over to view the body all day long at the makeshift wake in the bay of the firehouse.

The firefighters realized they could not keep the body there, so they called Campbell's Funeral Home. The funeral director told them that they could not accept the body until it was released by the medical examiner and that there would have to be an autopsy.

Somehow, on 9/11, a medical examiner showed up at the firehouse. He said, "I have to take the body. There will have to be an autopsy, and the way things are going it will be about three or four days before you can get the body back."

One of Mayor Giuliani's aides was standing nearby and said, "You don't understand! He's Jewish![66] We have to have the body back tomorrow!"

The body was released that same evening.

When Monsignor Delendick later asked Dr. Kelly how the examiner's office could work so quickly, she replied, "The men in the medical examiner's office respect you guys, but they are terrified of the rabbi." (Monsignor Delendick later talked to the medical examiner, who said, "I knew who he was. I couldn't keep him for three or four days. I knew I had to get him back right away.")

Father Judge was the only uniformed member of the FDNY killed on 9/11 who had an open-casket funeral.

Dr. Kelly and a couple of police officers broke into a Duane Reade drugstore on 9/11 to get supplies. Then they set up a field emergency room in the lobby. They anticipated they would be treating many people, but few showed up as most people were either killed or suffered comparatively minor injuries. When people were not seriously injured but were in need of hospital care, ambulances would take them to a more distant location to conserve resources of nearby hospitals for an anticipated flood of serious injuries that did not materialize.

After Monsignor Delendick escorted the bodies of Chief Ganci and Deputy Commissioner Feehan to the morgue, he went back to the WTC. He met several firefighters looking for their sons and brothers. Former President of the Uniformed Fire Fighters Association Jimmy Boyle told him that he was looking for his son, Michael, and Ed Henry's son. He met Michael Henry and told him that his father, Ed, was in the hospital.

Michael replied, "I know that. I'm looking for my brother."

Later, Monsignor Delendick met Ed Henry Jr. Ed Jr. said, "Listen! I'm looking for my brother."

Delendick finally saw the chance to give someone good news and he said, "I just ran into him. I saw Michael down the street!"

---

66   The Jewish religion requires that bodies be buried as soon as possible, usually the day after the person passes away.

Ed Jr. replied, "No! No! No! I'm looking for Joey!" The monsignor had forgotten that three Henry brothers were firefighters.

Around 9:00 p.m. Monsignor Delendick ran into the Ginley family members, close friends of his. The father and five sons were firefighters. One of the sons, Lt. John Ginley, died that day.

When the buildings collapsed, the board with locations of firefighting units and personnel was destroyed. "Riding lists" carried by officers and copies in the fire trucks in many cases were missing as officers were killed and trucks were buried and destroyed in the rubble. Additionally, many firefighters reported directly to Ground Zero and were not with their units. As a result, it was days before an accurate accounting could be made of those killed.

When Monsignor Delendick returned to the WTC site, he went to the FDNY command post, now located on the third floor of the World Financial Center (WFC) because there were two working telephone lines in an office there. The cafeteria was located on the same floor. Some of the firefighters and Delendick broke into the cafeteria and emptied the refrigerators. They liberated all of the sandwiches they could find and passed them out to emergency workers.

When fatigue overcame him after a long day of stress and physical activity, Monsignor Delendick returned to his rectory. He found his car mostly undamaged, but looking like it had been in a heavy snowstorm. The vehicle, parked near the entrance to the Brooklyn Battery Tunnel, was covered with a foot of debris and coated with gray powdery dust. He scraped the windows clean so he could see to drive home.

He arrived at the silent, lonely rectory at 3:30 a.m., exhausted. No one was up, no one to talk to. No one to share his feelings, his stresses, his pain at losing so many good friends. No one to offer comfort. Monsignor John Delendick sat down and cried.

For the first time he felt the loneliness of celibacy. "You come home and there's nobody there to greet you and ask if you are OK." Even to call his sister in New Jersey he'd have to wake her up. He went to bed, got up again at 6:30 a.m., and returned to Ground Zero.

On September 13, Bishop Tom Daily of the Diocese of Brooklyn called him and said, "I know you have a lot to do with the fire department. I'm giving you another priest for your parish at St. Michael's. He's a retired pastor, so he knows administration. He can take over when you're not there.

Don't worry about the parish. Do what you have to do. We'll worry about the parish!"

He spent the following days in pastoral care, talking to families hoping to find their loved ones, Oklahoma police who had come to help, firefighters looking for survivors and victims. He consoled people who were looking for their sons, brothers, fathers, and friends.

Mayor Giuliani told Monsignor Delendick to go around Ground Zero because there was a large number of priests and other clergy walking around.

The mayor said, "See if you can find out who they are and see if we can organize them."

The monsignor took a pen and pad and started walking around getting names, where they were from, and their affiliations. When he finished going around the area, he had many pages of names. He went back to where he had started, and there were so many new ones that he decided that it was not possible to organize them, especially since there was no way to determine their credibility. Later, perimeter checkpoints were set up to screen people and establish credentials.

One volunteer group that was approved set up a booth and passed out food to emergency workers. Monsignor Delendick was concerned when he saw young teenage girls from the group wearing shirts that said "Volunteer Ministers."

He stopped one of them and inquired, "How are you a minister?"

The young girl replied, "Oh, we took some courses on grief counseling."

Delendick said, "I could just see one of these cute young things stopping one of our guys from Rescue 2 and saying 'I'm here to help you!'"

He voiced his concerns to Richard Sheirer, the chief of the Office of Emergency Management. The young people were working in a very dangerous place. They were not properly dressed and not wearing hard hats. Further, he was worried what their reactions would be if they started seeing bodies and body parts. Sheirer directed that the young people stay in their food booths and not wear the "Volunteer Minister" shirts. The next day he called the monsignor and told him that the group had ignored his directive and had been ordered to leave the site. If they wanted to return, they would have to have approval from Monsignor Delendick.

The first funerals were held on Saturday, September 15. Monsignor Delendick went to Deputy Commissioner Feehan's funeral and conducted the Mass and preached at Chief Ganci's funeral that day.

A week after 9/11, the fire department, accompanied by Red Cross workers and firefighters, started bringing groups of wives, children, and parents of missing people to Ground Zero two or three times a day. They would leave by boat from the Brooklyn Navy Yard and dock at a marina near the World Trade Center.

En route he could hear chatter: "My son was in the military. He can take care of himself. He's stuck in a pocket. We're sure he's going to get out!"

They would take the groups to a corner at West and Liberty Streets where they could see the entire site. They would look at the scene and realization would hit them. Television could not show the totality of the disaster. Two 110-story buildings were now three stories high, collapsed into subbasements. There were no desks, no computers, no phones. Everything had disintegrated. The only remnants of the Twin Towers were miles of telephone and electrical wire and huge pieces of steel. Construction workers had expected to remove large pieces of concrete, but it had all disintegrated. Jet fuel burns at 2,600 degrees Fahrenheit. Bodies are cremated at 1,500 degrees. Clearly, many of the missing had been cremated.

When the groups arrived at Ground Zero, firefighters would point out where the buildings had been located. Monsignor Delendick would talk to the group, and he would then ask them to take a few minutes to just be quiet.

Then he told them, "Talk to your loved ones and let them know that you are here. Let them know you miss them."

A few minutes later, he would tell them, "Be very still. Let them answer you and tell you that they are OK and that they love you."

From there they would lead the group to a makeshift memorial for the FDNY, PAPD, and NYPD, where he would conduct a prayer service. People would leave stuffed animals and various mementos.

The trip back to the Navy Yard was much different. People would speak in hushed voices, or would be silent. When they noticed people sitting quietly by themselves, they would go over to console them and ensure they were all right.

Monsignor Delendick does not recall now how many memorial services and funerals he attended. A driver would pick him up every morning at 7 a.m. A fax each day would list memorial services, sometimes as many as fifteen. He would plan the day trying to attend those of people that he knew well, usually attending three each day. Occasionally he would take a day to go to Ground Zero, visit firehouses, or go to the fire department headquarters because he was exhausted from the stress of so many funerals.

The first two weeks he would visit support groups. A normal day started at 6:30 a.m. and usually lasted until midnight. After these groups became established, he gradually returned to his other duties.

In December 2001, Monsignor Delendick had a unique opportunity. He was able to join a group of three New York firefighters and two police officers going to Afghanistan. With the approval of General Tommy Franks and the U.S. State Department, they were on the first nonmilitary aircraft to land at Bagram Air Base. They were allowed on the ground only from sunup to sunset, as the local air controllers did not have compatible equipment to control their aircraft at night. The men visited soldiers and brought supplies and goodies to an orphanage near Kabul.

Visiting a children's hospital with about three hundred children, some victims of the war with Russia, they found few supplies or medications. Even the infant formula they brought would be of little use, as the pure water needed to mix it with was unavailable. Every other supply was polluted. When they visited a ward with about twenty children, a doctor told them, "I will guarantee you that within a week or two, 70 percent of these children will be dead."

In 2003 he made a similar trip to Iraq. When they left the country, they went by road to Amman, Jordan. They were warned of bandits along the way, and that if anyone in pickup trucks started chasing them they should not stop. They had an uneventful trip.

Monsignor Delendick described a theory that he read regarding the new "normal." He said that everyone in New York City, and perhaps elsewhere in our country, after 9/11 had a new "normal." When someone asks how you are, you usually reply, "I'm fine." Now, you still reply, "I'm fine." But now it is a different level of normal, because there is always the layer of sadness from 9/11 under the surface. Sometimes something will trigger that layer of sadness and bring it to the surface. This is the new way of being "normal."

Monsignor John Delendick is certain that Chief Peter Ganci saved his life when he ordered him to go north to the Chambers Street command post. Most of the people he had seen at the first command post had died. It appeared that Chief Ganci, Deputy Commissioner Feehan, and the others were on their way back to the field command post in the garage when the North Tower fell and they were struck and killed by a piece of steel.

Joey Henry, who the other Henry firefighter brothers were looking for at Ground Zero, was killed. Their father has recuperated from his injuries.

Monsignor David Cassato, Chaplain, NYPD
"Today, you have seen the worst in people and you have seen the best in people."

Father Brian Gordon on 9/11

On 9/11 Monsignor David Cassato had been a priest for twenty-nine years. He had grown up in Brooklyn and had a strong attraction to the church since he was a child. Police Commissioner Bernard Kerik had met him and knew he had formed a bond with local police officers supporting church activities, such as fiestas, for many years.

After they met, Commissioner Kerik said, "I wish I had an opening for a police chaplain."

A few months later, when a police chaplain retired, the commissioner's office called and offered him a chaplain's job. This presented a touchy situation, as normal procedure is for the bishop to nominate a priest. In spite of the protocol violation, Bishop Thomas Daily approved the request and David Cassato was appointed as a chaplain for the NYPD on June 18, 2001.

On September 11, 2001, Monsignor Cassato had a 9:30 a.m. appointment with Bishop Daily. After informing Monsignor Cassato that he was being transferred to St. Athanasius Parish in Brooklyn, the bishop cut the meeting short because of the attack on the city.

Bishop Daily said, "Go do your job with the police!"

Cassato left immediately with his driver, who had been waiting. He had an eerie feeling as they drove across the empty Brooklyn Bridge with no other vehicles or people. They drove directly to police headquarters, arriving there at 10:15 a.m., thirteen minutes before the North Tower fell. The headquarters was abandoned. Everyone had gone to the WTC. First he heard the noise and then watched in horror as the North Tower went down and a huge cloud of dust and debris formed two blocks away.

Monsignor Cassato, like most people, was unsure about what to do. By now many people were leaving Manhattan, walking over the bridges. He went to St. James Catholic Church, which had become a spontaneous relief center, just outside police headquarters. People were coming into the church. Some were looking for friends or family members. Some were in tears. Others just needed to talk to someone. He sat with people and talked with them, consoling those that were looking for missing relatives.

He heard a report that a chaplain had died. He left the church and was walking toward the WTC when he met a friend, Father Jamie John Gigantiello from Brooklyn. Gigantiello, learning that a chaplain had died and thinking that it might have been Monsignor Cassato, got a ride with a police officer to the WTC area. The two spent the remainder of the day ministering to people. First they worked at St. James Church, then they went to the Police Academy, where a command post had been established. They walked to St. Paul's Church, near Ground Zero. When they went in they saw Father Judge's body lying in front of the altar. Monsignor Cassato blessed the body.

Father Brian Gordon, a close friend of Father Judge, was there and said, "Today, you have seen the worst in people and you have seen the best in people."

Monsignor Cassato used that message in the homily at his parish the following Sunday.

When Mayor Giuliani heard that Monsignor Cassato was there, he asked him to join him. The mayor and the monsignor then went to St. Vincent's Hospital.

Mayor Giuliani asked hospital authorities, "What do you need here?"

They replied, "We need to release noncritical patients to make room for the expected flood of victims, and we need purified water." Giuliani approved the release of those patients and arranged for a supply of pure water. Then the men returned to police headquarters. The surge of victims to the hospital did not occur.

Monsignor Cassato went to the morgue, which was also expecting a lot of victims. Again, it didn't happen. He went to a location where people were reporting missing persons and assisted in consoling people there.

At 9:00 p.m., all police chaplains were ordered to report to the police headquarters. When Monsignor Cassato, Rabbi Alvin Kass, and Monsignor Robert Romano arrived, there was an assemblage of families of twenty-three missing police officers. Each of them met with family members, trying to talk, to console, and to give hope.

Cots were set up in the police department auditorium. Family members of missing police officers lived there for days.

Dead tired, Monsignor Cassato went back to the rectory at 2:30 a.m. The next morning the bishop's office called to see how he was doing. He replied that he was all right, then headed back to Ground Zero. Every day for weeks he went to the police headquarters auditorium to meet with families of the missing. He would say Mass every morning and would then, like Monsignor Delendick, escort groups of people who had lost loved ones to the site. They would board a fire boat then proceed to Ground Zero where they would survey the destruction while facing the crushing reality of their lost loved ones.

He tried to help them deal with the hard fact that their son or daughter, brother or sister, had died. It was a tremendous effort to accompany them to the "pit," to walk through the rubble, to face the raw grief of so many devastated families. It was also deeply traumatic and trying for him.

Monsignor Cassato conducted and preached at countless funerals, including those of firefighters, police officers, emergency workers, and employees of the World Trade Center. While most funerals of police officers were conducted by the parish of the deceased, Cassato was asked to conduct three of the police officer funerals and to preach the homily. He conducted two ceremonies apiece for two victims, NYPD Officers Robert Fazio, Thirteenth Precinct, and Santos Valentin Jr., assigned to the Emergency Service Unit. A memorial service was conducted while the men were missing, then a second service was held after their remains were found. He also presided at funerals of two firefighters, Manuel Mojica, Rescue 1, and Tom Casoria, Squad 1, who had been altar boys in his parish in their earlier years. He became very close to the family of Ronny Kloepfer, thirty-nine, an eighteen-year veteran of the NYPD and a sniper with the Emergency Service Unit. As the years passed, Monsignor Cassato has performed all of the Kloepfer family weddings, anniversary Masses, and baptisms.

He said, "In the tragedy of the moment comes a gift—the bonding of friendship. They are wonderful people!"

Ronald Kloepfer's mother still waits for closure. His remains have never been found.

At one of the funerals, Mayor Giuliani spoke and thanked the Catholic Church for its role in bringing solace to so many grieving families and for conducting memorial services and funerals.

He attended the funeral Mass at St. Patrick's Cathedral for police officer Moira Smith, the only female NYPD police officer killed on 9/11. She was seen helping an injured man out of the tower, then returned into the building and was killed as she assisted others to safety.

The monsignor described her husband, also a police officer, and her two-year-old daughter, when Officer Smith was posthumously awarded the NYPD Medal of Honor, "The little girl was dressed so beautifully. She was such a delightful child. Those are the things that pull on your heart—a beautiful child without a mother."

Police Commissioner Bernard Kerik asked Monsignor Cassato to appear at the first month's commemoration of 9/11. He and Rabbi Joseph Potasnik, an FDNY chaplain, joined arms and were televised nationally as they said a prayer over the site.

Some Arab Christian groups asked Monsignor Cassato to address them because they were worried about community reactions due to their Arab background. They wanted to assure people that they were appalled at the 9/11 attacks. He preached in their church in Bay Ridge in Brooklyn.

Later when Pope Benedict came to visit New York City and pray at the World Trade Center site in April 2008, Monsignor Cassato was again a participant in a television interview.

He reflected, "It was a very poignant sight, the day of remembrance there. It was very powerful to see him lay a wreath and pray there."

Monsignor Cassato remains deeply affected by 9/11. While he tries to block it out of his mind, he knows that 9/11 has marked his life. Each anniversary brings back memories of terror, chaos, people falling from the Twin Towers, and families waiting in vain for news of their missing loved ones. He found the first anniversary of 9/11 to be profoundly difficult and emotional.

At the reading of the names of the dead, he would think, "I knew that person."

Monsignor Cassato described his relationship with the NYPD by saying he thought it was the best job in the world. The police respected him, and it was an easy job. Then 9/11 happened. Although the job was no longer easy, the chaplains of all faiths in the police department earned even more respect, both within the NYPD and in the city for the work they did.

He said, "Not only have I ministered to the police officers, but they have ministered to me. They were incredible when my mother died in December 2009. The police officers were right there with me, going through the grief. Chief Esposito was especially helpful. He is an extraordinary person. We have become steadfast friends."

On June 3, 2010, the New York State Legislature passed a resolution commending Monsignor David Cassato on his receiving the Religious Community Service Award from the Council of Neighborhood Organizations, Inc.

FDNY firefighters working at Ground Zero-photo courtesy of FDNY

Chapter Fourteen
Jim and Michael Boyle, David Arce, the Haskell Brothers

"Did you find my daddy today?"

Meaghan Haskell to her uncle Ken

Thirty-seven-year old Michael Boyle, firefighter son of James Boyle, former two-term president of the Uniformed Firefighter Association, and his best friend, thirty-six-year-old David Arce, had just gone off duty on September 11, 2001, after having worked the night before.[67] Michael left a message on his father's phone at 8:35 a.m., saying that they were going to Queens to help his cousin, who was running for City Council, as September 11 was primary election day in New York. He said that they "would meet later." Instead, after they heard of the planes hitting the World Trade Center, even though they were off duty, they rode their company's fire truck, Engine 33, "riding heavy" (the term for off-duty firefighters accompanying the on-duty crew) and went to the scene of the action, not even taking time to change from civilian clothes into firefighter clothing.

---

67   Except as otherwise noted, this chapter is based on interviews with former Uniformed Firefighter Association President James Boyle, Mrs. Marge Arce, mother of FDNY firefighter David Arce, and firefighter Kenneth Haskell, brother of FDNY Captain Thomas and firefighter Timothy Haskell.

Michael's father, Jim, had retired from the FDNY and was now the operations officer of the Kings County District Attorney's office, working in his office, located near the Twin Towers. His window overlooked the site, and, as he saw smoke rising, someone shouted that a plane had hit one of the towers. Then, as he watched, a second plane struck the other tower. With Manhattan under attack, the building that he was in was being evacuated even though it wasn't in the WTC complex.

Jim Boyle had heard that after terrorists had set the truck bomb in the parking garage of the World Trade Center in 1993, they went to a nearby second-story music store with a good vantage point to watch the buildings when the explosives detonated. Thinking that if they did this again, he might be able to help apprehend them, he headed towards that store.

When he walked across the Brooklyn Bridge, he found bedlam as hundreds of frightened people rushed to escape the chaos in Manhattan. Although the bridge had been closed to all vehicle traffic except emergency vehicles, people were everywhere. He did not think the towers would fall— high rises don't do that, he thought as he approached the World Trade Center. However, the South Tower collapsed as he was on the corner of Broadway and Barclay St., about three blocks away. Fortunately, Jim was able to duck into the Woolworth building, where he was shielded from most of the effects of the immense cloud of drywall dust, ashes, paper, and debris.

Jim then proceeded down Vesey Street toward West Street and the fire department command post. As he neared the North Tower he saw debris falling and people jumping. Because of this he detoured north on Greenwich for a block to Barclay, then west to West Street. As he approached the command center, suddenly he was enveloped in the huge cloud of dust and debris as the second tower fell. The sudden tornadolike gush of wind knocked him off his feet. He couldn't see. He couldn't breathe. Cars were on fire. An engine and other parts from one of the planes were lying on the ground. Still wearing his suit, he crawled through the powdery dust and debris on hands and knees at first. Unable to see and engulfed by the blinding dust storm, he didn't really know where he was. As the immense cloud slowly settled, he realized he had lived through the disaster, his entire body covered with the fine powder. He waited for the cloud to dissipate. When he could finally stand, he found a place in a building with a sink and a hose where he could clean up a bit and rinse his eyes and face. He said, "I didn't know why I survived. I went and looked at the area. There was a brick and mortar telephone building there that took the blast from the north. It was damaged, but it held." He said, "If you went north you made it. If you went south you didn't make it."

Hoping that his son hadn't gone to the WTC, but knowing deep inside that he probably had, Jim went to look for him. He passed burning cars and an abandoned city bus and walked through the haze of what had begun as a gorgeous day in New York City. He slowly worked his way to the site, and after searching awhile he found his son's fire engine and located the "riding list" that showed who was on board for the last fatal trip. Michael's name was not on it. That gave him a bit of hope, but then he talked with the chauffeur who told him that his son, in fact, had been on the engine and was missing. The "pile," as it became known, was eight stories high. People were already starting to organize a rescue effort. Jim was hoping that someone had seen his son. He asked firefighter Peter Culkin from Engine Company 226, "Have you seen my son Mike?" Peter replied, "No, Jim, I'm sorry, I haven't seen your son."[68] Jim asked FDNY Chaplain John Delendick the same question and got the same answer. Hoping and praying whenever he saw someone that he knew, he asked the same question. He kept getting the same answer, "No, Jim. I'm sorry. I haven't seen your son."

Jim met Pete Hayden,[69] a good friend and now the firefighter official in charge of the rescue effort, as Peter Ganci and Ray Downey had been killed.

Pete said, "Everyone is dead!"

At 5:20 p.m. World Trade Center Building Seven, forty-seven stories high, collapsed, and those in the area again experienced the cloud of dust and the rushing wind, although not as severe as when the Twin Towers fell. By this time the collapse of Building Seven was expected and precautions had been taken to avoid further casualties.

Jim went to the new command post, set up after the original had been crushed, to see who had been found. He worked for fifteen hours searching for his son and other survivors, then he walked to Saint Peter's Catholic Church, where his friend Father Judge's body had been laid by the altar. Numb, he tried to compose himself and said some prayers. People there at first didn't realize that Jim's son was missing, but when they found out

---

68   Firefighter Peter Culkin, interview with the author.
69   Pete Hayden later became the Chief of Department, FDNY.

they were very kind. Jim wanted to be by himself for a while, so he slowly started to walk through the crowds of thousands of people towards Mike's firehouse—not that he could have taken any other means of transportation, as New York was shut down. With a sinking feeling in his stomach, he passed Canal Street, then a bit later Bleecker Street. Nearing Washington Square, the center of the New York University campus, he turned and arrived at Mike's firehouse. The surviving firefighters were very considerate. (Seven firefighters assigned to Engine 33, Jim's son's truck, and three firefighters from Ladder 9, also stationed in this firehouse, were missing.) The firefighters there helped him clean up and wipe the dirt and debris from his clothes and shoes.

Lieutenant Warren Smith, from Ladder 9, described his experience and the chaos and confusion.[70] Collocated with Engine 33, he and his men heard a plane flying low overhead followed by a loud "boom." Some of the men thought that it was a sonic boom, but when they looked down the street where they could see the Twin Towers, they saw what had happened. Minutes later they were on their way to the World Trade Center. When they arrived at the scene, he ordered the chauffeur to park some distance away from the Twin Towers so that the rig wouldn't be hit by debris that was falling after the planes struck. While many other fire trucks were crushed when the towers fell, this ladder truck was destroyed, instead, by fire caused by flying debris when the towers collapsed. Lieutenant Smith, avoiding falling bodies and debris, led his men to the command post in the North Tower and was given orders to go into the building and do what they could.

He said, "We were given no specific orders or instructions at this time. No floor. No specific job. No chief to report to. No nothing. It was then that I realized how chaotic and desperate our situation was."

Realizing that they could not use elevators and would have to climb stairs, he directed his men to stay together. While climbing, they passed other firefighters loaded with heavy gear. Many needed oxygen, and some were experiencing chest pains. Lieutenant Smith was aware that many of these firefighters, although they may have been in excellent condition, were running up the stairs carrying loads approaching one hundred pounds

---

70   Transcript of Safety Battalion interview with Lieutenant Smith, December 4, 2001.

and had overexerted themselves. Lieutenant Smith insisted his men pace themselves, and he stopped them several times to ensure they remained together and were not becoming exhausted.

As they passed civilians descending the stairways, they asked the people evacuating the building to keep to the right and tried to reassure them that they would be okay. Some civilians that seemed to be fire safety directors or officials representing their offices remained, and many offered water to the firefighters who were straining and sweating in their exertion under their heavy loads and wearing their bulky firefighting clothing. He described the evacuation as orderly, with no sign of panic. When they got to the thirty-third floor, he started to report to a battalion chief that was there, but before he could get to him, the building shook as the South Tower fell. Thinking that their building was hit again, the firefighters ran for cover in a stairwell, and when the building quit shaking, Lieutenant Smith asked the battalion chief what they should do. The chief got on the radio and received the order to evacuate. The electricity had gone out, which slowed their descent in semidarkness.

Lieutenant Smith ordered the firefighters to drop unnecessary gear and instructed other firefighters who had not received the evacuation order to follow along. Around the eleventh floor, their downward progress ground to a halt in the stairwell that they were using when a firefighter tapped him on the shoulder and told him that a different stairway was clear. He directed his men and others to that stairway.

Those that followed made it to safety. Many of those that either didn't get those instructions or proceeded on the original stairway—which was blocked at the lobby by debris—didn't make it. When they reached the lobby, Lieutenant Smith felt that they had to get away from the building, and get away quickly.[71] There was a battalion chief with a bullhorn yelling at all those exiting the building to go north. As the South Tower had already collapsed, it would have meant going through or around the debris if they had gone south. About a minute later, when they were about three or four blocks away, the second tower fell. When they heard the roar, they started to run, and within a few seconds they were caught in the cloud of dust and "utter darkness."

---

71   Lieutenant Warren Smith's letter to family and friends, September 11, 2001.

Later when the dust settled, Lieutenant Smith linked up with the men of his company that he could find and got medical attention for two who needed it. Covered with dust and grime, they made their way to a small warehouse where people helped clean them off and gave them water. There they were also able to telephone their families and let them know that they were all right. Then they went to a nearby firehouse, where they learned of the totality of the disaster. Finally they returned to their own fire station, wrongly anticipating that the missing firefighters would link up with them.

Much later and with little hope left, Jim Boyle also arrived at the same firehouse. He went to his son's locker and recovered the wallet that his son, Mike, had left along with the keys to his fiancée's car, which Mike had used to come to work the night before. He called his wife and told her, "It doesn't look good." He was exhausted by now, having been on his feet for fifteen or more hours. He had walked from his office across the Brooklyn Bridge to the World Trade Center, then to St. Peter's Church, and then to Mike's firehouse. In the hours that he had spent walking around the site of the disaster, it was very difficult to get from one place to another; he had to detour around massive piles of debris, seven or more stories high.

Now at last, using the car keys and firefighter badge that his son had left, Jim drove home. He got no sleep, his rest shattered by countless phone calls. People called him asking for help. Television reporters called. He had to contact his children living in different parts of the country and arrange for them to come to the city. They found out later that Mike and David had been at least to the thirty-ninth floor with their company. When their remains were found on January 23, 2002, together with three other members of their company, they were fifty-seven feet below ground level.

Michael Boyle and David Arce, lifelong friends, had grown up together. They lived around the corner and attended school together. Michael was an athletic person and a marathon runner. His goal was to run the 2001 New York Marathon in under three hours, a time that he had previously attained some years earlier. Michael was also one of five members of a baseball team sponsored by a local bar. The team had been eliminated from a local competition, resulting in all of them being back at their jobs. All five were killed.

Marge Arce, David's mother, is a volunteer guide at the Tribute Center across the street from Ground Zero, which honors the memories of those killed at the World Trade Center on 9/11. She says that being a guide does not provide her with closure; still, it is something that she has to do. Philosophically she says, "You have a choice. You can sit down or you can stand up. I choose to stand up."

Jim Boyle said, "It still seems unreal and yet, after all these years, I still dwell on the event every day. Each morning when I awake I have a picture of Michael in front of me and I say a prayer. Each night the procedure is repeated as I close my eyes."

Jim Boyle and Marge Arce, along with O'Hurley's Bar in Manhattan, sponsor a foundation in memory of their sons. The money raised is used to support firefighters and their families in times of need. In one instance, money was given to the widow of a firefighter. The foundation received a letter from the thankful woman, who told them that she did not have a stove and had used the money to purchase one.

The Haskell Brothers

Firefighting was inbred in the Haskell family. The Haskell brothers' father was medically retired from the NYFD in 1979 after ten years of service due to a heart condition. He later died. All three of his sons became firefighters, and on September 11, 2001, thirty-seven-year-old Tommy, the oldest son, was a captain awaiting promotion to battalion chief and was acting in a temporary capacity "UFO" (until further orders). Thirty-four-year-old firefighter Timothy was a member of the elite Special Operations Command Squad 18.

Firefighter Kenneth was the youngest of the Haskell firefighters. Before transferring to the FDNY, he served as an NYPD policeman for three years. On the morning of 9/11, Ken was off duty. He was remodeling his home and was at a tile store owned by a cousin when he first heard of the airplanes hitting the WTC. He immediately went to his fire station. Police, controlling traffic, let him pass when he showed them his firefighter's uniform. After arriving at the fire station, he and others commandeered[72] a city

---

72   City bus drivers fully cooperated to provide rides to off-duty firefighters to go to the World Trade Center.

transit bus to get a ride to the WTC. They stopped at firehouses along the way to pick up more off-duty firefighters who had responded to the "total recall." When they reached the Manhattan Bridge, the bus was full and they were travelling slowly because of the traffic and people, covered with soot and dust, walking across the bridge from Manhattan after leaving the scene of destruction. They were delayed for a time because of concerns that there might be other attacks. A rumor circulated, later proved to be false, that there was another plane inbound to the New York City area. As they approached Ground Zero, the North Tower collapsed.

Ken knew that his brothers were working, and he correctly assumed that both of them had been dispatched to the WTC. Tommy had responded to the South Tower, the first to fall, with Ladder 132 from nearby Brooklyn, while Tim had been dispatched to the site with his squad in Manhattan. Tim Haskell and Danny Murphy found a man experiencing chest pains and apparently having a heart attack. They gave him oxygen, then Tim went further into the tower to answer a "Mayday!" call while a Port Authority policeman took care of the heart attack victim. Danny was just outside the building and was blown off his feet when it collapsed, but he survived. Tim's body was found four days after 9/11.

Ken Haskell found chaos when he arrived at Ground Zero. Off-duty firefighters, not knowing where their crews were, immediately went to work doing what needed to be done. There were explosions in WTC Building Five, and rumors circulated they might be caused by follow-up attacks. It turned out that the building was being used by U.S. Customs to store confiscated explosives, which "cooked off" as all five floors of the building were on fire. Large sections of the WTC Building Seven facade, which had been set on fire by flaming debris from the nearby towers, were also falling into the debris-littered street.

During the time that he worked at the site, the discovery of two bodies brought back vivid memories for Ken. The first was that of a man who apparently had been on the airplane that struck the building. The body looked as though it had gone through a meat slicer. The remains included half of his head, one arm, and part of his torso. His one eye was open and the rest of the torso looked almost undamaged—everything else was missing. At least he died instantly, Ken thought. The other body was that of a young woman, probably in her mid-twenties. She was apparently asphyxiated, as there were no apparent traumatic injuries. When they cleaned off the dust and debris, they found that she was well dressed and looked like a successful woman with a bright future suddenly cut short. In addition to the deaths of his brothers, Ken remains haunted by the memories of a woman and a man that he didn't even know.

Ken worked at the site every day for two weeks. As they continued to search for victims, Battalion Chief Thomas Haskell's eight-year old daughter, Meghan, would ask her Uncle Ken, "Did you find my daddy today?" Her father, Captain Thomas Haskell, had been assigned to Ladder 132 in Brooklyn, one of the first companies to respond to the disaster. As a high school athlete at Seaford High, Thomas was an all-star player on the football team at Seaford in Long Island. His three daughters, Meaghan, Erin, and Tara, were ages eight, five, and two at the time he was killed on 9/11.[73]

The first day that Ken took off was to attend his brother's closed-casket funeral. Ken had asked those who found Tim's body if the body was intact. He was assured that it was. Although clearly disturbed that Tommy's remains had not yet been located, Ken felt some relief that Tim's body was intact. Captain Tommy Haskell was posthumously promoted to battalion chief. His body was never found. Six members of Tommy Haskell's former unit, Ladder 132, died. Three officers from Division 15, Tommy's temporary assignment, were killed. Seven firefighters were lost from Timothy Haskell's Rescue Squad 18 on September 11, 2001.

Seaford High School, on Long Island, has an annual candlelight memorial service honoring the five graduates of the school that were killed on 9/11. These are the two Haskell brothers, Lieutenant Glenn Perry, Ladder 25, and two employees of the Cantor Fitzgerald securities firm (Robert Sliwack and Michael Wittenstein).

Four of the fifteen firefighters from this firehouse that worked at the WTC after 9/11 have cancer, possibly a result of their work on the "pile." These relatively young men have thyroid, prostate, non-Hodgkin lymphoma, and leukemia cancers.

In October 2005, after Hurricane Katrina hit, Ken went with a group of firefighters to New Orleans to help. In New Orleans the firefighters would work twenty-four hours on and then twenty-four hours off. During their off-duty time they helped clean flooded houses. He said the devastation

73   Information on Thomas Haskell from newsday.com/911/victimsearch.

there appeared worse in a way than 9/11 because it encompassed such a wide area, whereas in New York it was limited to a few blocks.

Ken met President Bush five times, the first time at the one year commemoration of 9/11. His most memorable meeting was when he did a scripture reading at a Mass at the White House. The president's entire cabinet, including Vice President Cheney and Secretary of State Colin Powell, were present.

Ken Haskell is currently assigned to Truck 175, collocated with Engine 332. He has been a chauffeur since 1995. Ken and his wife have two sons.

FDNY at Ground Zero-photo courtesy of FDNY

Chapter Fifteen
Michael Weinstock

"Tragically, some people didn't understand that this wasn't the time for watching. This was the time for running."

Michael Weinstock

Tuesday morning, September 11, 2001, Michael Weinstock was in bed in his Brooklyn apartment near the East River listening to the radio on the first day of his weeklong vacation.[74] He had worked his way up from being homeless and sleeping in his car during his senior year of high school. He was now a successful young lawyer and had recently been appointed an assistant district attorney in Brooklyn, New York.

Michael heard that a plane had hit one of the Twin Towers. He reluctantly admits that he didn't immediately jump out of bed when he heard the news report. As a boy, he had read that a small plane had once hit the Empire State Building at the tail end of World War II. Because of the strength of the building, the structure itself was barely damaged. Michael assumed that a small plane had likely hit one of the towers. While he was lying in bed, however, he began to hear genuine fear in the voices of the people on the radio. He jumped out of bed and ran to the window.

He was shocked to see the volume of smoke that was pouring out of the North Tower of the World Trade Center. A cold chill suddenly went

---

74   Michael Weinstock interviews with the author.

through him. Having recently completed a course on high-rise fires at the volunteer fire academy, he immediately realized the enormity of the situation. Weinstock instinctively knew this was worse than any high-rise fire in modern history. He dressed hurriedly, grabbed his trauma bag filled with emergency medical supplies, put on his boots and a fire department T-shirt, and rushed out of the building toward the North Tower a few blocks away.

As a senior in high school, Michael had a neighbor who was a member of the local volunteer fire department. She had a pager, a blue light for her car, and a badge. She was also allowed to attend the local movie theater for free. All of these things were appealing to a seventeen-year-old boy. He also knew that if he joined the fire department, it would infuriate his mother, who had absolutely forbidden him to join. On his eighteenth birthday, Michael joined the Great Neck Vigilant Volunteer Fire Department on Long Island without telling his mother. A few months earlier, Jonathan Ielpi, a high school classmate, had also joined the fire department. Lee Ielpi, his father, was a retired New York City firefighter. Michael and Jonathan quickly became best friends.

Michael's mother had very serious problems with alcohol and depression. His father had moved away when Michael was very young and was not involved with the family. As Michael's family situation deteriorated, his life became intolerable. His grades suffered and money was scarce. In desperation, Michael left home. He asked friends if they might have a couch or extra bed where he could sleep. With regrets, his friends declined for various reasons. Some explained that they simply didn't have the space. Others explained that they had dysfunctional families in their own right. For a number of months, Michael stayed in a vacant apartment. After being caught and chased away, he slept in his car. Soon after joining the Vigilant Fire Department, however, Michael's life began to change. Without being asked, the men and women of the fire department offered their support. Some offered their couches. One family had a spare bedroom. A couple of the firefighters made sure Michael came over to their homes regularly for a hot meal.

Michael desperately wanted to go to college, but with the turmoil at home, his grades were poor. Since he did not have a home, he was using the mailing address of Mrs. Pearl, a lovely woman who had taught his tenth-grade English class and one of the few people who understood the gravity of Michael's situation. After rejection letters from ten different schools,

Michael was hardly enthusiastic about the one outstanding application to the University of Iowa. It was, without question, one of the most prestigious public universities in the country. One afternoon there was a message waiting for Michael at the firehouse.

It read, "Call Mrs. Pearl, GREAT NEWS!" He immediately called her back.

Mrs. Pearl shouted into the receiver. "I have some great news! You got into the University of Iowa!"

Michael couldn't believe her. He made her repeat herself over and over again. He asked, "How in the world could I have possibly been accepted at such a great school?"

Michael fully recognized the immediate significance of the moment. He was no longer straddling the line of homelessness. In a few short weeks, he would be living in a dormitory and creating a schedule of classes like thousands of other students. He was about to live a "normal" lifestyle as he had always dreamed. He would no longer be forced to navigate the unpredictable peaks and valleys of a parent with a severe drinking problem.

Michael says, "I will always remember the moment I was accepted, because it was such a difficult and painful experience to be rejected by college after college. I was also terrified that every single school would turn me down and I would find myself completely homeless and living in the park. While I was standing there in the firehouse, listening to Mrs. Pearl promise me that she was telling me the truth and swear to me that it wasn't some sort of cruel hoax, I suddenly felt like the guy that just won a Cadillac on The Price is Right. In a single moment, I understood that my life had changed dramatically. I felt like the luckiest person in New York City."

Although the University of Iowa is an enormous school with more than thirty thousand students, there aren't many native New Yorkers.

When Michael is asked why he chose the school, he provides a matter-of-fact response. "Firstly, I got in."

Just as importantly, he adds, "I could afford it. It was the cheapest school in the Big Ten, by far. Since my parents weren't going to be helping out, I needed to choose a school that I could afford."

Michael sometimes provides a little bit more information. "I needed to choose a place that was far away. I didn't want any surprise visits. If phone calls were considered long distance, even better."

A few weeks after Michael enrolled and was living in the dormitories, he paid a visit to the admissions office, where he met the woman who had approved his application. He learned why he had been accepted at the University of Iowa, despite his lackluster high school grades.

When Michael was a senior in high school, he completed an internship at the environmental organization Greenpeace. His supervisor at Greenpeace promised to write a letter of recommendation, but kept procrastinating. Finally, his beloved English teacher, Mrs. Pearl, wrote a strong letter of recommendation on Greenpeace stationery, signed it, and sent a copy to the Greenpeace supervisor. With the Greenpeace supervisor's approval, they used the letter in his applications. When he later asked the admissions officer why he had been accepted with his poor grades, she replied that she was an environmentalist, and because of the extraordinary Greenpeace letter, she decided to take a chance on him.

Michael always had a part-time job. He became a county certified lifeguard in high school because it paid two dollars an hour more than other part-time jobs in the area. Michael was hired by a local fitness club that had an indoor pool. A lifeguard was required by law even though the pool was only four feet deep. The manager didn't mind if Michael kept his clothes on and did his homework at work. He talked at length with retirees who came to use the pool. They enjoyed giving Michael advice about choosing the right college and the factors he should consider if he was genuinely interested in attending law school afterwards. The gym opened at 5:30 in the morning, giving Michael the opportunity to work before going to school. Thanks to his job at the health club and his friends from the firehouse, Michael was able to save more than $6,000 for his first year of college. He also received a $3,000 scholarship for his first year from the Great Neck Student Aid Fund, which provides money for disadvantaged students from Great Neck.

When Michael wasn't lifeguarding or volunteering with the firehouse, he was involved with local political campaigns. He had a passion for politics, and even when things were unbelievably difficult at home, he managed to get involved with local political campaigns. In high school, he began volunteering for neighborhood people who he admired. After developing a reputation as a young man with a good sense of humor who always kept his word, he would occasionally be offered a job in a political campaign that paid a few dollars. It was usually more lucrative to work as a lifeguard than in politics, but Michael tried to find the right balance. After his first year of law school, he worked on a campaign that made national news.

Michael had accepted a summer job with the New York City Law Department when he heard through friends that Carolyn McCarthy, a local woman from Long Island, would be announcing a long-shot bid to unseat her congressman. Sadly, her husband had been killed and her son was very seriously wounded a few years earlier when a gunman opened fire on the Long Island Railroad with an assault weapon. After the trial of the shooter, Carolyn McCarthy later became well known for championing "common sense" gun control laws involving machine guns and assault weapons. She stood next to President Clinton when the assault weapons ban became law. When her local congressman voted to repeal the law, she decided to run against him.

At first, her campaign didn't have any money and was not taken seriously. Nonetheless, Michael interviewed with Carolyn in her living room and liked her immediately. He gave up the summer Law Department job and accepted an offer to work for the campaign full time. It was agreed that he would be given a small salary if the campaign was successful in raising money and becoming viable. Otherwise, it would be a full-time volunteer position.

Michael was initially given the role of scheduler. He worked with McCarthy and her campaign manager and decided what events she should attend. The days would frequently begin at diners before 7:00 a.m. and continue in television studios past 11:00 p.m. For Michael it was a dream come true. She jokingly called him "my bodyguard" and he called her "Aunt Carolyn." During the course of the campaign, Michael appeared in photographs with her in People, Good Housekeeping, and George magazines, along with many newspapers and television shows.

The other employees on the campaign knew Michael was a law student and some knew he was a volunteer firefighter, but nobody knew he had been living out of his car only four or five years earlier. McCarthy, however, spent enough time with Michael to draw certain conclusions.

On more than one occasion, she pulled Michael aside and told him "I know that you don't come from a wealthy family like the other young people volunteering on the campaign. Here's twenty dollars for gas. It's our secret."

Eventually, the campaign did indeed raise enough money to become "viable." The campaign moved out of Carolyn's home and into a storefront. Michael was promoted from scheduler to work exclusively on issues, bringing in experts and arranging briefings to inform her and the staff on issues other than guns. He arranged briefings on campaign finance reform, health care, Social Security reform, and the Israeli-Palestinian conflict. Taped above Michael's desk there was a sign that read in large block letters: "It's more than guns, stupid!" This sign made its way into one of the newspaper articles written about the campaign.

On Election Day, Carolyn McCarthy beat the incumbent with a landslide victory of more than 17 percent. That night, Congresswoman-elect Carolyn McCarthy addressed the assembled group of staffers and volunteers. Even though there were more than two hundred people gathered in the room, Michael was only one of three or four people addressed individually.

"You were one of the people with me from the very beginning" she told him. "You were there in my living room when nobody took us seriously. I will always remember how hard you worked on this campaign and how dedicated you were at all hours of the day and night. Thank you!"

During his sophomore year in college, Robert and Martha Klein, parents of Alex, another volunteer firefighter, asked Michael if he would house sit for them while they were on vacation in December. Michael eagerly agreed. When they returned after a week, their son informed them that Michael didn't have a place to stay, and they invited him to stay for the holidays. Then they invited him to stay during the summer when he was home from college. For the next six years, until he graduated from law school and could afford his own place, Michael Weinstock had a place to stay when he wasn't in school. The Kleins became proxy parents. Robert even gave Michael the same lecture on sex, drugs, and alcohol that he had given his own children. When Michael graduated from law school, the Kleins bought him a beautiful navy blue suit from Brooks Brothers. In the beginning of the McCarthy political campaign, all the staffers were asked to provide Carolyn a list of wealthy friends and family members who might contribute to the campaign. Michael placed Alex's Uncle Ron on the list and Carolyn called him and asked for money. He contributed $5,000 and introduced Carolyn to his boss, Michael Bloomberg, who later became mayor of New York City. He also contributed $5,000 to Carolyn McCarthy's campaign.

When Michael applied to law school, he expected another round of applications and rejections just as humiliating and exhausting as his college application process. Instead, he encountered the exact opposite. Michael applied to six schools and was accepted at five of them. Most importantly, however, Michael was accepted at St. John's Law School, the school that was his first choice.

When Michael was a boy, Mario Cuomo was governor. He delivered beautiful speeches about doing well and striving for excellence. He talked about the beauty of New York's outer boroughs and the satisfaction gained from helping others. For a boy with no father around, Mario Cuomo, a proud graduate of St. John's University, seemed to speak to him personally.

If Michael had been accepted at Harvard, he would have thought to himself, "This is nice, but it's not St. John's."

St. John's was also famous because it had the highest percentage of students passing the bar exam in the country.

Getting accepted at St. John's without the emotional or financial support of a family was so backbreaking difficult that Michael considered it the end of his incredibly tough journey, rather than the beginning. Naively, he failed to realize that the academic responsibilities of law school were an entirely new and equally important endeavor. Michael coasted on the joy of his admissions accomplishment and neglected his studies. While his fellow students were staying up late and memorizing cases, Michael discovered a love of literature. Instead of learning the fundamental rules of civil procedure or the foundations of corporations, Michael was reading To Kill a Mockingbird and other classic works of fiction. He was reasonably certain he could attend class, do a little reading here and there, and have no trouble securing a "gentleman's C." He was entirely mistaken. Michael earned a "gentleman's F," along with a D or two.

He was called in to meet the professor whose class he was failing. When he arrived in the administrative area on the top floor, he saw a commotion going on around an elderly gentleman.

He overheard a security guard say, "I don't know. Maybe it's serious. Perhaps we should call an ambulance."

Michael said, "I'm a firefighter and an EMT. Can I give you a hand?"

The security guard looked him over and brought him into an office, where he found a man slumped over in his chair not feeling well.

The man complained of indigestion and said, "I just need some seltzer and some privacy. It's not a big deal."

Michael replied, "All right. I just want to take your vital signs."

He immediately determined the man was having a heart attack. Michael slipped a note to a bystander demanding that they call 911 and ask for an Advanced Care Life Support ambulance needed to treat a man having a heart attack verified by an EMT. The ambulance arrived, treated the man, and took him to a hospital. Michael was surprised to find that the man, Dr. Patrick J. Rohan, was not only a professor but had been the dean of the law school for ten years. Fifty years earlier, the future dean had graduated from law school with the future Governor Cuomo. Both gentlemen tied for first place in their class. During the course of his career, Rohan published fifty-two books on condominium and cooperative apartment law.

Two months later, after he had recuperated from his heart attack, Dean Rohan called Michael into his office and announced, "You saved my life!"

Michael replied, "No, I just helped out."

The dean said, "Ten more minutes and I would have died. I had no intention of going to the hospital. None! And I wouldn't let anyone call for help. I'd like to take you to dinner."

Michael, not having money to eat very well anyway, readily agreed. Dean Rohan became Michael's mentor and a father figure. Following his guidance, Michael study habits and grades improved, and he graduated from St. John's Law School. The dean called a friend who was the district attorney of Brooklyn and who, at his urging, hired Michael as an assistant district attorney. Michael, because of his experiences at home, asked to be assigned to the sex crimes and domestic violence bureau. There he worked with hundreds of women and girls who were victims of abuse.

When Dean Rohan retired in 2009, there was a special Mass held in his honor at St. Patrick's Cathedral in Manhattan. The event was festive.

Before the Mass, Dean Rohan introduced Michael to Governor Cuomo. "Mario, this is the young man who saved my life a few years back. I'd like him to sit next to you and Matilda during the service, if you don't mind. You were a big influence on Michael when he was a boy."

After the Mass there was a party at the Cornell Club nearby. Three people spoke at the party. Governor Cuomo spoke first, Dean Rohan spoke second, and Michael Weinstock spoke last. When Dean Rohan passed away, Michael Weinstock was a pallbearer at his funeral.

Although he no longer lived in Great Neck, on September 11, 2001, Michael had not yet resigned as a volunteer firefighter, and he still had his equipment. Now, with smoke pouring out of the World Trade Center, he ran into the street and flagged down a passing ambulance. As they passed through the Brooklyn Battery Tunnel, the second plane hit the South Tower.

When they arrived on the scene, a federal agent said, "This is a crime scene. Do not disturb the bodies!"

Michael said that it broke his heart, but try as he might, the driver could not get to the staging area without driving over bodies. Torsos, limbs, and heads of passengers, many of which already had tire tracks from previous vehicles, along with parts of the plane were strewn over the area. When they arrived in a staging area a block away from the South Tower, they started to load equipment that they might need onto a stretcher.

Unexpectedly, they heard an ominous rumble heard by so many others at the WTC that day. The ambulance driver and Michael looked up and saw the top floors collapsing. They made eye contact and then ran, along with other bystanders, as fast as they could, into the nearest building. Some people, not understanding the danger they were in, watched as though they were seeing a movie, not realizing their actions in the next ten seconds would determine whether they lived or died. Their bodies were pulverized beyond recognition.

"Tragically, some people didn't understand that this wasn't the time for watching," Michael said, "This was the time for running."

The ambulance that he came in was destroyed.

Within seconds, every window in the building went dark as though suddenly painted black by a band of graffiti artists. Clouds of dust completely obscured the sun and covered the windows. Michael found himself in the dark, marble lobby of an old building. A handful of flashlights were found. Three or four firefighters, six or seven policemen, a couple of emergency medical technicians, and a lot of scared civilians, some of them injured, were in the building.

Michael, along with the crew from the ambulance, started treating some of the injured civilians. They found some bottled water set up for a meeting and used it to help clean wounds.

After a few minutes, a policeman held up his hand, gathered about twenty-five civilians in a group, and said, "Ladies and gentlemen! Give me your attention! There is a staging area being put together in Battery Park. I want everyone to form a single file and we'll take a walk over there."

Michael, who had learned in training that you should not move people in an emergency situation unless you are absolutely sure you are moving them from an area of danger to an area of safety, tapped him on the shoulder and said, "Officer, we don't know what the hell is going on out there and what is going to be happening in a few minutes. This is a nice, safe old building with a big marble lobby near the elevators. I think we should have everyone sit down and wait for about twenty-five minutes. After we know it is safe, we'll move everyone over to Battery Park."

The police officer, without even looking around to see who was giving the advice, again raised his hand and addressed the group, "Ladies and gentlemen! We have a change of plans. This is a nice, safe, strong building. We're going to sit here for at least twenty-five minutes. When we know it's safe outside, we'll move."

The officer's voice gave away just the slightest hint of a smile as he spoke. The inkling of levity was well received by the assembled crowd in a moment that was absolutely surreal and unquestionably frightening.

After a few more minutes, Michael looked outside. He tried to open the door. With difficulty, he was finally able to push the door partly open through the concrete, broken glass, and other rubble. Outside it was eerily quiet, when earlier it had been a cacophony of noise. He was surprised to see that it was snowing. But this was September on a warm day, and the snow was warm as it fell to the pavement, cars, and some trees in the area.

"Thank goodness! This is a dream. Thank God!" Michael thought.

This was not a fleeting thought and he was relieved. All of the terror and nervousness that he had been experiencing left him.

In the surreal, eerie world, he thought, "In a few moments, I'll wake up and I'll be in my bed and realize that this has all been a passing dream."

He reached out his hands and started spinning in circles for a few seconds, collecting what he thought was warm snow in his hands. Then he heard other doors open as other people forced them open against piles of debris and started to venture out.

He thought, "Damn! Maybe it's not a dream. I had better continue to treat people just in case it isn't."

He hurried out to treat more of the injured people. A few minutes later he again heard the same frightening rumble as the second tower started

210

to fall. He had another very close call but quickly ducked into another building close by. The people that had remained in the other building at Michael's suggestion were out of danger. Again, venturing out when it seemed safe, Michael started treating injured people. Michael worked for two more hours, then, when a lot of firefighters arrived and there wasn't much need for him, he started back to his apartment in Brooklyn.

As he walked along, one thing stood out in his mind was the sight of immigrant vendors standing by their carts giving away bottles of water, iced tea, and soda to the throngs of dirty, scared people as they escaped the chaos.

He said, "It is a testament to the character of these people. They didn't run. They stayed and gave away their goods. It was their way of helping."

Walking across the Manhattan Bridge, he saw people lying on the deck of the bridge helping other pedestrians climb over up so they could get up to the bridge quickly to make their way to safety.

"It was a beautiful moment," Michael said, "watching strangers of different ethnic backgrounds helping each other. People, terrified and covered with soot and dust, were not pushing, shoving, and panicking. There was grace and dignity that day. It made me very proud to be a New Yorker. It didn't matter the color or size or appearance of the people who approached. Everyone got a hand."

Going across the bridge, he met a couple, Rupert and Kiri Rogers, visiting from New Zealand.

They started chatting and Michael told them, "What you see (people helping one another) is the beauty of New York. That's why this city is so special, not just because it has tall buildings, but because of the grace that you are seeing among the people right now."

As they walked, the three people found a woman who had collapsed on the bridge and was having a heart attack. The New Zealand couple helped get the woman up on Michael's shoulders and, with the help of other people, they carried her back to Manhattan and put her in a police van. Michael gave the woman his phone number in the district attorney's office. Thereafter, when the woman was in the hospital and she had a panic attack, she would call Michael. Even if he was in the middle of a trial, he would visit her in the hospital before he went to bed that evening.

When Michael returned to his Great Neck firehouse a few hours later, he met firefighters who he knew.

He said, "Everything is OK. Right?"

The men looked away and didn't answer directly.

Then one of his close friends called him aside and said, "Michael, I have to talk to you."

The two men went aside and his friend said, "I have to let you know that Jonathan Ielpi is missing."

Jonathan Ielpi was the assistant chief of the Volunteer Vigilant Fire Department in Great Neck, as well as being a full-time firefighter in the New York City Fire Department. More importantly, he was Michael's best friend since high school. The entire crew of Jonathan's truck had been killed. Michael heard the words, but he refused to absorb them. He pretended to accept the words he was being told, but at first he didn't believe that Jonathan could really be dead. Slowly, as time passed, the realization came to him that Jonathan would not be coming back.

Michael, along with his volunteer fire department, joined Lee Ielpi, Jonathan's father, and worked at the site every day for a week until he had to go back to work at the district attorney's office. His fire department was given good assignments, partly because Jonathan had been the assistant chief of the Great Neck department and partly because Lee Ielpi, the retired FDNY firefighter, was such a prominent individual among those working at Ground Zero. One day the Great Neck Vigilant Volunteers were given the honor of working at the top of the "pile."

When Michael returned to work, the district attorney, Joe Hynes, informed him that he would not be charged vacation time for the week that he had spent at the World Trade Center site. With a great deal of discretion, he also transferred Michael to a less emotionally taxing department than the domestic abuse bureau to which he had been assigned, so he could recover from the trauma.

Jonathan Ielpi's body was found among the rubble of the Twin Towers three months after he was killed.

Rupert and Kiri Rogers, the couple from New Zealand, invited Michael to visit them on the first anniversary of September 11, 2001. During that visit, Michael was brought to the nation's Parliament, where he was honored by Helen Clark, the prime minister of New Zealand.

Michael Weinstock, once homeless and broke at age eighteen, is now a successful defense attorney in New York City. His mother has since died and relations with his father have improved.

NYC Urban Search and Rescue teams continue search for survivors amidst wreckage at WTC-photo by Andrea Booher FEMA News Photo

Chapter Sixteen
Search and Rescue

"Now what do we do?"

Firefighter Peter Culkin

Engine 226 is located on State Street in Brooklyn, four and a half miles away across the Hudson River from the Twin Towers.[75] Because it is located near Manhattan, Engine 226 is often dispatched to Manhattan to fight fires. On 9/11, Engine 226's crew, composed of five men, was one of the first fire trucks to arrive at the site of the World Trade Center. When it was dispatched, the crew was initially directed to the site; then, as they were en route, they were ordered to report to the North Tower. Off-duty Engine 226 firefighter Peter Culkin was returning from walking his son to kindergarten when his sister-in-law called him to tell him the planes had hit the Twin Towers. He immediately contacted his wife, Beth, at work and asked her to come home so he could go to the World Trade Center. While he waited, he collected some personal gear that he thought might be needed as he kept an eye on the television to see what was happening.

He saw immediately this was a catastrophic event. As he watched on television before the second plane hit and flames engulfed the building, he

---

75   Except as otherwise noted this chapter is based on interviews with FDNY Lieutenants Peter Culkin and William Reddan and firefighters Chuck Pettignano and Duncan Cooke.

spotted a large plume of smoke coming out of the windows and assumed that it would be an all-day operation.

He said, "At this point I was handcuffed to my home with our two-and-a-half-year-old daughter, Gillian, while Beth was working at a hospital in Brooklyn as a psychologist. I had to wait for her to come home before I could go anywhere. So even though I was nearby in Brooklyn, it took time to get out the door."

When Beth arrived, Peter drove to the fire station through roads choked with traffic, police checkpoints, and general confusion in the streets from the disaster.

The first tower fell while he was in his car. Peter recalls people trying to communicate from their cars, sometimes using hand gestures as they inched along. An Asian man in a car next to him seemed to be trying to tell him, with gestures, that he was usually in one of the towers. Peter could see the plume of smoke coming from the towers, and as he drove under it about 10:00 a.m., the plume became darker and wider.

He arrived at the firehouse around 10:30 a.m. The engine and its crew had already been dispatched to the scene. The firehouse was deserted except for two relatively new firefighters serving a period of training at the fire station (Ralph Vitiello and Tom Chiancone). They had also been off duty and had come in. The three men gathered as much firefighting gear as they could find and prepared for the difficult and long stretch of work ahead. They filled an orange medical bag with respirators, since their regular masks were on the dispatched truck. They packed up firefighter helmets, coats, and boots and headed off on foot. They went through the Fulton Street Mall, past Macy's to Flatbush Avenue, where they were slowed by a flow of pedestrians fleeing the city. When they arrived at the base of the Manhattan Bridge, several city buses were transporting firefighters across the bridge.

They boarded a bus that had been commandeered by other firefighters and headed for the towers. Once across, they found that the area looked like a military encampment or holding area. There were busloads of fire-fighters, fire trucks, and other miscellaneous vehicles filled with people, all eager to go to the World Trade Center. They were being held up partly because the senior authorities were still struggling for control of the situation and partly because of the possibility that more attacks were coming. There was a rumor that there was an unidentified airplane headed towards their location. Some firefighters heard reports of people like Father Judge being killed, and they all realized that this was a major, ongoing event.

Meanwhile, hundreds of firefighters were forced into simply waiting, just standing around and wondering what was happening. Unofficial communications were primarily from cell phones. Some firefighters worried about family members in downtown Manhattan. One firefighter had talked to his sister, who had been in one of the towers, and found out, thankfully, that she was on her way home.

Frightened people streaming by shouted to the waiting firefighters, saying, "God bless you! God bless you! Be careful!"

After several false starts—"we're going," "we're not going"— the buses finally started rolling.

Military jets roared overhead. While giving the waiting firefighters confidence, they also underlined the seriousness of the situation.

Peter Culkin, Ralph Vitiello, and Tom Chiancone got off the bus and started walking south into what looked like a snowstorm in September. Peter remembers taking his shoes off so he could put on his firefighter boots. He tied the laces together and hung the shoes on a wrought iron fence, thinking he would come back for them later. He never was able to recover them and later joked that someone probably sold his shoes on eBay.

When they arrived, both towers had already fallen. WTC Building Seven, which housed the City's Emergency Operations Center and command post, was on fire with eight floors already burning. There were major problems with water pressure in the system being used to fight fires in the buildings surrounding the fallen Twin Towers. The destruction of these buildings had severely damaged the water main. The only available water on the west side was that coming through the fire department's fire boats. Peter, Tom, and Ralph joined the group of firefighters assembling in this blizzardlike atmosphere and waited an anxious, interminable half hour, ready to do their part to get into the action. They talked to each other while they impatiently waited, sharing what little information they had. They were sure they had lost many friends, but they didn't know who, and they hoped that their comrades from Engine 226 had somehow survived the collapse of the two towers.

Finally given the go-ahead, they got on a ladder truck and went to the other side of the devastated area. Here they found a completely different world. No more "blizzard." Now the sun was again shining and the sky was a brilliant blue. The massive clouds of dust and smoke were blowing southeast toward Brooklyn, leaving the west side clear. This gave the firefighters relief from breathing the polluted dust and smoke they had been exposed to earlier.

Now they found themselves in another staging area. There were many firefighters, some equipped with whatever tools they were able to carry, and again they were forced to wait for something to happen, somebody to order them to proceed, someone to tell them what to do, and unsure why they were being held back. Volunteers in the area were bringing sandwiches and drinks to the waiting men. They weren't really hungry but it was already well past lunchtime. They didn't know how much longer they might be on the site, so each had a sandwich offered by the compassionate bystanders.

Finally WTC Building Seven, which had been fully engulfed in flames, fell. It became clear that they had been forced to wait so that more firefighters, more of their friends, and more of their leaders wouldn't be killed or injured by the expected collapse of that building. Peter and the two probies stayed together and walked over towards Stuyvesant High School. There, he recognized Jim Boyle, a retired firefighter and former president of the New York City Fire Fighter Union. Jim told Peter that his son, Michael, who had previously worked at the Engine 226 firehouse, was missing, and he asked Peter if he had seen him. Peter replied that he had not. While Jim Boyle was clearly distraught, he was holding himself together. A friend of Peter's, Jerry Rogan, a lieutenant at the time, told him that his brother, firefighter Matthew, from Ladder Company 11 was missing.

They walked along the Hudson River toward Battery Park and sneaked around the side and came into the World Trade Center complex. They entered the complex near an indoor/outdoor atrium restaurant, where Peter and his sister had eaten lunch at outdoor tables in the past. The building had survived but with much damage. Then he saw a sight that he'll never forget—linen tablecloths neatly set with wine glasses, napkins, and silverware, all covered with a thick layer of dust. To enter the site, they went through a fitness center in the American Express building and stepped gingerly through a smashed plate glass window into an eerie setting.

They felt as though they had just stepped off of a space ship onto the surface of the moon. Everything was coated with that layer of dust. Nothing was intact. Their surroundings were just shredded and pulverized with torn wires, twisted metal, glass, massive chunks of concrete, and debris everywhere. It was strangely, eerily quiet. Cranes quickly started the search for possible survivors while firefighters manned hoses, stomping out remaining fires, but everything was quiet. There were no automobiles, no horns blowing, no street noise. Peter remembers only the sound of his footsteps as he climbed through the rubble, dust, and debris of the fallen World Trade Center, searching for his comrades.

When they finally reached the heart of the area, they felt a silent helplessness.

There was no one to report to, no one to give them direction, and Peter thought, "Now what do we do?"

A primary concern was searching for their comrades from Engine 226, but where would they start?

He said, "I just started poking around. The only productive thing that I remember doing was going through a temporary office trailer on a construction site that had been blown over on its side to make sure that there was no one in there. There was a pair of 'boat shoes,' and I hoped the guy who owned them had gone home."

Later he found a man's foot. A bare foot, no shoe, no sock, isolated with no body, no other body parts. Later there was a more sophisticated procedure for handling remains, but at that moment the men had to act quickly on their own. They put the foot into a cardboard box so that it could be preserved and indentified later.

The rest of their day was spent trying to find their missing crew and helping out where needed, not really knowing what else to do. They called their engine house to see if they could get an update on what was happening and hopefully link up with their comrades that had gone earlier. A lieutenant at the fire station told them he thought the others might have gone to the New York Telephone Company Building, so they headed over to that building just north of the towers to look for them. Going into the phone company, Peter's flashlight had stopped working, but one of the others had a light stick and, using it, they followed a fire hose leading into the building, hoping that their companions were there. When they got to the end of the hose at the third or fourth floor, they found the nozzle, which had been turned off, next to a wall that looked like it had exploded. They now had some hope that their friends had survived, since there was no sign of any one around. Perhaps their missing crew had activated this hose line but had already left. Since the hose nozzle was turned off, they thought the men were probably OK. The building was no longer on fire, although it had been damaged by debris. The damage might have occurred when Building Seven next door collapsed. The three men left the building and went back to do whatever they could to help out. At this point a number of iron workers had arrived. Lights were being set up. Cutting torches were being rushed into use to start disassembling the "pile" to search for possible survivors and to recover remains of those that had been murdered. The mounds of debris were everywhere, fifteen, twenty, thirty feet or more high depending on where you were. The scene resembled pictures they had seen of Berlin after it had been bombed during World War II.

Sometime after midnight, Peter and Tom Chiancone wanted to reconnect with their firehouse. They walked to the Brooklyn Bridge, exhausted and frustrated after the day's events and their inability to do much visible work at the site of the devastation. Much more important was their sinking feeling that the crew of Engine 226 would not join them at the firehouse. Ralph Vitiello, a U.S. Marine reservist, stayed at the site throughout the night. A police van at the bridge gave the worn-out men a ride to the firehouse. There they found exhausted men, those that had been off duty and had come in and worked all day, just laid out everywhere, resting, trying to sleep, guys talking to their wives. That night, in a small fire station intended to provide minimal space for five or six men at a time, there were men sleeping on a bench, lying on the floor, in chairs—anywhere they could find a spot to try to rest. The on-duty Engine 226 crew was not there.

Peter said, "We kind of knew during the day that the engine crew might have been killed, but we did not accept it at this point."

Their quest searching for their friends was not over, and for the next few days they held out hope that, somehow, the men might be found alive, trapped in the rubble. Four or five days later they came to the final, grim realization that no one would not be found alive. They later determined that the men had been working their way upstairs in the North Tower when it fell. An audio tape was heard in which Lieutenant Wallace, detailed to Engine Company 226 that day, was responding to a request from a chief for a hose line, and he was heard saying that he was on his way up in the North Tower. None of their bodies were ever recovered, although search crews later found some identification for Dave DeRubbio.

No one wanted to go home, and most didn't go home for the next few days. For the next two weeks Peter and the other firefighters from the State

Street firehouse worked about ten twenty-four-hour shifts, some at the station and some at the site, catching sleep whenever and wherever they could. Policemen from the nearby Dean Street station would transport the firefighters to and from the site until their truck was repaired. The fire engine itself was intact, although it was badly damaged and the windshield had been blown out. A massive amount of New York Fire Department equipment had been damaged or destroyed. A huge backlog of work orders resulted in long delays for repairs. Finally, the men of Engine Company 226 cleaned up and restored their "rig" to operable status. Later they weren't sure that this was a good idea when they learned that the coating of dust and grime on their truck may have been badly polluted with numerous toxic materials. Even today, they wonder if their future health may be affected by the events of September 11, 2001.

The only good news was that the driver or "chauffeur" of Engine 226, although injured, had survived. Firefighter Tom Casatelli walked back to his fire station and then to a nearby hospital to be treated for his injuries. Suffering from post traumatic stress disorder, he retired from the fire department.[76] After treatment his condition has greatly improved. He now owns a restaurant in Brooklyn and was recently married.

Peter Culkin continues his career with the New York Fire Department. In November 2003 he was promoted to lieutenant and now is assigned to Ladder Company 163 in Queens. Tom Chiancone has also been promoted to lieutenant.

Inspired by the events of September 11, 2001, Ralph Vitiello was deployed with the U.S. Marine Corps and served two tours of duty in Iraq before returning to his job as a New York City firefighter.

The men of Engine Company 226 have erected a memorial to the deceased firefighters in the firehouse containing firefighter coats with the names of the missing on them.

As Mother's Day 2002 approached, the men of Engine Company 226 wanted to do something for the mothers of the firefighters from their station who had died on 9/11, so they presented them with bouquets of flowers.

The next year one of the firefighters said, "Let's take them to lunch."

So they arranged a luncheon on a date near Mother's Day which has now become a tradition for this fire station, and each year around Mother's Day

---

76   Firefighter Charlie Stephen, interview, September 11, 2007.

they go out to lunch. Peter said that they do this partly out of a sense of duty for their comrades and partly because they have developed a relationship with the mothers of their friends that were murdered on September 11, and they enjoy their company. They remain in contact with the women and continue to assist them whenever possible.

Lieutenant William Reddan
"Funny, it was like a lifetime ago, yet it was like yesterday."
Lieutenant William Reddan

Firefighter Bill Reddan was assigned to Squad One, located on Union Street in Brooklyn. Squad One can get to the site of the World Trade Center in as little as five to ten minutes and was one of the first fire companies to respond that day. Bill was on vacation. His wife, a private nurse, had recently had a baby, and Bill was at home caring for the baby.

Each borough in New York City, except Staten Island, has a squad specially trained, equipped, and staffed with firefighters. While their primary mission is to rescue trapped firefighters, they also routinely work with FDNY engine and ladder companies rescuing people trapped in fires and other types of emergencies. Their training includes disposing of hazardous materials and working with specialized equipment for both rescue and routine firefighting operations. Men assigned to squads have at least two years' prior experience and must come highly recommended by their former organizations.

Bill Reddan's mother-in-law called him and frantically said, "Look out the window!" (Bill's Brooklyn apartment had an excellent view of the World Trade Center.) When he saw the billowing smoke, Bill immediately called his wife and asked her to come home.

He said, "Look, honey, I have to go!"

She tried to convince him that he didn't have to respond because he was on vacation, but he was adamant. She quickly left her job and came home. Bill rushed to the Squad One firehouse, where two other men, also off duty, had come in. The crew on duty had already gone to the World Trade Center. The three men collected their equipment, stopped a fire department truck equipped to do electrical work, and asked for a ride to the city. While this truck had no emergency lights and sirens, it had FDNY markings and passed checkpoints without difficulty. They crossed the Brooklyn Bridge, clogged by the mass of pedestrians, many covered with grime, some helping injured people who were escaping from the collapse of the South Tower. With no vehicle traffic going into the city, the police waved them through. On the Manhattan side of the bridge as they approached City Hall a few blocks from the World Trade Center, they were shocked as they watched the North Tower fall. Bill realized that if they had arrived just a few moments earlier, they probably would have been killed. The men borrowed masks from nearby fire trucks and then walked into the immense cloud of chalky dust to search for survivors.

Bill joined firefighter Steve Brown. The men found burning fire trucks and did their best to put those fires out.

People were screaming, "There are people trapped over there!"

He said, "We'd run over to see what we could do, but the reports were unfounded. We figured that people would be trapped all over the place, but they weren't. They either made it or they didn't. Those who didn't get out were pulverized. They try to butter it up, you know, they say that they died. But they were murdered."

The men heard reports that people were trapped in Building Seven. They entered the structure from the northeast corner. While the building looked like it was still sound, in reality, the southwest side of the building had been destroyed.

Bill said, "So we went in and started searching. We were with Chief Brown at the time, and another chief came along and told us to get out of the building because it was compromised. There was a lot of emotion flying around. Chief Brown said, 'You don't know what you're talking about! There are reports of people trapped. We're going to go get them.' We started up the stairs. Suddenly, we heard a rumble, like a heavy collapse inside the place. We ran out of there as fast as we could!"

A few hours later World Trade Center Building Seven, which had housed New York City's Emergency Operations Center, also collapsed.

The men then went to the west side, where they joined some other units and "started crawling into crevasses, looking for people."

He said they found the remains of some people, but "there was nothing that we could do."

A few injured victims were found by other people, but Bill and the men with him from Squad One found no survivors.

Bill Reddan stayed at the site until noon the next day, when he was ordered to go home and rest. He realizes that if he hadn't been on vacation, he, too, would have been killed on September 11. As it was, the firefighter who replaced Bill while he was on vacation died.

Asked how he felt about that, he replied, "Survivor's guilt? Yeah. I went through all of that. Lot of pain, but you know…"

Even though years have passed, Bill says about the events of that day, "Funny, it was like a lifetime ago, yet it was like yesterday."

Squad One lost eleven firefighters that day.

Both Bill Reddan and Steve Brown were later promoted to lieutenant.

Chuck Pettignano

After the second plane hit the Twin Towers, Squad 61, located in the Bronx, was anxious to go, and the crew kept asking their officer, Lieutenant Pete Runfola, to head to the World Trade Center.

There was a report of more planes missing, however, so the dispatcher told them to "sit tight!"

The crew members kept saying, "Let's just get on the rig and go!"

Lieutenant Runfola kept his composure and replied, "Take it easy. Relax. We'll go when the time is right."

By the time they were dispatched, around 9:30 a.m., traffic was at a standstill.

The men actually had to walk in front of the fire truck to direct traffic, "You! Move your car over here! You! Pull over there!"

By the time they finally arrived, half an hour later, the second tower had already collapsed. It had been a beautiful day. When they arrived, though, it was black as night with the smoke and dust from the fallen towers.

The men went to work looking for people that were trapped. They found an NYPD policeman named Esposito, in World Trade Center Seven, pinned down by debris from the floor above that had collapsed. Firefighters Chuck Pettignano and Tom Day freed the officer, who had a badly injured knee, and carried him down the stairs. Then Pettignano took him, with the policeman's arm over his shoulder, about ten blocks to an Emergency Medical Service bus.

Pettignano returned to Ground Zero and the crew went into the Marriott Hotel. They found a gruesome scene, with body parts spread around. They spent about forty minutes there but did not find anyone alive. Later they worked at the site, mostly in the tunnels that ran under the Twin Towers, searching for victims.

The crew realized that but for Lieutenant Runfola remaining calm, and the ensuing delay, they would very likely have been killed when the towers fell.

Chuck Pettignano often thought about Lieutenant Runfola telling his men, "Take it easy. Relax. We'll go when the time is right!"

He suffered from "survivor's guilt" for awhile, and for many years he did not speak to anyone, not even his wife, about his experiences at Ground Zero. He wore a mask when he worked at the site and does not have breathing problems.

WTC Clean up operations-Michael Rieger FEMA News Photo

Chapter Seventeen
Port Authority Police Department (PAPD)

"We are involved in a tidal wave and it is our job not to drown! We have to bring order out of chaos!"

James Nachstein, the PAPD chief of operations during the 1993 attack on the World Trade Center

The Port Authority Police Department is the twenty-seventh largest police department in the United States. It is responsible for police functions at all major transportation facilities and the World Trade Center in the New York City urban area.[77]

Chief Christopher Trucillo was a PAPD sergeant at one of the airports in February 1993 when the terrorists placed a truck bomb in the parking garage. He responded to the site with Fred Morrone, later the superintendent of police. The PAPD officers that had been involved in the 1993 bomb attack on the Twin Towers had expected that the stricken tower would fall. Because it didn't, they were lulled into a false sense of security on 9/11 and thought that the towers were indestructible.

Prior to 9/11, Chief Trucillo was the commander of the PAPD Internal Affairs Division. Trucillo often kidded his brother-in-law, Antonio Rocha,

---

77   Except as otherwise noted this chapter is based on interviews with PAPD Chiefs (retired) Christopher Trucillo and Joseph Morris and Mrs. Thelma Stuart, widow of PAPD Officer Walwyn Stuart.

working on the fifty-sixth floor of the North Tower, because his office was located on a higher floor and had a better view. In August 2001 Rocha went to work for Cantor Fitzgerald on the 105th floor of the building. He then ribbed Trucillo about having a better "room with a view." In July 2001 Trucillo's office was moved to the Port Authority headquarters in Jersey City, New Jersey, because World Trade Center real estate had become so valuable.

The Trucillo and Rocha families had planned to go to Cabo San Lucas, Mexico, for a vacation together. They were scheduled to leave on September 15, 2001. A week earlier, Chief of Department James Romito called Trucillo and asked him and two other officers to attend a two-day conference in Atlantic City, New Jersey, starting on Monday, September 10.

They enjoyed the first day, and on the morning of September 11, as they were coming out of an elevator of the Sheraton Hotel across from the Convention Center, they saw the fifty contestants for the Miss America contest posing on a spiral staircase.

Trucillo turned to his colleagues and said, "What could be better than this? No work, fifty beautiful women, and a gorgeous day!"

They were just having their first cup of coffee at breakfast when the pagers started going off. Something had hit the World Trade Center. They initially thought it was a small plane.

The men rushed back to their rooms to watch the scene unfold on television. Realizing the magnitude of the situation, they immediately started packing. As Trucillo was throwing his belongings into a suitcase, his sister, Marilyn Rocha, phoned him. She had just received a phone call from her husband, Antonio, trapped on the upper floors of the tower, saying that he loved her. He asked her to tell their children that he loved them, too. The three men ran to their police cruiser and raced back to their headquarters in Jersey City, New Jersey.

Inspector Joseph Morris joined the Port Authority Police Department in 1972. Prior to 9/11, he had served in the Lincoln Tunnel, PATH Command, bus and marine terminal commands, as well as at headquarters, the Criminal Investigations Bureau, and the Special Investigations Unit. On September 11, he was commanding the PAPD unit at LaGuardia International Airport in New York City.

Early that morning he was in his office when a man suddenly shouted, "A plane just crashed into the World Trade Center!"

Morris turned to the TV to see the upper stories of the North Tower engulfed in flames. He had worked at the Trade Center after the February 1993 attack, and with more than twenty years of experience, he knew what would be needed.

He yelled out to Lieutenant Ed Dowling, "Round up all the free bodies we can spare! We're going to the World Trade Center!"

Minutes later he was racing toward Manhattan with seventeen police officers and detectives in a convoy of seven vehicles, including marked and unmarked sedans and the airport's Emergency Service Unit truck.

One of the men with him was Lieutenant Emilio Sepulveda, who had been a police officer, then later a sergeant, and had worked at the WTC for nine years, being directly involved in the 1993 bombing recovery operations with then-Lieutenant Morris. With sirens wailing, they raced down the Brooklyn-Queens Expressway, then crossed the Williamsburg Bridge toward Manhattan. En route, they saw the second airliner smash through the South Tower and immediately realized they were under a terrorist attack. Inspector Morris recalled his earlier experience when terrorists struck in 1993.

He was with James Nachstein, the PAPD chief of operations, who, during the rescue operations, told him, "Joe, we hope the training kicks in. We are involved in a tidal wave and it is our job not to drown! We have to bring order out of chaos!"

Anticipating security requirements and additional manpower needs at the World Trade Center and the airports, Morris directed the LaGuardia airport police unit to have the afternoon shift report in immediately. He knew Chief James Romito would have responded from Port Authority Police headquarters in Jersey City, New Jersey, so he radioed the central police desk to confirm the location of the "rally (meeting) point," but the police desk was unable to contact anyone at the site. As he approached the World Trade Center, Inspector Morris saw objects falling from the towers, so he diverted the convoy down West Broadway and parked at Barclay Street a block away to have the cover of adjacent buildings north of the complex. There they responded down Barclay Street to West Street to meet the Port Authority incident command vehicle. PAPD contingency plans called for the rally point to be located at Vesey and West streets. (Contingency plans had been revised after the 1993 terrorist bombing and again prior to the millennium celebrations.) When they arrived, the PAPD incident command bus and about 50 PA police officers from the Newark airport had already assembled there.

NYPD First Deputy Commissioner Joseph Dunne and Port Authority Inspector General Robert Van Etten were there. Dunne asked who was in command of the Port Authority Police, and Van Etten responded that Inspector Morris was the senior police officer present. Dunne then asked if the bridges and tunnels into the city had been closed off. Morris confirmed that these approaches had been closed and that emergency vehicles coming from New Jersey would use the Holland Tunnel New Jersey Plaza as a staging point for WTC response.

Inspector Morris ordered PAPD lieutenants and sergeants to divide the men into groups of four or five men, each with a supervisor for rescue operations. He learned from Sergeant Joseph Poland that Superintendent of Police Director Fred Morrone, Chief of Department James Romito, a twenty-nine-year veteran of the PAPD, and Inspector Anthony Infante, a twenty-one-year veteran and commanding officer of Port Authority police at JFK Airport, had gone into the North Tower to meet with Port Authority Executive Director Neil Levin and other Port Authority executives at the sixty-fourth floor operations center. The chief's and inspector's actions mirrored those they took after the 1993 bombing. Now, however, the situation had changed. After the previous bombing people were calmly evacuated from the building, and casualties were escorted to waiting ambulances on West Street. While there were approximately one thousand people injured in the 1993 bombing, most of those suffered smoke and dust inhalation. This time the situation was total disaster. Instead of one building affected, the entire World Trade Center complex was involved. Thousands of people were killed and injured by falling debris, fire, explosion, and then the collapse of the buildings as well as smoke and dust inhalation. Carnage was everywhere.

Unable to contact the World Trade Center PAPD command desk, Morris told his men to remain at the command post. He and Lieutenant Sepulveda started south toward the North Tower, with the intention of reporting to the PAPD/FDNY lobby incident command desk. Inspector Morris observed that few civilians were present in the street adjacent to the North Tower and Building Five of the complex, leaving mostly firefighters, police, and other emergency workers to handle the worsening situation.

Inspector Morris described the scene: People and debris were on the ground and falling from the towers. As their bodies struck the street and the roof of the north bridge over West Street, a loud thud was heard, similar to pumpkins smashing. Blood splattered the windows. As they approached the walking bridge connecting World Trade Center Building Five to the financial center, he looked up and was shocked to see more black objects starting to cascade from the South Tower as it started to collapse.

The two men ran together north about sixty yards. Morris then dove into the PAPD incident command bus as he was being immersed in a cloud of dust and debris he describes as "a warm whiteout blizzard of fine granulated powder that invaded everything." The lieutenant continued to run and was not seen the rest of the day. Lt. Sepulveda was listed as missing and believed dead until early the next morning, when he reported that he had been overtaken by the cloud of dust and had collapsed. He luckily was picked up by the crew of a fleeing ambulance and taken for medical treatment in Brooklyn. Emergency workers in the area ran and dove for cover. All were shocked by the massive damage and carnage.

Whether people lived or died depended on where they were. Port Authority Police Officer George Howard, forty-four years old, from Hicksville, New York, with sixteen years' service and assigned to JFK Airport, had been off duty but rushed to the site when he first heard of the plane hitting the North Tower. He was forty feet away from Morris in the southbound lanes of West Street when the South Tower fell. He was killed by falling debris. His body was one of the first recovered that afternoon.

Port Authority Police Officer Joseph Szczepanski was on duty at another PATH train station and commandeered a cab to respond to the WTC. He was on the WTC concourse at the top of the long escalator leading down to the WTC station turnstile level, directing people to safety from the complex, when the South Tower collapsed. He jumped over the wall onto the escalator, a drop in excess of fifteen feet and found himself in total darkness, choking on smoke and dust. When he recovered from his jump, he used his flashlight to get other victims together. Then, forming a human chain, he led four other people to safety.

Inspector Morris said, "There were no computers, no desks. Everything was pulverized. The only things not pulverized were plastic ID cards and rugs. Concrete was turned to powder. Paper was everywhere. Paper was part of the white blizzard."

Captain Whitaker, the police commander of the WTC, came to the incident command vehicle located just north of Vesey Street in the northbound West Street lane headed in a southbound direction. The captain warned people he believed the North Tower was also going to fall. The avalanche of debris and rubble had piled up around the command vehicle to the front windshield of the vehicle. It wouldn't start until Officers Frank Accardi and Tom Kennedy improvised cleaning the air filter at a fire hydrant. They moved the bus two blocks north, saving it from destruction when the North tower fell. Two days later, Officer Accardi, the operator of the command vehicle, told Inspector Morris, "I'll never forget the look on your face when you pushed yourself up off the floor after diving into the vehicle." Morris asked, "Was it fear?" "No," Frank replied, "but it was a look of great concern."

The Port Authority policemen assembled at the new command post on West Street. Supervisors had started to account for personnel and plan rescue operations when the North Tower collapsed. Morris and the others jumped back into the bus as a new avalanche of debris and clouds of pulverized dust enveloped the area. When the dust settled again, they moved the command post vehicle north on West Street to a location north of Chambers Street outside of Manhattan Borough Community College and set up operations in the college gym.

Sixty-three-year-old PAPD Superintendent of Police Fred Morrone was a retired New Jersey state trooper. He had been last seen in an emergency stairwell near the thirtieth floor of the North Tower. He was speaking on his cell phone with Michael Scott, Port Authority assistant public safety office, when the tower collapsed. His body was never found.

Chief Romito was with Captain Kathy Mazza and three other Port Authority Police personnel using a chair to carry an obese woman down the stairs when the tower fell. Fire Chief Picciotto, trapped for hours in the same stairwell when the tower fell, was within six feet of Chief Romito. He was shocked to hear later from Inspector Morris that Romito had been killed. Chief Romito was respected as one of the smartest and most experienced men in the department and a man that was able to get things done.

Chief Morris said, "If you wanted to know history of the department operations and practices or if you wanted something done, you called Jim Romito. He was one of the smartest men I ever knew."

Captain Kathy Mazza, forty-six years old, from Farmingdale, New York, was the first female commander of the Port Authority Police Academy. Prior to joining the Port Authority Police Department, Captain Mazza had been a cardiac nurse at St. Francis hospital in Roslyn, Long Island. Recognizing that her mother was experiencing the symptoms of an oncoming heart attack, Kathy insisted that she go to a hospital where stents were emplaced, saving her life. When her mother suggested that she should not leave nursing to go to the PAPD, Kathy said that she would bring her skills with her. She had defibrillation devices installed by the PAPD in key locations, resulting in at least fourteen lives being saved prior to 9/11 and many more later. When she had open heart surgery, she asked the surgeons to take photographs of her heart. She later displayed these on a wall in her office and kidded people who said she didn't have a heart by saying, "Oh yes I do. There is a photograph of it right there!"

When Kathy heard the Twin Towers had been struck, she gathered up four of her subordinates, including thirty-nine-year-old Lieutenant Robert Cirri and Officer James Parham (a thirty-three-year-old former marine and an instructor at the PAPD Academy), and said, "Come on! Let's go!"

She drove with them through the Holland Tunnel to the World Trade Center and immediately started helping people escape. Forty-five-year-old Officer Stephen Huczko, a fifteen-year veteran from Bethlehem, New Jersey, assigned to the Newark Airport, had been at the Police Academy interviewing with Captain Mazza for a police academy instructor's position when the towers were struck. He responded to the WTC with the academy officers.

One survivor described the bottleneck at the exit of the North Tower on the plaza level because a door wouldn't open after the South Tower had collapsed. Captain Mazza used her handgun to shoot the hardened plate glass window out, allowing trapped people to escape.

A survivor said later, "She saved my life!"

Mazza and her crew went up the stairwell to rescue others after the plaza level was clear of persons escaping the carnage.

Inspector Joseph Morris was put in charge of the PAPD rescue and recovery effort later on the afternoon of September 11. His first priority was to establish command and control and meet manpower requirements. PAPD Chief Thomas Farrell had been on disability leave due to a serious back injury. He responded from his home in central New Jersey to PAPD police headquarters in Jersey City. He conferred with Inspector Morris on police personnel needs at the WTC site as well as other Port Authority transportation facilities in the New York/New Jersey metropolitan area, all of which had been placed at the highest terrorist threat level. Police personnel on the entire force were placed on twelve-hour days with all scheduled time off cancelled. No excused time for officers was permitted. Most Port Authority Police officers wanted to work at the site. There were 1,267 officers remaining after the thirty-seven who had been killed, but manpower requirements, including those at the WTC site—"the pile," as the disaster area was frequently called—were in excess of 2,100 officers. Police officers were still needed at the three airports, four bridges, two tunnels, the PATH train system, New York and New Jersey port pier facilities, and bus terminals. Morris decided to limit the number of officers working at the WTC to two hundred. Men and women normally on medical leave or absent for other personal reasons, if physically able, worked where they could at administrative duties or lobby facilities to free others for field duties. As a result, a normal medical absence rate of sixty to seventy people was cut to ten or fifteen.

Throughout the department, the 3:00–11:00 p.m. shift was eliminated and personnel were split between the two remaining shifts. At the WTC site, Lieutenant John Ryan and Lieutenant William Keegan were hand-picked by Morris to represent the Port Authority at the interagency WTC site command post tent located at the West and Vesey streets intersection. They were selected for their knowledge and leadership capabilities, defined by their strong personalities. Sergeant John Flynn, one of the department's emergency services experts, and Lieutenant Mark Winslow were assigned to formulate and coordinate emergency services rescue and recovery operations at the site. Inspector Morris worked there every day until September 26, when he was promoted to chief of the department. After his promotion he maintained direct supervision over PAPD operations at the site.

The Port Authority Medical Department and risk management personnel resources provided expertise in selecting proper rescue and safety equipment, such as respirator masks, for those who worked at the site. Lieutenant Ryan became known as the "Pile Nazi" and later "Pit Nazi" because of his insistence that workers wear their issued respirators—a policy that unquestionably reduced casualties among the Port Authority police working at the site.

After three weeks, the department officers got a day off every second week, then months later, a day every week. In spite of the grueling work and long hours, few complained.

"It is an amazing police department!" Morris said.

At 4:45 every morning he would stop at the Port Authority agency command post in Jersey City to check on the events of the night before and then proceed to the site, where he would remain until relieved at 7:00 p.m. by Inspector Gene Ceccarelli or Captain Anthony R. Whitaker.

In May 2002, the WTC recovery operations came to an end and the site became a construction site. In July 2003, after a number of new police classes had graduated from the police academy, placing 543 new officers on the force, the twelve-hour tours ended.

The remains of Captain Kathy Mazza, Lieutenant Robert Cirri, and Officer James Parham were found together five months later, buried in debris five levels below ground, along with those of Chief James Romito, Paul Laczinski, and Police Officer Stephen Huczko. The remains of a sixth person, an invalid woman strapped to a chair, were also found with them. Lieutenant Cirri, who was familiar with the World Trade Center, had apparently been leading the group to a seldom used exit door in the northwest emergency stairwell when the North Tower collapsed.[78] Chief Joseph Morris was notified early one Saturday morning when Chief Romito's and Captain Mazza's bodies were found. He immediately responded to the site. He went down where the remains were located with a medical examiner and helped carry both bodies out between two lines of assembled police, fire, and construction workers, as had become the practice when the remains of a first responder were identified and removed. While carrying Mazza's remains out of the cavern, he thought, "Kathy, I didn't know you were this heavy." When they brought the remains to the field morgue, it was discovered her remains were entangled with those of Officer Steven Huczko.

Lieutenant Cirri's wedding ring was returned to his wife, Eileen, at the funeral service conducted after her husband's body was recovered in March 2002.[79] Eileen Cirri, already a registered nurse, went to law school after 9/11 and now works for the Medicaid Fraud Department of the federal government.[80]

---

78   Eileen Cirri interview with author March 30, 2011.
79   Ibid.
80   Ibid.

Walwyn Stuart's performance on 9/11 was typical of PAPD policemen. On Monday evening, September 10, 2001, his wife, Thelma, was pleased to see her twenty-eight-year-old husband playing with their daughter, Amanda. Walwyn had been troubled for weeks with nightmares.

He described a recent one to Thelma as dreaming he had been injured and was lying on the floor at work with his legs crushed. In all of them something was happening that might cost him his job. Now, though, Walwyn was at peace, enjoying time with Amanda. He loved his little girl and was planning her first birthday party, two weeks off.

Walwyn, youngest of seven children, felt it was his calling to become a policeman. He had worked as an undercover detective for the NYPD in drug-infested neighborhoods in Harlem. Later he decided it was time to find a safer job, and was hired as an officer for the Port Authority Police Department and assigned to the Port Authority Trans-Hudson (PATH) train system. On September 11, 2001 he had just returned from vacation and was substituting for thirty-eight-year-old Donald J. McIntyre, a fourteen-year member of the force. (Although he was technically off duty, Officer McIntyre had arranged a shift change and was also present that day.)

Witnesses reported that after the South Tower, where he was stationed, was struck, Officer Stuart commandeered the last PATH train and directed passengers to stay aboard the train as he ordered the train's engineer to move the train out of the area. Other people said that he was later seen helping injured people.

Thelma, meanwhile, arrived at her job at the Administration for Children's Services, three blocks from the World Trade Center. When she debarked from the subway train, she asked a policeman what was happening. His reply was that a plane had hit the building. From a distance she was horrified to see people jumping from the tower that had just been struck.

Both Walwyn Stuart and Donald McIntyre died that morning in the performance of their duties. Although his remains were never recovered, some of Walwyn's personal effects, including his service revolver and handcuffs, were found in the rubble of the South Tower.

Many people in the World Trade Center that morning used cell phones to contact loved ones to let them know that they were all right, or, in many cases, to express their love and to say good-bye. Walwyn could not call Thelma because he had, atypically, left his cell phone, wallet, wedding ring, ID card, necklace, and car keys in his locker at work. Thelma feels that with all of the uncharacteristic things that he had done, Walwyn had a premonition that something bad was going to happen.

Amanda doesn't want to talk about her father, saying, "If he can't come back, I don't want to talk about him!"

Despite the chaotic situation, able civilian workers also helped those needing assistance. Port Authority employee Jeffrey Gertler was in his office on the eighty-eighth floor of the North Tower when American Airlines Flight 11 struck the tower between the ninety-third and ninety-ninth floors at 8:47 a.m.[81] As the staff was evacuating down one of the stairwells, he saw that fifty-six-year-old Judith A. Reiss, a temporary Port Authority employee from Kearny, New Jersey, with asthma, was having difficulty breathing. He assisted her as they descended, stopping along the way so she could rest and catch her breath. When they reached the eleventh floor, firefighters ordered him, over his objections, to leave the woman with them. He comforted her and told her that he would wait for her outside the building, then he did as he was told and continued down the stairs, leaving the building minutes before it fell. Judith Reiss was killed when the building fell.[82]

Raymond Finnegan and William Lipke, of the Port Authority, saved another Port Authority Engineering Department employee, Cynthia Ford, carrying her when necessary down from the fortieth floor of the North Tower. Upset and hyperventilating, she likely would not have made it out of the building without their assistance. They brought her to Emergency Medical Service personnel just as the South Tower fell.[83]

Barbara Iannacone-Ramos was assisting World Trade Center Mall tenants and customers evacuate when she found an injured woman lying on the floor after being burned and struck by debris. Iannacone-Ramos got the woman to her feet and rushed her to the police desk, where she was given medical attention and taken to a hospital. She then assisted the police in evacuating other people until the police ordered her to leave before the collapse of the South Tower.[84]

---

81   The 9/11 Commission Report, p. 285.
82   Thememoryhole.org, Port Authority Awards.
83   Ibid.
84   Ibid.

Mark Hanna and Frank Varriano helped Moe Lipson, an eighty-nine-year-old worker, all the way down to the lobby and to an ambulance outside the North Tower minutes before it fell.[85]

Port Authority officers and personnel, many off duty, some retired, came to the World Trade Center and the headquarters. Upon his return to PAPD headquarters from Atlantic City, Chief Trucillo realized that establishing the status of personnel on duty was critical in the chaos, so he began to try to account for everyone. He tried to determine from each command which of their people had responded to the site. He found "controlled chaos." When he directed some people to remain in the headquarters to help, he ran into resistance, as they all wanted to go to the site to help with the rescue and recovery effort.

He assembled everyone in the conference room and explained, "I understand what you want to do and where you want to be, but I have something more important. We need to reach out and help the families of our people who have no information. Even if we don't know the status of their loved ones right now, we must let them know that we are here, and that when we get information we will let them know."

Barbara Mahon, a medically retired PAPD detective, was one of those that came in to help. Trucillo asked her to work for him. Since that day, Barbara has been totally dedicated to the families of the thirty-seven Port Authority police officers that were killed on that day.

Inspector Joseph Morris was put in charge of the PAPD rescue and recovery effort later on the afternoon of September 11. His first priority was to establish command and control and meet manpower requirements.

Kathy Mazza's parents had a monument placed in a park in Long Island to honor her. Regrettably, it was twice vandalized by teenagers who didn't know who she was or why the monument was there. It has been moved to a more secure location in nearby Allan Park. A street in Massapequa, Long Island, has also been named Captain Kathy Mazza Way after her.[86] Kathy Mazza is survived by her husband, retired Police Officer Christopher Delosh, her mother, Rose Mazza and three brothers.

Antonio Rocha, Chief Trucillo's brother-in-law, who worked for Cantor Fitzgerald on the 105th floor of the North Tower, was killed. His body was recovered five days later.

---

85   Ibid.
86   Rose Mazza, mother of Kathy Mazza, interview.

The Port Authority of New York and New Jersey lost eighty-four people on September 11, thirty-seven of whom were police officers. This was the largest one-day loss of any police department in the history of United States law enforcement. An estimated twenty-five thousand people were evacuated from the Twin Towers before they collapsed.

The PAPD union requested that the only police officers that would get the PAPD Medal of Honor were those that died that day. Deserving officers received commendation medals and other recognition.

When the recovery effort ended, the PAPD arranged a debriefing and counseling session with psychologists for the officers. The two-day session was held at a hotel, with spouses attending the second day. Posttraumatic stress syndrome was recognized and treatment was made available for the men and women who needed it. The department later received an award and worldwide recognition for this program.

Chief Christopher Trucillo kept a copy of the 9/11 report in his office so that he could refer to it and would always be reminded of the commission's criticism and recommendations.

He said, "My vision is that we should be the best counterterrorism department in the country. Everything that the PAPD is responsible for—bridges, tunnels, trains, and airports—is a potential terrorist target. We also have to do regular police work."

The PAPD Emergency Service Unit (ESU) was expanded from ten officers to 157. Officers were trained in special procedures such as use of heavy weapons, decontamination, and poison detection. A "robust" motorcycle squad was established to maintain a visible presence at the bridges and tunnels—not to write tickets, but rather to "eyeball" people, looking for people who didn't fit. PAPD was one of the first departments in the country to develop a behavioral assessment training program, which was given to every police officer in the department. They are taught to look for the traits and body indicators that might indicate hostile intent. The PAPD also partners with the Department of Homeland Security and brings in the latest technology to test it. They help the Department of Homeland Security by advising that agency about procedures to use at bridges, tunnels, airports, etc.

Chief Trucillo said, "We had to change the culture to ensure that every police officer in the Port Authority understands that their primary mission is counterterrorism and never take their eyes off the ball."

Searching for victims - photo courtesy of FDNY

Chapter Eighteen
Band of Dads

"Finding my son is my mission!"

Lee Ielpi

Twenty-nine-year-old Jonathan Ielpi, stationed at Squad 288 in Queens, would call his father, Lee, several times every day just to chat.[87] On the morning of September 11, however, he called to tell him about the plane hitting the North Tower of the World Trade Center. As they were talking, Lee heard the firehouse tone alarm in the background, signaling the crew that they were being dispatched. Jonathan told his dad that they were going to the World Trade Center.

Lee said, "OK, be careful!"

That was his last conversation with Jonathan.

Retired firefighter Lee Ielpi, a combat veteran of Vietnam and twenty-six-year veteran of the FDNY, is the father of two boys and two girls. During most of his career Lee was assigned to Rescue Two, "Best of the Best," which covered the entire borough of Brooklyn. Lee has earned many awards, but is most proud of two. He received a Class B Award for bravery after he and another fireman chased down a robber who had stabbed a priest. They cornered the robber in a parking lot, where he was apprehended by police. Lee also received an "Above and Beyond the Call of Duty" medal, awarded

---

87   This chapter is based on interviews with FDNY firefighter (retired) Lee Ielpi.

to thirty-five of the eleven thousand New York firefighters each year. Once, on the spur of a moment, Lee took a test that would have put him on the promotion list to lieutenant. Without studying, he missed passing by two points. This frightened him. Had he been promoted, he would have had to leave his company and battalion and never return. He never took another test.

Shortly after Lee's conversation with Jonathan, a "total recall" alert went out to all emergency responders in New York City, requiring them to report for duty. Lee immediately started to drive his other son, Brendan, to his firehouse. Brendan had recently graduated from college with two degrees. He was a "probie" with only four months of service with the FDNY.

As they were leaving home, the South Tower was struck by the second airplane. Arriving at Ladder 110, Brendan's company, on the Brooklyn side of the Brooklyn Bridge, Lee parked his car near the station and got a ride with a policeman across the bridge to City Hall, arriving a half hour after the towers had fallen. Lee hurried down West Street towards the disaster looking for his son. Jonathan had been sent to the South Tower, but Lee did not know that.

Now, almost unable to see because of the blinding cloud of smoke, ash, and powder, Lee worked his way closer to the site. He met other fathers and brothers of firefighters, including retired Uniformed Firefighter Association President Jimmy Boyle and Battalion Chief Lyons, looking for their sons. He met Battalion Chief Joe Downey and Captain Chuck Downey looking for their father, Deputy Fire Chief, Special Operations Command, Ray Downey.

He met a friend, Fire Officer Henry MacDonald, executive assistant to Deputy Commissioner William Feehan, who asked, "Lee! Hey! Did you see my brother?"

Lee replied, "No, did you see Squad 288? My son is here."

MacDonald answered, "No, let's go!"

The two men set out to search for the missing firefighters.

The rubble-strewn streets were a scene of complete disaster. Lee described it as "worse than the worst horror movies you have ever seen!"

Pandemonium! Chaos! As they went to the command post, the men passed wounded people walking away from the site. They passed six fire trucks parked under a large arch that had been crushed by debris from the falling building. Lee, wearing moccasins, shorts, and a short-sleeved

T-shirt, had gone to the site expecting to help people. He did not anticipate that the buildings would fall. Lee found a HazMat (Hazardous Material) truck, equipped to handle explosives and toxic material, under a walkway with the engine still running. Concerned about carbon monoxide buildup in a confined area, he turned off the engine.

Starting to look for victims, Lee crawled into a hole in the debris only to be burned on his stomach by a piece of hot steel. Realizing that it made no sense to go into this situation dressed as he was, he searched around and found a building with two cargo doors open. In disbelief and not understanding why they were there, he found inside a treasure trove of firefighter "turnout coats," boots, and helmets. He quickly found boots that fit and a turnout coat and helmet. Now properly clothed, he continued the work of an experienced firefighter searching for victims.

The only road into the devastation was clogged with vehicles and wreckage. He found Fire Department Staff Chief Frank Cruther and offered to clear the road so that construction equipment could be brought in. Given the go-ahead, a civilian construction supervisor who had overheard the conversation offered to bring in heavy equipment including "clamshell grapples" capable of lifting the crushed and damaged vehicles out of the way. The civilian contractor suggested that he "hot-wire" one piece of equipment owned by someone else. His offer was quickly accepted, and the clearing operation got under way. The contractor's men moved the cars, including a chief's undamaged automobile, and put them on the sidewalk around the corner. Rescue Company 2 and Squad 1 had parked their rigs on the south side of Liberty and West streets. All members of both crews were killed inside the towers when they fell.

Lee felt a rush of relief when he recognized some firefighters from Jonathan's unit, Squad 288, who had been off duty and rushed to the site. He thought, "Great!" but when the men saw him, they hung their heads. His optimism turned to dread as he realized what that meant. Lee kept looking and hoping.

He met Tony Belasari and asked, "Tony, did you find the squad?"

"No, Lee," Tony said. "We don't know where they are."

World Trade Center Building Seven crashed to the ground in another roaring cloud of debris around 5:20 p.m. The building had been expected to fall and had been cleared of people hours earlier. The firefighters, police, and other emergency workers watched as it fell straight down and then went back to work searching for both the living and the dead.

Lee called a friend and asked him to pick up his daughter-in-law and his two grandchildren and bring them to his home to be with his wife, Anne. Afraid of what he might find with a mother that had probably lost her son, a wife her husband, and two young children their father, Lee was reluctant to go home that night. Finally, exhausted, dirty, and worried, he drove home, arriving around midnight.

As he walked into the home, his ten-year-old grandson, Andrew, asked, "Did you find my daddy?"

Lee replied, "No, but we're going to keep on looking."

The next morning, and every morning for the next nine months, Lee returned to the site. A group of eight fathers soon formed what became known as "the Band of Dads," all but one retired firefighters. Jack Lynch, an Irish immigrant working for the Metropolitan Transit Authority, was the only exception. Another, Lieutenant Dennis Oberg, immediately retired, reasoning that if he remained on active duty he wouldn't be able to look for his son, also named Dennis.

The Band of Dads was soon equipped with walkie-talkies and other essential firefighter equipment. They would meet in a parking lot and divide up into small groups to search in different areas. Although nonemergency personnel were not permitted on the site, these seasoned men were not only welcomed but were frequently asked by fire department personnel to help in specific tasks. Their presence was also a morale boost for others working there. Firefighters later told them that when they considered not returning to the site and they would see the dads working, they were inspired to stay on the job. The men met and worked every day for nine months until the recovery effort was officially ended.

Lee Ielpi was asked to help out at the newly formed 9/11 Families Association, formed to act as a conduit for information to the families of victims.

He agreed but said, "I'm not leaving the site. Finding my son is my mission." Every day, Lee would work during the day at the site, and, when finished, would go to the 9/11 Families office to work there.

Shortly after arriving home exactly three months after September 11, Lee Ielpi received a phone call asking him to return to the site of the World Trade Center. His son's body had been found. Lee and Brendan, his other son, returned to the site. Tradition is that "the firehouse that loses a firefighter brings him out." The site was silent as construction equipment stopped; for a brief moment the mission had changed. Led by Lee Ielpi and Brendan, Squad 288 carried the stretcher bearing Jonathan's remains up the ramp leading seventy feet up from the bedrock that had supported the Twin Towers. Firefighters, policemen, and volunteers lined each side and saluted the fallen firefighter as he was carried past.

Lee felt fortunate. Jonathan's body was one of only 174 of the people murdered at the World Trade Center whose bodies were found intact. Lee worked every day helping the other members of the Band of Dads look for their sons and other victims.

"How could I leave," Lee said, "when the others hadn't found their sons?"

Jonathan Ielpi left a widow and four children, two boys and two girls. When he first told his father that he wanted to be a firefighter, Lee suggested that he take both the New York City police and firefighter tests. He easily passed both, but the waiting time to be called up as a firefighter was much longer than that for policemen. He served in the NYPD for two years before becoming a firefighter. He was also assistant chief of the Great Neck Long Island Vigilant Volunteer Fire Department. North High School, of Great Neck, where he played hockey, has retired number 16, the number on his hockey jersey. Jonathan's life revolved around his family and the fire department. He and his family loved camping, fishing, and hiking.

Once again, in almost the same scenario, Jack Lynch, an Irish immigrant and the only nonfirefighter in the "Band of Dads," had returned home after a long day searching for the band's sons. In March 2002 the remains of firefighter Michael Lynch were found. His badly damaged body was identified by some papers in his coat pocket. Ielpi, who was still at the site, went to a quiet spot and phoned Jack.

Jack asked, "What is it, Lee?"

Lee, trying to keep the situation calm, answered, "Just come back. We don't know for sure yet."

When Lynch arrived, Lee informed him, "Jack, listen! We have Michael, but you shouldn't look."

Jack replied, "I want to…" and Lee interrupted him and said, "You shouldn't look."

Jack obeyed and avoided looking at the remains of his son. Then he phoned his family and they arrived. Once again, the equipment stopped. All was silent. The long, narrow ramp was lined with firefighters, workers, and police saluting as the battered remains of Michael Lynch, Engine 40, were carried up the ramp by his family and his company, his mother at her son's side. A woman's body was found next to Michael Lynch's and it appeared that he was trying to rescue her when they were killed.

The remains of Lieutenant Dennis Oberg, Ladder 105, were never found. His shoes were found in the company's truck.

John Vigiano, who lost two sons, showed up every day at Ground Zero. The body of his policeman son, Joseph was found, but John Junior's remains have never been located.

Joseph Angelini Sr.'s body was found near the pedestrian bridge. Joseph Senior was killed when the North Tower collapsed as he was looking for his son. His son's body was never found.

Jimmy Boyle's son, Michael, was killed.

Deputy Fire Chief Ray Downey, one of the senior fire officials at that time, was killed. His remains were found and he was laid to rest on May 20, 2002.

Fire Officer Henry MacDonald's brother, firefighter Tommy MacDonald, escaped injury.

Six "probies" in Brendan Ielpi's class were also killed on September 11, 2001.

The Tribute Center

Jennifer Adams, a Miami native who had "fallen in love with the city," had previously worked in the Twin Towers. She decided to stay in New York when her company moved out of town. After 9/11, she volunteered to work at a tent at the site giving out boots, equipment, coffee, hot chocolate, and compassion to the workers. Jennifer, with her strong financial background with an investment banking company, heard about the 9/11 Families Association and agreed to volunteer with them for two or three months.

When the search for victims formally ended in May 2002, Lee Ielpi went to work full time for the 9/11 Families Association. At this point the mission of the association evolved, and plans were developed for a Tribute Center honoring victims of the terrorist attack. Later Jennifer became a full-time employee and became the chief executive officer of the Tribute Center. Jennifer suggested that the association reorganize to match its new mission and lease a vacant storefront directly across the street from the World Trade Center site. The association also acquired office space in an office building overlooking the site. Governor George Pataki offered the state's financial assistance.

Open since September, 2006, this impressive center has had over 1,300,000 visitors from 120 countries. Filled with thousands of photographs and other memorabilia, the Tribute Center offers visitors an opportunity to share their thoughts, prayers, and, often, tears as they view both the photographs of that tragic day and pictures of victims and heroes. It is open seven days a week. Walking tours are conducted seven days a week, with six tours on Saturday.

Ielpi said, "We can't change what has happened, but we can do something to enlighten our young."

President Bush and Bob Beckwith-photo courtesy of Bob Beckwith

Chapter Nineteen
Recovery Operations

Firefighter Bob Beckwith
"Well, I can hear you! The rest of the world can hear you, and the people that knocked these buildings down will hear all of us soon!"

President George W. Bush

Sixty-nine-year-old Bob Beckwith's grandson was hit by a car while riding his bike near his home.[88] After the ambulance came, he went to the hospital to see how his grandson, who had suffered a broken arm, was doing. When Beckwith, a retired firefighter, returned home, he heard on the radio that a small plane had hit one of the Twin Towers. He switched on the TV, and when he saw the tower that had been hit, he wondered, "How could a plane crash into the World Trade Center on such a clear day?" Then he saw the second plane hit the South Tower.

After being assured that his grandson would be all right, he considered going to Ground Zero. His family talked him out of it, saying that at his age he should leave the rescue and firefighting to younger people.

Two days later Bob learned that Michael Boyle, son of James Boyle (former president of the Uniformed Fire Fighter Association), was missing, and he said, "That's it! I'm going down there."

---

88   Firefighter (retired) Bob Beckwith, interviews with author.

On the morning of September 14th, Bob started toward Ground Zero. He heard that all bridges and tunnels to Manhattan were closed, and at the Williamsburg Bridge he found the way blocked by orange traffic cones. When he saw police cars going between the cones and crossing the bridge, he followed them and then parked at the Engine 55 firehouse about a mile from Ground Zero. He was stopped when he reached a checkpoint manned by police at the perimeter. He was wearing his helmet and showed his ID. They let him pass. He came to another barricade manned by National Guard soldiers and was told, "I don't care who you are, you're not going through." He "lied a bit" and told them he was supposed to be there, was running late, and would be in a lot trouble if he didn't report in. The soldiers relented and let him pass.

He joined hundreds of other volunteers, including firefighters, police reserves, National Guard members, ironworkers, and dog handlers with their dogs, and spent all day digging in the rubble, hoping to find survivors, without success. He and other workers, using shovels, uncovered a fire truck pumper covered with rubble and debris near the North Tower to see if there were any firefighters or people under it, as some had dove under trucks for shelter as the towers started to fall. They would dig for a while, and then someone would bring dogs over to help search. They found no one there. Finally a crane lifted the badly crushed pumper out of the rubble.

In the late afternoon, the firefighters heard that President Bush was coming to the site. A little later Bob heard the crowd shouting, "USA! USA! USA!" and, as he thought the president might be approaching, he went over to the truck that they had recovered since it was near the Command Center. He climbed up on it so he would have a good vantage point to see the area where some microphones had been set up.

A man in civilian clothes came over, brushed off some of the dirt near where he was standing, and asked if the truck was safe for someone to stand on. Bob, thinking the man was a Secret Service agent, replied that it was. The man then said, "Show me," and asked Bob to jump up and down on it, which he did. The "Secret Service agent" told him to help someone else that would be coming get up on the truck. He told Bob that after the other man got up, he should get down. As Bob says, "When the Secret Service asks you to do something, you do it." Bob anticipated that the president would go to the nearby command center, where the microphones had been set up, and that perhaps another Secret Service person or "politician" would be coming up on the truck. Then he saw the president coming toward the nearby command post. Beckwith was surprised to see the president turn and come directly toward the fire truck that he was standing on. Bob helped President Bush up and asked him if he was all right. The president replied that he was, and so Bob, as instructed, started down. The president asked, "Where are you going?" and Bob answered, "I was told to get down." President Bush said, "No! You stay right here!" and he put his arm around Bob's shoulder. A photograph of the two men was later featured on the cover of Time magazine.

When President Bush started to speak, people on one side of the crowd stopped chanting "USA!" and instead started chanting, "We can't hear you! We can't hear you!"

A worker at the site handed the president a megaphone, and President Bush made his famous speech, saying, "Well, I can hear you! The rest of the world can hear you, and the people that knocked these buildings down will hear all of us soon!"

That short speech drew tremendous applause from the hundreds of workers, lifting the spirits of volunteers who had worked endless hours in the devastation to find survivors and to recover remains. When the president had finished talking, Bob helped him down from the fire truck, and someone handed the president a flag to wave. A big man, later identified as New York Governor George Pataki, picked Bob up and lifted him off the truck. Minutes later, a Secret Service agent came over and tapped Bob on the shoulder and said, "President Bush asked me to give you this" and handed him the flag that the president had held.

By then it was late, and he had worked all day, Bob decided to go home. He returned to the Engine 55 firehouse in Little Italy where he had parked his car. He stopped in the firehouse, which lost five firefighters, paid his condolences, and then went home. He thought to himself, "Who will believe all this?" But as he approached his home, neighbors told him that he had been on television. Cameras from a long distance away had captured the event.

That night, the head of the firefighters' union called Bob Beckwith and asked him not to go back to the site, and to let younger people handle the recovery. He was asked if his uniform still fit, and he replied that it did. The union leader asked him, instead, to attend as many of the funerals and memorial services as he could. Bob did that, often going to three or four funerals or services each day during the weeks ahead.

Later, because of this event, Bob Beckwith gave talks in many places, including Holland, Ireland, and during three trips to Germany. Honorariums he was paid for these presentations were all donated to the firefighters' Burn Foundation, which treats severe burn cases for people from all walks of life. He also received a letter from a man named Karl Rove, thanking him for helping him. He was the man Beckwith thought was a Secret Service agent.

Firefighter Jim Fortmeyer

Firefighter Jim Fortmeyer had worked a twelve-hour shift the night before 9/11 at Engine 275 in Queens.[89] Just after he returned to his fire station, Ladder Company 125, also in Queens, he watched television as the second plane hit the World Trade Center. A few days later, he was sent to the site, where he initially worked for over a month. The "pile" was still hot when he arrived, with fires still smoldering and much of the water available for extinguishing fires pumped by fireboats from the Hudson River. When people working at the pile found bodies, mostly pulverized, there would be a short ceremony, and they would be gently carried out in a Stokes basket.

Off and on, Jim spent several months working on the pile. He and others at his firehouse, and many other firehouses, were replaced by volunteer firefighters, both full time and part time, and firefighters from other communities. He describes the volunteers, many only nineteen or twenty years old, as eager to work and "ready to take on the world." There were problems, especially at first, but in spite of these, they did credible work and relieved the regular firefighters to work at the site. The volunteers were not familiar with the areas where they worked, but were able to use "route books" to find the locations where they were dispatched.

Jim felt fortunate that he did not work at the site the day the planes hit, as many of the firefighters and other workers there suffered ill affects afterward. Some returned to their work stations with eyes red and crusted, and many suffered lung problems. Jim wore a respirator when he worked at Ground Zero and has had no ill effects.

---

89   James Fortmeyer interview with author.

252

Janet McGuire—American Red Cross

Janet McGuire and her husband, Bernard (Bernie), were both working for the public affairs office of the American Red Cross in Tampa, Florida, on September 11, 2001.[90] The Tampa chapter, in conjunction with the coast guard, fire department, and other local authorities, was preparing to start a mass casualty drill involving a hypothetical ship in Tampa Bay. They were ready to start the exercise when Bernie phoned to tell her that a plane had struck one of the Twin Towers in the World Trade Center. Minutes later he called back to tell her that a second plane had struck the other tower.

A cold chill went through her as she realized that our nation was under attack. With more than one hundred volunteers standing by to participate in the exercise, she immediately called the director at the Disaster Operations Center (DOC) and asked that the exercise be cancelled. People might think that Tampa was also under attack if they suddenly saw fire trucks, ambulances, and police cars congregating downtown.

The DOC, anticipating a tropical storm during the next few days, already had volunteers, computers, and communications equipment ready to go into action. It was activated immediately. In the next week, the DOC received one call about the storm—and ten thousand calls from people inquiring about loved ones in New York or Washington, D.C. During the following weekend, the National Red Cross headquarters asked Janet if she and her husband would be willing to go to New York to assist. They immediately agreed.

The Red Cross set up two respite centers at Ground Zero, one in a building donated for use by St. John's University, the other at the Marriott Financial Center Hotel on the opposite side of the site. The respite centers provided a place to decompress for firefighters, police officers, and other emergency workers. Gourmet meals, donated by New Yorkers, were served around the clock. The centers responded, providing cots, recliners, computer access, gloves, boots, and socks, among other items. Workers would typically wear out two pairs of boots in a week because of the metal shards, concrete rubble, and heat from smoldering fires. Perhaps more importantly, there was always someone standing by with a smile and a hug.

The biggest problem that the respite centers had was convincing these dedicated workers to take a break. Most were reluctant to leave their

---

90   Janet McGuire interviews with the author.

backbreaking, somber jobs of searching for human remains. Respite center workers could tell when remains had been found. The mood would change and become even more serious as site workers came in to take a short break.

When they saw the Red Cross pins or other items, people in New York would make it a point to say "Thanks for what you are doing!" Janet and Bernie were riding a subway train when a young woman worked her way over to them and offered her thanks. Janet could see that the woman was distraught, and she asked if she was all right. The woman, named Rosie, broke into tears and explained that on 9/11 she had been running late to her new job in the World Trade Center. She couldn't understand why people were fleeing the building when suddenly a body crashed to the pavement next to her. Now, not only deeply troubled by the trauma of that day, she didn't have a job, as the office where she was to have worked had been destroyed. She had no way to pay her rent, couldn't get back into her apartment, and was afraid that she would lose her place to live. She didn't know what to do. Janet told her that she may qualify for assistance and told her to go to the Family Assistance Center. Bernie took the Red Cross pin off his lapel and pinned it on hers. He told her, "Now every time you think that you are alone, just touch the pin. We're going to be here and we want to make sure that you are okay." Janet said, "I wish I knew how this was going to turn out."

Later that day Janet saw a woman who looked like Rosie, but she was puzzled because she knew that it was necessary to go through a number of checkpoints and Rosie didn't have credentials. Later that evening at dinner, the respite center's manager told Janet, "Something strange happened today." He explained how a policeman brought a young woman in saying that she needed help. The manager started to explain that she had to go to the Family Assistance Center on the other side of town when she saw the Red Cross pin from the Tampa chapter. He asked Rosie where she got the pin. After she explained, the manager called the Family Assistance Center, which sent a representative over to interview the troubled woman. They came to the Respite Center and arranged aid for her and helped her find a new job. Janet learned how it all turned out.

Red Cross workers at the site were required to wear hard hats, gloves, respirators, and Red Cross vests. When entering the Respite Centers, all personnel had to observe decontamination procedures, where a hand sanitation station was set up, boots and shoes were cleaned, and dust particles were vacuumed or brushed from clothing.

A Family Assistance Center was also set up at Pier 94 on the Hudson River at Fifty-Fourth Street. This location provided all types of services for families of victims of the terrorist attack. Originally called the Compassion Center and set up in an armory, the Red Cross worked with the City of New York to find a more comfortable space for grieving families. The Family Assistance Center was then relocated to Pier 94. The facility was the size of two football fields and staffed by many different agencies, including the FBI, DNA collection facilities, and spiritual consultants—ministers, priests, and rabbis—representing all denominations. Child care facilities were available for people applying for assistance.

The center had hundreds of notes on the walls from people missing loved ones, some from children asking Daddy to "hold on!" Therapy dogs helped relieve the anxiety and stress of those people. Relatives of victims of the Oklahoma bombing sent a myriad of teddy bears.

Janet McGuire doesn't believe that she suffered posttraumatic stress, but knew she had developed a deep sense of empathy for the victims and their families. She had to take a year off from work because of digestive problems, although she can't be certain whether her time at Ground Zero was the cause. Although she wore a respirator, she could still smell the noxious odors from the site.

The Red Cross provided disaster assistance in New York City, Washington, D.C., and Shanksville, Pennsylvania, where United Airlines Flight 93 crashed on 9/11. The organization served more than fourteen million meals and snacks to emergency workers and people affected by the trauma of 9/11. It deployed 292 emergency response vehicles, opened sixty shelters for 3,554 families, and helped 59,217 families and individuals, including 537 from foreign countries. A total of 57,434 Red Cross employees and volunteers from all fifty states participated in the operation.[91]

Firefighter Danny Prince

Firefighter Danny Prince, assigned to the FDNY Safety Battalion, was in Minnesota on September 10, 2001.[92] His brother, an Agent Orange victim from Vietnam service, was in poor shape and was about to be sent to

---

91   www.redcross.org/911recovery.
92   Firefighter (retired) Danny Prince interview by the author.

a nursing home in the Twin Cities. Dan wanted to check out the facility to make sure his brother would be comfortable and receive good medical care. He couldn't have been more pleased with the facility.

The following morning he was devastated when he saw what was happening in New York. He went to the airport to try to get back, but all flights nationwide had been cancelled. Emotional, he was shown on local television as he pleaded for a way to get back to the city. The young daughter of a Minnesota firefighter saw him on TV and had her father contact him because her class at the Countryside Elementary School in Edina, Minnesota, wanted to send some cards to his fire station. They sent beautiful cards to the Safety Battalion, which had lost four firefighters.

It took Prince three days to find a way to get back to New York. Six local firefighters from Minneapolis and Cottage Grove, Minnesota, volunteered to go to New York and arranged a flight to Connecticut for themselves and Dan. They then went to work at Ground Zero.

Later, each time Dan returned to Minnesota to see his brother and father, also in a nursing home, he would go to visit the second-grade class at Countryside School. He was asked if he would visit the class on the first anniversary of 9/11. Initially, he thought that he should be at the ceremonies in New York on that date, but his wife suggested that since he had been in Minnesota when the WTC was attacked, it would be appropriate to be there on the first anniversary. When he attended, the class made him an honorary second grader.

Later, when a ceremony was planned at the Metrodome, the Minnesota Twins' stadium, to honor 9/11 heroes and victims, Dan was asked to throw out the first pitch. He asked if arrangements could be made to bring his father and brother to the game. Authorities picked the two up, brought them to the game, and gave Dan tickets so that twenty relatives and friends of his could also attend. This was the last time that the three men enjoyed each other's company together. Dan's brother passed away two months later, and his father died two years later.

Wounded Warriors

The retired firefighters who support wounded warriors from Iraq and Afghanistan have a relationship based on mutual respect with these men.

They completely understand these men are not looking for sympathy or pity. Their overwhelming desire is to be able to return to their military units.

The firefighters who visit Walter Reed Army and Bethesda Naval hospital in Washington, D.C. also support wounded warriors in the New York City area. A fishing trip off Breezy Point in Brooklyn included a soldier who had lost his legs. The firefighters ran into difficulty moving the soldier through a narrow doorway on the fishing boat, so one of them said, "Let's cross our hands, use the fireman's carry, and carry him through the door. Someone can collapse the wheelchair and bring it through."

As they were carrying the soldier, one of the New York firefighters, a Yankee fan, looked up and said, "Is that a Boston Red Sox cap he's wearing? Let's throw the son of a bitch overboard!"

The soldier laughed and replied, "You firemen are spectacular!"[93]

---

93   FDNY Captain (retired) George McGann interview with the author.

911 firefighter funeral-photo courtesy of FDNY

Epilogue

"Let us strive on to finish the work we are in; to bind up the nation's wounds; to care for him who shall have borne the battle, and for his widow, and his orphan—to do all which may achieve and cherish a just, and a lasting peace, among ourselves, and with all nations."

Abraham Lincoln in his second inaugural address

After the terrible terrorist attacks of September 11, 2001, our country faltered for a relatively short time. New York City was, as one might expect, hit the hardest. At first its losses appeared to be staggering. A total of 2,749 people, including 343 FDNY firefighters, thirty-seven PAPD and twenty-three NYPD police officers, were killed in the attack on New York City, with the remains of less than half of those identified.[94] While the terrorists had undoubtedly expected that attacks on the World Trade Center, the Pentagon, and the foiled attack by the plane that crashed in Shanksville, Pennsylvania, would stifle our economy and our national will, this terrorism had only a short-term effect. Many small businesses were underinsured or didn't have insurance at all. Most didn't have business interruption insurance. Two thousand school trips were cancelled. Marathon runners were offered priority consideration to run in the 2002 race if they did not participate in the November 2001 New York City Marathon. Cab drivers and local restaurants, many of which depended on lunch revenues to stay in business, lost business because tourism was down and the World Trade Center employees weren't there. Rents in unregulated apartments in Manhattan fell by an average of 18 percent.

---

94   Marge Arce, Tribute Center, interview by the author.

By the Christmas shopping season, however, long lines and pedestrian gridlock had come back to New York City. Hotels saw increased business and even, on occasion, were filled to capacity, albeit at reduced rates. The House of Representatives and the Senate provided New York City with $8.2 billion to help in the recovery process.[95] The rest of the country, not affected as much, also recovered. The stock market rebounded.

The offices of the commissioner and chief of the New York City Fire Department have much memorabilia, including photographs, baseball caps, and plaques coming from all over the world. Commissioner Cassano said that after 9/11, people visited from all across the country. Everyone was very supportive. "They gave us a tremendous amount of support, and we needed it. We don't forget what people did for us after September 11. We needed a lot of help. It was a difficult time and we got a lot of support early on. We have really recovered and learned from the things that we did on September 11. We've improved our response times. We've improved our operations, our communications, and our training. On September 11 we lost 4,400 years of experience. The FDNY suffered more losses in one day than it had in the previous fifty years. The fire department has had over a 50 percent personnel turnover since 9/11. Since that day, the department has hired almost six thousand new firefighters in an organization with a total strength of eleven thousand people."

Important changes have been made in the FDNY to better prepare it for any type of mass casualty situation, whether it be terrorist or natural disaster. Instead of the modest two-room computer office that served as the Emergency Operations Center (EOC), the FDNY now has a state-of-the-art facility that serves as a model for other large cities throughout the country. The well-trained staff can watch live video feeds from all major TV stations in the New York area. The exact location of all fire department ambulances is constantly tracked. When the emergency room of a hospital has a backup, this is immediately known and ambulances can be sent to other emergency facilities at other hospitals. When an emergency such as a fire occurs, the EOC can instantly pull up data on the building. As an example, if a fire should occur in a Laundromat, responding firefighters are alerted that the floor of the facility may have a heavy load and that responding

---

95   New York Times Index, 2001, pp. 1189–1190.

firefighters should be aware that a fire-weakened floor could collapse while they are fighting the fire.

Other important changes have been made in the procedures followed in fighting large fires and catastrophic events. Senior leaders can monitor events directly in real time from the EOC. In the January 2009 "Miracle on the Hudson," when an airplane made an emergency landing in the Hudson River after suffering engine failure due to bird strikes, the chief of the FDNY was able to keep the "incident commander" on the scene informed of developments as they happened because he could simultaneously monitor police reports, TV video, and had the liaison from other emergency services instantly available.

Additionally, new procedures have been instituted to limit unnecessary exposure of fire department personnel. Firefighters, policemen, emergency medical technicians, and indeed civilians want to help. On 9/11, many brave people responded even when they were off duty, some from relatively long distances. Tragically many of these heroes died that day. Firefighters came into their fire stations after the primary equipment had already been dispatched and scavenged whatever equipment they could find. When they arrived, they weren't with the companies that they had trained with; they often had no specific job and, as noted in earlier chapters, often didn't know what to do when they finally got to the site. Under the new policies, fire crews are no longer permitted to "ride heavy." Trained people will be needed to respond to "everyday" emergencies. People still have heart attacks. Fires still occur. Other emergencies will happen. All emergency workers cannot go to the scene of a single action, even if it is a major catastrophe.

The states of New Jersey and New York, where the Port Authority works, committed $300 million for new counterterrorism efforts by that agency. Improvements include training an additional five hundred PAPD officers, which has expanded the force to 1,600 personnel. The Port Authority has also implemented a $500 million plan to improve security at New York/New Jersey airports, bridges, and tunnels.[96]

A New England Journal of Medicine report published in April 2010 indicated that 13 percent of the eleven thousand firefighters who did not smoke and had worked at the WTC site during the two weeks after 9/11 scored below normal on breathing tests. David Prezant, the fire depart-

---

96   The Chief: the Civil Employees Weekly, May 28, 2004.

ment's chief medical officer, stated that the normal loss of lung function was equivalent to that caused by aging for twelve years.[97]

FDNY Chief Edward Kilduff said that heart attacks used to be the fire department's primary health concern; now it is cancer. Both the FDNY and NYPD report a number of cancer deaths of relatively young men that are linked to work at Ground Zero on and after 9/11. Additionally, prescriptions drugs to treat these chronic diseases, such as leukemia, prostate cancer, and non-Hodgkin lymphoma, are extremely expensive, often with copayments of up to $1,500 per month. Firefighters who worked at Ground Zero get a baseline physical examination when they retire. This is followed up with a complete physical examination every other year. All firefighters are issued personal breathing apparatus.[98]

Yet, in spite of the improvement of the New York Fire Department, its resources, its training, its better communications and equipment, Commissioner Cassano worries about the threat of further terrorist attacks against our country. He is very aware that New York City would be a primary, if not the most likely, target for another 9/11 type attack.

The probability of future terrorist attacks, both outside and inside of the United States will most certainly result in more people stepping up to the plate and risking their lives as heroes in the war against terror. A number of terrorist attacks, mostly unsuccessful, have been attempted since 9/11, and our country remains vulnerable. Future terrorist attacks can take many forms, including aircraft used as missiles, aircraft bombings (such as the "shoe" and "underwear" bombing attempts), car bombings (such as the attempted SUV car bombing in Times Square) so prevalent in the Mideast, political assassinations, reservoir poisonings, and possibly even the use of weapons of mass destruction.

The actions of the people, firefighters, police officers, emergency medical personnel, and civilians, on September 11, 2001, demonstrated the will and fortitude of the American people. This same will and fortitude will again be demonstrated if our country is again endangered, whether it be by hurricanes, floods, blizzards, or terrorist actions.

---

97   "Study: Time doesn't heal lung damage from 9/11," Jacksonville (FL) Times Union, April 8, 2010.

98   FDNY Chief of Department Edward Kilduff, interview.

Glossary

Chauffeur—The driver of a New York City Fire Department fire engine.

Clamshell grapple—A large tracked vehicle with a "clamshell" crane that can pick up large items.

Engine—A fire engine that normally carries a crew of six and fire hoses to a fire. The engine's crew is primarily responsible for putting out fires. An engine company is usually called an "engine" in firefighter language. An "engine" is not called a "truck."

FDNY—Fire Department of New York.

Ground Zero—The site where the Twin Towers were struck and fell became known as "Ground Zero."

Halligan—A tool (named after its inventor) used by firefighters to break down doors and open areas. The tool is a combination crowbar, wedge, and pry bar. One end of it can be hit with a sledgehammer to assist as needed.

HazMat—Short for "hazardous material," which could include explosives, biological, chemical, or other materials.

Jumpers—People who jumped to their deaths from the stricken Twin Towers to avoid being incinerated.

Ladder—A fire engine that carries a crew of six firefighters and ladders. The ladder crew's primary function is to access a burning building and rescue potential victims. A ladder company is usually called a "ladder" or "truck" in firefighter language.

Motor Pump Operator—The motor pump operator, or MPO, operates the motorized pump on an engine to pump water on fires. The MPO is also the "chauffeur."

"Mutual"—A mutual exchange of shifts of duty. FDNY firefighter shifts are typically 9:00 a.m. to 6:00 p.m. and 6:00 p.m. to 9:00 a.m. A "mutual" usually results in a firefighter pulling a 24-hour shift so another firefighter can have time off. The fire fighter being replaced "repays" his or her replacement at another time.

NYPD—New York Police Department.

OEM—Office of Emergency Management.

PAPD—Port Authority of New York and New Jersey Police Department.

"Pile"—The mountain of rubble at the World Trade Center after the terrorist attack on 9/11.

The Pit—The hole created by the collapse of the Twin Towers.

Probie—A firefighter trainee on probation until he or she has successfully completed initial training and a supervised first assignment with a firefighting company.

Relocation—When a ladder or engine company is called out for a fire, another similar company may be directed to relocate to that company's firehouse to cover during its absence.

"Ride Heavy—Extra firefighters riding to a fire although they are not scheduled or required to do so. On 9/11 many firefighters "rode heavy" after the planes hit the Twin Towers during a shift change. Many of those going off duty volunteered to go to the scene of the action. Others off duty also joined their comrades.

Riding Lists—A list of firefighters on each fire truck committed to a fire. One copy is placed in the glove compartment of the apparatus, and the fire officer assigned to the committed unit carries a second copy.

Standpipe—A pipe installed in buildings of seven or more stories and designed to allow firefighters to connect to a hydrant to furnish water throughout a building. These buildings usually also have an emergency water supply on the roof of the building.

Stokes or Stokes Basket—A long, narrow, metal or plastic mesh "basket" (named after its inventor) used by firefighters as a stretcher to carry injured people.

Squad—A squad has special tools that engine and ladder companies don't normally carry. The crews are charged with augmenting engine and ladder companies as needed and to rescue potential victims and firefighters.

Survivor's Guilt—A guilty feeling that many people experience after losing friends or family members in a situation where they were also in danger.

Tone Alarm—A very loud, shrill alarm at firehouses to alert firefighters that they are being dispatched.

Total Recall—In major emergencies, all available FDNY personnel are directed to report to their duty stations.

Truck—A truck is also known as a "ladder" and is a fire truck equipped with a ladder reaching one hundred feet or a tower ladder reaching seventy-five or ninety-five feet. A tower ladder has a boom at the end that is capable of raising a firefighter to the top. A ladder crew is responsible for rescuing people and venting, entering, and searching burning buildings, or "VES."

Turnout Coats—Protective coats worn by firefighters when fighting fires and in other dangerous situations.

UFO—"Until Further Orders," or temporary duties assigned to personnel, often newly promoted, while awaiting permanent orders.

WTC—World Trade Center.

Bibliography

National Commission on Terrorist Attacks on the United States. The 9/11 Commission Report. 2004. Available at http://www.9-11commission.gov/report/911Report.pdf . Accessed January 23, 2011.

Dwyer, J., and K. Flynn. 102 Minutes. New York: Times Books, 2005.

Langewiesche, W. American Ground: Unbuilding the World Trade Center. New York: North Point Press, 2002.

Klein, H. "September 11 Observances Around the Borough." Brooklyn Courier Life, September 7, 2007.

Halberstam, D. Firehouse. New York: Hyperion, 2002.

Kreuscher, G. R. Fireman. United States of America, 2008.

Stewart, J. B. Heart of a Soldier. New York: Simon & Schuster, 2002.

Carbone, G. "The Miracle of Ladder 6 and Josephine." Providence Journal Company, 2002. Available at http://www.projo.com/words/st20021016.htm. Accessed January 23, 2011.

Picciotto, R., and D. Palsner. Last Man Down: A Firefighter's Story of Survival and Escape from the World Trade Center. New York: Berkley Publishing, 2002.

Giuliani, R., and K. Kurson. Leadership. New York: Miramax Books, 2002.

New York Times. New York Times Index 2001, A Book of Records. New York: New York Times Company, 2001.

Feister, J. B., and J. Zawadzinksi. No Greater Love: Chaplain Mychal Judge, O.F.M, Available at http://www.americancatholic.org/messenger/dec2001/feature2.asp. Accessed January 23, 2011.

The staff of the New York Times. Portraits 9/11/01: The Collected Portraits of Grief from the New York Times. New York: Henry Holt and Company, 2002.

Smith, D. Report from Ground Zero. New York: Penguin Books, 2003.

Murphy, D. September 11: An Oral History. New York: Random House, 2002.

Flood, J. The Fires. New York: Riverhead Books, 2010.

Kerik, B. B. The Lost Son: A Life in Pursuit of Justice. New York: HarperCollins, 2001.

The World Trade Center. Available at www.skyscraper.org/TALLEST_TOWERS/t_wtc.htm. Accessed January 25, 2011.

Author's Notes

A retired FDNY fire fighter selling antique glass bottles at a street market in Brooklyn was the unlikely catalyst for a journey that has led through the past and present ranks of New York City's fire and police departments and the Port Authority of New York and New Jersey, from top to bottom. "Fireman Jack" Fortmeyer's conversation with my wife, Barbara, which led to my introduction to a retired firefighters' monthly breakfast meeting, including some who had been at the Twin Towers that day, led in turn to a cascade of interest and cooperation. Similar help from NYPD and Port Authority police officers combined to make this book possible.

Mayor Rudy Giuliani, Congressman Peter T. King, and FDNY Commissioner Sal Cassano, among so many others, were very gracious with their assistance.

People ask why I wrote Ordinary People: Extraordinary Heroes. It's because after this decade or more since 9/11, too many Americans have perhaps relegated those vicious, tragic events at "Ground Zero" to history, rather than adopting the "Never Again!" view that will keep alive the active precautions, both personal and governmental, that will prevent a recurrence. The wonderful people interviewed in this book, and the many families who lost loved ones on 9/11 will never forget, and neither must we. That subsequent foreign terrorist attempts have been unsuccessful (such as shoe bombers, underwear grenadiers and SUV dynamiters in Times Square) should give us no assurance. Most of us are more concerned about jobs, the economy and family problems at home every day than we are of an event seemingly long past. Terrorism is a war, not an event. In these days, with a world full of violence, we can no longer underestimate the massive threat to our nation that we face as part of life. It is there, and it is real, happening elsewhere in the world whether we think about it or not.

The events of 9/11, as related in the experiences of those who agreed to be interviewed for this book, are a part of our nation's "living history." The experiences of men and women, who lived through 9/11, faced death at close range and came forward to tell about it in their own words, demonstrate once again that courage is alive and vibrant in today's American society. The reputation of firefighters and police officers as those who run TOWARD danger to save the lives of others at the risk of their own is reaffirmed to their lasting credit.

Many of the stories in these pages were revealed for the first time by people who had declined previous interviews over the years. Others needed intervening years before being ready to relate their traumatic experiences to others. When I told them that we were seeking to keep the day alive in the minds of our countrymen, responses came back instantly that said, in so many words, "I remember 9/11 every day since it happened, and I'll remember it each day for the rest of my life." Some interviews were more difficult than others. None were easy. Accounts opened up long buried emotions, and the depths of sadness often showed themselves in tears. The sixty firefighters, police officers and civilians I interviewed are still living with that unforgettable day. Many who were interviewed had been medically retired for Line of Duty injuries and conditions which disqualified them for full duty in their demanding professions.

America is in good hands thanks to people like this. It's up to all of us to keep it that way.

Will G. Merrill Jr.